John Millhouse, Anderson William

Practical Mercantile Correspondence

Collection of modern Letters of Businness

John Millhouse, Anderson William

Practical Mercantile Correspondence

Collection of modern Letters of Businness

ISBN/EAN: 9783337136666

Printed in Europe, USA, Canada, Australia, Japan

Cover: Foto ©ninafisch / pixelio.de

More available books at **www.hansebooks.com**

PRACTICAL
MERCANTILE CORRESPONDENCE,

COLLECTION OF

MODERN LETTERS OF BUSINESS,

WITH

an **APPENDIX**

CONTAINING

PRO FORMA INVOICES, ACCOUNT SALES, BILLS OF LADING,

AND BILLS OF EXCHANGE,

ALSO

AN EXPLANATION OF THE GERMAN CHAIN RULE,

AS APPLICABLE TO THE CALCULATION

OF EXCHANGES.

BY **WILLIAM ANDERSON**,

WITH ITALIAN NOTES

BY **JHON MILLHOUSE.**

THIRD EDITION

MILAN,
MDCCCLXXII.

CONTENTS.

Preliminary Observations . . . . Page 1
Analytical Index . . . . » 6

Commercial Correspondence.

Letter. I. Advice to a person commencing business . . . » 17
    II. Ditto . . . . » 19

Circulars.

   III. House of general agency established . . . . . » 22
   IV. Death of partner . . . . » 23
   V. Change in firm . . . . » 23
   VI. Broker's circular . . . . » 24
   VII. House of agency . . . . » 24
   VIII. Dissolution of partnership . . . . » 25
   IX. Firms—two united . . . . » 25
   X. English agent abroad, letter from . . . . . . » 26
   XI. Death of partner . . . . » 26
   XII. New partner admitted . . . . » 27
   XIII. Merchants and agents, new establishment of . » 27
   XIV. Ship and insurance broker . . . . » 28
   XV. American agency for collection of debts and settlement
       of affairs . . . . » 28
   XVI. Wine, spirit and ale merchant . . . . » 30
   XVII. Death of partner . . . . » 30
   XVIII. Stationer succeeding to business . . . . . . » 31
   XIX. Death of partner, and change of firm . . . . » 31
   XX. Death of partner—admission of a new one . . » 32
   XXI. New establishment . . . . » 32
   XXII. Retirement of partner—alteration in firm . . » 33
   XXIII. Son taken into partnership . . . . » 33
   XXIV. Clerk admitted as partner . . . . » 33
   XXV. Intention to establish a foreign branch of a London
       house . . . . » 34
   XXVI. Recommendation of new firm . . . . » 34

CONTENTS.

Lett. XXVII. Establishment of new firm . . . . . . Page 35
XXVIII. Old firm retire—new firm commence . . . . » 35
XXIX. Circular of new firm . . . . » 36
XXX. Announcement of new firm . . . . » 36
XXXI. Failure, notice of . . . . » 36
XXXII. Suspension of payments, notice of . . . . . » 37
XXXIII. Dissolution of partnership . . . . » 37
XXXIV. Ibid . . . . » 38
XXXV. New firms . . . . » 38
XXXVI. Rates of interest in public funds . . . . » 38

Letters of Introduction.

XXXVII. To Bristol in favour of a nephew of an old connexion » 39
XXXVIII. To Bombay   »   a mercantile house . . . » 40
XXXIX. To Liverpool   »   son of partner . . . . » 40
XL. To London   »   agent . . . . » 40
XLI. To Hamburg   »   and invalid friend wishing to
                           obtain employment abroad » 41
XLII. To Liverpool   »   partner of Paris house . » 41
XLIII. To Oporto   »   captain of vessel . . . » 42

Letters of Introduction and Credit.

XLIV. To Bristol in favour of American merchant . . » 42
XLV. To Manchester   »   agent of German house » 42
XLVI. To Falmouth   »   a person on his way to
                           Portugal . . . . » 43

Letters of Credit. (On a place.)

XLVII. On Plymouth in favour of a merchant . . . » 43
XLVIII. On Paris   »   a nobleman . . . » 44

General Correspondence.

Series   Page
1. XLIX—LXI. Adventure in cotton 44-50
2. LXII—LXXI. Wine trade-exchanges-order for hare skins-
   order for insurance 50-55
3. LXXII—LXXX. Remittance 55-59
4. LXXXI—XCII. Joint speculation in tobacco 60-64
5. XCIII—XCV. Dishonored bill 65
6. XCVI—CXLVI. Trade between Fayal and London in fruit,
   wine, etc. 65-92
7. CXLVII—CLI. Speculation in exchanges 93-95

CONTENTS.

Series	Page
8. CLII—CLVI. Adventure in flax	95-98
9. CLVII—CLVIII. Miscellaneous business—particular averages recovered	99-101
10. CLIX—CLXIV. Order for copper sheathing	104-106
11. CLXV—CXC. Ship detained for repairs, and part of cargo sold	106-115
12. CXCI—CXCVI. Exchange operations	116-115
13. CXCVII-CCI. Loss of ship—recovery from underwriters	120-123
14. CCII—CCIX. Bill dishonored at Rio de Janeiro . . .	123-126
15. CCX—CCXIII. Order for cargo of coals	126-128
16. CCXIV—CCXVII. Sales of fruit by auction	129-130
17. CCXVIII—CCXXII. Security required and given for dishonored draft	130-132
18. CCXXIII—CCXXV. Orders for British manufactured goods	132-133
19. CCXXVI—CCXXIX. Payment of a quarterly pension .	133-134
20. CCXXX—CCXXXI. Order for sugars on joint-account .	134-135
21. CCXXXII—CCXXXVII. Cargo seized by customs at Charleston	136-138
22. CCXXXVIII—CCXL. Sale of British manufactured goods in America	139-140
23. CCXLI—CCXLII. Reports of markets	141-146
24. CCXLIII—CCXLIV. Goods and letters not received . .	148-149
25. CCXLV—CCXLVII. Bill dishonored at Axbridge . . .	149-150
26. CCXLVIII—CCL. General business	150-152
27. CCLI—CCLIII. Orders for hemp from Riga	153-153
28. CCLIV-CCLVI. Agreement for dividing commission . .	154-155
29. CCLVII—CCLXX. Oporto wine trade—insurance—loss of ship—recovery	155-162
30. CCLXXIII—CCLXXIVI. Consignments of wool	163-165
— CCLXXVIII—CCCIX. Miscellaneous Letters	165-183
Appendix	183

PREFACE TO THE FIRST LONDON EDITION

The following sheets (1) have been compiled with a view (2) to supply a deficiency that has hitherto (3) existed in our literature.

It appears a remarkable anomaly that, in a country so eminently commercial as Great-Britain, the initiatory studies of young men destined for mercantile life (4) should be so notoriously neglected.

Our literature, copious enough in almost every other branch, affords (5) abundant facility for an appropriate course of tuition (6) and study for the liberal professions and the arts: but to the young merchant, it proffers little assistance of the kind (7) required. We have excellent dictionaries of commerce, and works (8) of practical utility in this department; but none, that I have met (9) with, calculated to form the youthful mind (10) to habits of business (11), and familiarise it with the objects to which his future energies are to be directed.

Nothing, I conceive, can better conduce to this end (12) than a collection of genuine commercial letters, of recent dates, adapted at once (13) to form the style and to afford a correct insight (14) into the business of the counting house (15). In fact, the utility of such a collection has been long acknowledged (16); and its want felt (17) as well by the young gentlemen themselves, as by those tutors who profess to give their pupils a commercial education.

The few books of the kind that have existed are now out of print (18), and not one of those which have chanced to fall into my

---

(1) Seguenti fogli. (2) With a view to supply a deficiency, all'intento di sovvenire a un difetto. (3) Finora. (4) Vita. (5) Ramo, somministra. (6) Istruzione. (7) Genere. (8) Opere. (9) Ch'io m'abbia incontrato. (10) Lo spirito giovanile, della gioventù. (11) Affari. (12) Better conduce to this end, meglio contribuire a questo scopo. (13) Al tempo stesso. (14) To afford a correct insight into the business, a presentare un colpo d' occhio giusto, (una descrizione corretta) degli affari. (15) Banco, studio di negoziante. (16) Riconosciuta, ammessa. (17) Its want felt, il bisogno di essa sentito. (18) Are now out of print, sono ora esauriti, non se ne trova più alcuna copia.

PREFACE TO THE FIRST LONDON EDITION

hands (1), appeared to me well adapted to answer (2) the end proposed. They were defective in arrangement, or in diversity of subject; they were too incorrect in style for the present improved (3) and improving age; and from the (4) absence of explanatory notes, could not be sufficiently intelligible to those totally unacquainted (5) with the nature of business.

Indeed (6) it is a matter of surprise, when we consider the rapid progress of publication within (7) the last few years, that this deficiency has not sooner, be supplied. Nor can I find (8) any more probable reasons for it than the following (9).

1st. The difficulty of procuring materials for the work, and which no single house of business could supply.

2dly. The want of time, or of that portion, however (10) small, of literary taste (11) and acquirements, which may be considered necessary to prepare it for the press (12).

The former (13) cause will operate in the case of men (14) devoted to literary pursuits, who besides would be inadequate to the task (15), from their ignorance of business; the latter (16) in that of merchants themselves.

The difficulty alluded to is much greater than the reader may imagine.

Merchants are, usually, and from a very proper feeling (17), averse to suffering their correspondence to be made public; and when they have, in some few (18) instances, permitted a small selection to be made, for the exclusive use of a private academy, they have limited the favor to old (19) letters and commonplace (20) subjects; fearing that any correspondence of a personal nature, or particularly interesting from the peculiarity or delicacy of the transactions involved (which for such a purpose must be the more valuable) would be recognised, whatever attempts might be made to disguise it.

Having a large mass of correspondence at my command, I have been enabled (21) to overcome this difficulty; and with the aid of

---

(1) Which have chanced to fall into my hands, che mi capitarono tra le mani. (2) To answer the end, corrispondere al fine, raggiungere lo scopo. (3) For the present improved and improving age, pel progresso di questo secolo del perfezionamenti. (4) From the absence, a cagione dell'assenza. (5) Totally unacquainted with, del tutto ignari di. (6) In vero. (7) Within the last few years, in questi ultimi anni. (8) Trovare, assegnare. (9) Seguenti. (10) However small, per quanto piccola. (11) Literary taste and acquirements, gusto e cognizioni in fatto di letteratura. (12) Stampa. (13) The former cause, la prima cagione, la prima di queste due cagioni. (14) Men devoted to literary pursuits, i cultori delle belle lettere. (15) Inadequate to the task, inetti all'assunto, all'opera. (16) L'altra, la seconda. (17) Sentimento. (18) In some few instances, in alcuni pochi casi. (19) Antiche. (20) Triti. (21) I have been enabled to overcome, fui posto in grado di superare

some letters obtained through (1) the kindness of my friends * to submit to the public the following collection.

I have endeavoured (2) to correct the diction, when necessary, in order (3) to render theim fair (4) examples of the commercial style; avoiding (5) some inelegancies, and some ungrammatical and quaint (6) expressions, which, though frequently met with, are by no means (7) to be commended, or admitted into such examples as are intended to be placed in the hands of the pupil at the commercial academy, or the youth (8) who has just taken his seat at the counting-house desk (9). How far (10) I have succeeded in this attempt, the reader will determine.

I have been careful (11) to select simple transactions, and have in many cases, given the entire correspondence relating to them, in order to show (12) distinctly the common routine of business. At the same time I have endeavoured to introduce as much variety as my plan would allow (13), to obviate the monotony and dryness (14) that are inseparable from the common-place occurrences of the counting-house.

In a few instances, I have given the correspondence on one side (15) only, for the following reasons.

1st. In order not to swell my book to too large a size (16).

2nd. Because, in some transactions, the reply (17) is of necessity, merely an echo of the letter.

3rd. To afford so the young aspirant to commercial attainments the opportunity of writing answers, by way of exercise.

In short (18) it has been my principal objet to furnish an appropriate Exercise-book for the use of schools; and I will venture to suggest that every pupil destined for mercantile life should be required to copy the following sheets from beginning to end.

Foreigners desirous of acquiring the english commercial style, may employ themselves very profitably in a similar manner.

The Appendix is a new feature in a work of this kind. In it will

---

(1) Obtained through the kindness of my friends, ottenute dalla gentilezza de' miei amici. (2) I have endeavoured to, ho procurato di. (3) Al fine di. (4) Fair examples, begli esempi, degni modelli. (5) Evitando, scansando. (6) Quaint expressions, espressioni stravaganti, fuor del comune uso. (7) By no means, in nessun conto. (8) Giovane, giovanetto. (9) Scrittojo. (10) Sino a qual punto. (11) Sollecito, diligente. (12) Mostrare, far vedere. (13) Consentiva. (14) Aridità, tedio. (15) The correspondence on one side only, la corrispondenza di una delle parti soltanto, il carteggio di un solo dei corrispondenti. (16) Not to swell my book to too large a size, per non accrescere di soverchio la mole del libro. (17) Risposta. (18) In breve.

* The names, of course, are altered, and some little disguise has been resorted to in regard to the dates.

PREFACE TO THE FIRST LONDON EDITION.

be found some useful information on subjects intimately connected with mercantile affairs, and which I have endeavoured to place in a clear point of view, to render them intelligible to my youthful readers (1).

The explanation of the German Chain Rule cannot fail (2) to prove serviceable, since the utility of that Rule is unquestionable, and it is little known (3) in this country.

---

(1) Youthful readers, giovani lettori. (2) Cannot fail to prove serviceable, non può non tornar giovevole. (3) Conosciuta.

PRELIMINARY OBSERVATIONS.

The proper characteristics of the commercial style are neatness (1) and perspicuity. Brevity also is desiderable, as far as (2) may be consistent with the latter quality; for a waste of words is a waste of time, both to him who writes and to him who reads (3) a letter.

To attain (4) all this, I would recommend that the several subjects to be treated of, should be kept (5) perfectly distinct.

In replying to a letter, follow the same order that is observed therein (6), discussing one subject fully (7) and in a separate paragraph, before you proceed to the next (8).

The want of a proper division of a letter into paragraphs, and a neglect of punctuation, will scarcely fail to render it confused*.

It is a point of chief importance, that all orders given should be clear and explicit; and if their execution depend upon any contingency, the correspondent must have full directions how to act under any change of circumstances that may be contemplated: this is necessary to obviate misunderstandings (9) and disputes.

With the same view (10) it is usual, especially in important matters to recapitulate the principal subjects of the letter replied to. In this, however, merchants have also another object, which is to render their letter-books (11), as far as possible, a history of their transactions, for the advantage of a ready reference after a lapse of years, and for production in court (12) with the better effect, in case of litigation.

Accordingly, every letter should speak as it were, for itself, and give all the necessary particulars of the transactions to which it refers. For the same reason, merchants seldom (13) arrange any important business verbally, or if they do, a letter is immediately written stating (14) the nature of the arrangement (15) made

---

(1) Semplicità, purezza. (2) Per quanto. (3) A waste of words is a waste of time, both to him who writes and to him who reads, aprecar parole è sprecar tempo, al per chi scrive che per chi legge. (4) Conseguire. (5) Should be kept, s'abbiano a mantenere, tenere. (6) In essa. (7) Pienamente. (8) Susseguente. (9) Malintesi. (10) Allo stesso intento. (11) Libri di lettere. (12) In giudicio, al tribunale. (13) Di rado. (14) Constatante. (15) Aggiustamento, convenzione.

* Persons who are conscious of being deficient in style, would do well to study the principles of composition in *Justin Brennan's Composition and Punctuation*.

Anderson.

which is thus placed on record (1) in the letter-book, and is corroborated by the answer of the party concerned.

In the practice of letter-writing, there are some points to be observed, which will very materially facilitate (2) the performance of the duties of a corresponding clerk (3), and which I shall briefly notice.

In the first place, it is a matter of course (4) that every letter, as soon as (5) read, is folded (6) neatly and evenly, and endorsed (7) with the name and date, and date of receipt, a blank (8) being left for the date of reply.

Thus for instance

Hamburg, 10th Aug. 18—.
BERENBERG, GOSSLER & Co.
Received 16th Aug.
Answered

Or thus:

18—.
BERENBERG, GOSSLER & Co.
Hamburgh, 10th Aug.
Received 16th do.
Answered.

This practice is universal; but I would recommend further (9) the following, which, as far as I know, is by no means common.

Fold the letter in such a manner as to leave a blank space at the bottom of the side which is indorsed as above; or if the sheet be filled, attach to is a slip (10) of paper with gumwater (11), or a white wafer (12). Then let the principal subjects of the letter be briefly noted thereon (13); thus, for example:

Remittance of L. 1500,
Bill of Lading, 10 bales of wool,
per Fortuna.
Account sales, 10 pipes of wine,
ex Sallust.
Markets
Proposed adventure to Bahia on joint account.

---

(1) Placed on record, registrata. (2) Will very materially facilitate the performance, agevoleranno d'assai l'adempimento. (3) Commesso. (4) It is a matter of course, già s'intende, è ben naturale. (5) As soon as, appena. (6) Piegata. (7) Attergata. (8) Spazio vuoto. (9) Oltracciò. (10) A slip of paper, un pezzo di carta. (11) Acqua di gomma. (12) Obbiadino bianco. (13) Sopra di esso.

PRELIMINARY OBSERVATIONS.

Now by merely looking through (1) the letters, as they lie in the parcel, without untying the tape (2), you have an index of their contents *.

These notes should be made at once (3) when the letter is endorsed; for delay (4) in this, as in every thing else, occasions tenfold (5) trouble.

In the letter-book a similar plan may be adopted, as the subject of each paragraph may be noted in the margin. As a means of instant reference from one letter to another, to the same address, whether preceding or following without turning back to the index, I recommend, that as soon as a letter is copied, or the machine copy pasted (6) in, the folio of the last (7) letter, to the same party, be noted immediately under the name of the place in the margin. At the same time, note in the margin of the last letter the folio of the one just entered (8).

The numbers may be placed together thus, $\frac{340}{372}$, or the upper one (9) may be noted at the commencement, and the lower (10) at the conclusion of each (11) letter.

This mode will be found (12) particularly serviceable in large establishments, where two letter-books, with one index, are kept in use at once; as either book (13) may, by this means, be searched (14) without the index, or with only one reference to it.

In regard to giving instructions for answering any particular points that may occur, the practice of merchants varies very much. Some open their letters in the presence of their corresponding clerks, read them aloud (15), and state at once what kind of reply is to be given to each; excepting of course (16), cases which require consideration and private consultation among the partners (17). Others read their letters by themselves (18) and note with a pencil (19), or communicate verbally, on handing them (20) to the clerk, their wishes in regard to the replies. Whichever (21) plan be adopted, the young correspondent ought to feel (22) certain that he fully comprehends

---

(1) By merely looking through, semplicemente scorrendo coll'occhio, percorrendo collo sguardo. (2) Without untying the tape, senza sciogliere la fettuccia, slacciare il nastro. (3) Tosto, subito. (4) L'indugiare. (5) Dieci volte maggiore. (6) Incollata. (7) Ultima. (8) Registrata. (9) The upper one, il superiore. (10) L'inferiore. (11) Ciascuna. (12) Trovato. (13) Either book may, o l'uno o l'altro libro, ciascuno dei due libri può. (14) Esaminato, consultato. (15) Read them aloud, le leggono forte, ad alta voce. (16) Naturalmente. (17) Among the partners, tra i soci. (18) By themselves, da sè stessi, da soli. (19) Matita, lapis. (20) On handing them, nel consegnarle, passarle. (21) Qualsivoglia. (22) Ought to feel certain, dovrebbe essere ben sicuro.

* It is the practice, in some large houses, to keep an index to their correspondence in a book, which some may consider a preferable mode.

PRELIMINARY OBSERVATIONS.

his employer's (1) instructions before he attempts to commit them to paper (2); and it is better to ask questions beforehand (3), than to have to amend (4) his letter when written. When he receives directions verbally, he should note them immediately in a memorandum book, kept for that purpose. If he can take them in short hand (5), so much the better; but note them he must, unless endowed with a singularly retentive memory.

Indeed, a juvenile clerk, having every thing to learn, will do well to take notes of every occurrence that passes before him; by which means, he will lay by a stock (6) of useful information on commercial subjects, and of precedents for his future guidance; he will greatly enhance (7) the value of his services, and gain the good opinion of his employers, to whom it must ever be gratifying to see him steady (8), intelligent, and perfectly *au courant des affaires*.

NOTE, SECOND LONDON EDITION.

There are some minor points connected with Mercantile Correspondence which are not undeserving (9) of notice. It must frequently happen that the clerk is hurried (10) in making up his letters for the post, and then it is that vexations mistakes (11) occur, such as misdirecting (12) of letters, omitting enclosures (13), and such quotations of prices (14), etc., as are unavoidably left to the last (15). To prevent this it is a good practice to note in one corner (16) of the front page every enclosure that is to go with the letters, and to affix a slight (17) mark in the margin opposite to every blank. All the blanks being first carefully filled up, the letters should be handed to the copying-clerk, and being received back from the press sufficiently

---

(1) His employer's instructions, le istruzioni del suo principale. (2) To commit them to paper, metterle in iscritto. (3) Anticipatamente, preventivamente, in prevenzione. (4) Correggere. (5) Stenografia. (6) Will lay by a stock of, accumulerà un fondo, farà tesoro d'una quantità di. (7) Will greatly enhance, aumenterà d'assai. (8) Posato, giudizioso. (9) Immeritevoli. (10) Is hurried in making up, ha fretta nel completare. (11) Vexatious mistakes, rincrescevoli sbagli, aviste. (12) Dirigere male, sbagliare l'indirizzo. (13) Alligati. (14) Quotations of prices, indicazioni di prezzi. (15) As are unavoidably left to the last, che è pur d'uopo lasciare per ultimo. (16) Angolo. (17) Piccolo, leggero.

PRELIMINARY OBSERVATIONS.

dry for folding, the correspondent proceeds to this last process, first consulting the note in the corner to be certain that he has the inclosures correct. We must be careful, too, that no invoice (1), account-sales (2), or other document requiring the signature of the firm (3) be sent off (4) without it. All letters copied by hand ought to be marked in some uniform manner; and none should be folded that does not bear (5) the usual evidence of its having been copied.

The mere mechanical folding of a letter is not, as some persons unaccustomed to correspondence may imagine, a matter of little or no importance; — far from it! Indeed there is something offensive and redolent (6) of vulgarity in a letter clumsily (7) put together, ill-directed, or besmeared (8) with wax or wafer in the awkward (9) attempt to seal it (10). The commercial clerk and man of business must therefore study to acquire both a neat and a rapid method of making up his letters, and this is best accomplished by the aid of a paper-knife (11) and a thin slip (12) of mahogany, with which, in some counting houses, each clerk is furnished.

In shape (13) a letter should be neither too square (14) nor too oblong, and large in proportion to the enclosures, so as not to appear clumsily thick (15). The address (16) should be distinctly written and neatly placed; not straggling (17) too near the top (18), nor yet crowded too near the bottom (19); and, finally, the seal or wafer must not obliterate any portion of the writing.

---

(1) Fattura. (2) Conti di vendita. (3) Ditta, casa. (4) Sent off, spedito. (5) Porti, abbia. (6) Redolent of, che sente, che sa di. (7) Goffamente, alla carlona. (8) Imbrattata. (9) Goffo. (10) Sigillarla. (11) Paper-knife, stecca. (12) A thin slip, un pezzetto sottile. (13) In shape, quanto alla forma. (14) Quadrata. (15) Grossa. (16) Indirizzo. (17) Not straggling, non fuorviando, uscendo di linea, di riga. (18) Too near the top, troppo presso la cima, troppo insù. (19) Not yet crowded too near the bottom, e nemmeno troppo verso il fondo, troppo in giù.

ANALYTICAL INDEX

TO CORRESPONDENCE

Advice to persons commencing business, I, 17, II, 19.

Circulars.

Advances on consignments offered and expected, XIII, 27.
Agent, American, XV, 28.
    for settling claims, recovery of debts, and legal business, XV, 28.
    English, abroad, as attorney, solicitor, and general agent, X, 26.
    general, commencing in the Mauritius, III, 22.
            at Pernambuco, VII, 24.
            at London, XIII, 27.
    Intending to commence at Rio, XXV, 34.
    established, XXVI, 34.
    new firm, XXVII, 35.

Broker for colonial produce, commencing in London, VI, 24.
Ship and Insurance, XIV, 28.

Commencing business, see *Agent* and *Broker*.
    wine merchant, XVI, 30.
    stationer, XVIII, 31.

Death of partner, no alteration of firm, IV, 25; XVII, 30.
    change of firm, in consequence of, V, 23; XIX, 31.
    announcement of, XI, 26.
    new partnership in consequence of, XX, 32.
Dissolution of partnership announced, between house in London and
    house abroad, VIII, 25.
    signature used in liquidation, notice of, VIII, 25; XXXIII, 37;
        XXXIV, 38.
    announcement of, XXXIII, 37.
        new firm, XXXV, 38.

ANALYTICAL INDEX.

Failure, notice of, XXXI 36; XXXII, 37.
     trustees appointed, XXXI, 36.
Firms, two united, IX, 25.
 new, announcement of, XX, 32; XXVII, 35; XXVIII, 35; XXIX 36; XXXV, 38.
 announcement of, in new connexion, XXX, 36.
 alteration in, XXII, 33.
 old, extinction of, XXVIII, 35.
French, Funds, Table showing the rate of interest of, XXXVI, 38.

Liquidation, See *Dissolution of Partnership*.

Partner, nephew admitted, XII, 27.
 retirement of, XXII, 33.
 clerk admitted, XXIV, 33.

 See *Dissolution of Partnership* and *Death of Partner*.
Procuration, signature by, XXIX, 36.

Letters of Introduction.

XXXVII-XLIII, 39-42.

Letters of Introduction and Credit.

XLIV—XLVI, 42-43.

Letters of Credit.

XLVI—XLVIII, 43-44.

General Correspondence.

Acceptance, bill sent for, CCXLV, 142.
 declined on ground of irregularity, CIII, 68.
 for honor, CIV, 69.
 of bill advised, CVII, 70.
 advice of, CCLXXXV, 169.
Account current, transmitted, CXXI, 79; CXLVI, 93; CL, 95; CXCIX, 121; CCXLIX, 151; CCXCV, 174; CCC, 176; CCCVIII, 181.
 receipt of, acknowledged, CXXII, 79.
Account final, CXLVI, 92.
Account sales, of cotton, LX, 49.
 receipt of, LXI, 50.
 of specie, CXVIII, 76.

ANALYTICAL INDEX.

Account sales of fruit, CXXI, 78.
    of wine, CXXXVII, 87.
    of cork, CCLXIX, 161.
    of wood, CCLXXVII, 165; CCCVI, 180.
    of bullion, CCXCIX, 176.
    of sundries, CCCVIII, 181.
Acknowledgment of receipt of bill of lading and invoice. LVI, 47.
    goods received, LVIII, 48; CXVIII, 76.
    remittance, LXI, 50, LXXVI, 58; LXXIX, 59; CLVII, 99; CCLXV, 159.
    account-sales, LXI, 50.
    advice, LXXXIV, 61; CXXXVIII, 83.
    instructions received, as to consignment of tobacco, LXXXV, 62.
    advice of limits being too low, as to price of tobacco, LXXXIX, 63.
    account-sales, CXLV, 92; CLVI, 98.
    receipt of security, CCXX, 131.
    recommendation, CCXLVIII, 150.
    bill of lading and invoice, CCLXXVI, 164.
    of sugar, CCLXXXVII, 170.
Advances on fruit declined, CXI, 72; CXIV, 74.
    further declined, CXL, 89.
    made on ship to be charged, CXCIX, 122.
    on freight, CCXCVIII, 176.
    requested for friend, CCCIV, 178.
Advice of price of cotton at Liverpool, L, 45.
    to foreign house of consignment, LII, 46.
    of purchase and shipment of goods, LIII, 46; LIV, 47.
    of shipment of goods, LV, 47; LXIX, 54.
    of goods arrived, LVIII, 48; LIX, 49.
    of sales, LX, 49.
    of prices of wine, LXIII, 52.
    of sailing under convoy, LXIV, 52.
    of insurance effected, LXV, 52; LXVII, 53; LXXI, 55; CXXXV, 86.
    of bill drawn, LXV, 52; CCCV, 179.
    of arrival under convoy, LXVIII, 54.
    of premium recovered, LXIX, 54.
    of payment to banker, LXXVI, 58.
    of acceptance of drafts, LXXX, 59.
    of tobacco purchased, LXXXIII, 67.
    of speculation being relinquished, LXXXVIII, 63.
    of irregularity in CIII, 68.
    of intended shipment, CXVI, 75.
    of sale by auction, CLXXIV, 110; CLXXV, 110.
    of goods recovered, and sales effected, CCXXXVII, 138.
    See *Markets.*

ANALYTICAL INDEX. 2

Agency, fire insurance, application for, CCLXXVIII, 165; CCLXXX, 166.
   marine insurance, application for, CCLXXIX, 166.
Allowance required for difference in quality of sugar, CLVIII, 103.
Anticipation, proposal to draw in, CXXXIX, 88.
Application, see *Agency*.
Arrival of ship, advised, LXVIII, 54; CXVIII, 76; CXXXIX, 88; CXC, 115.
   under convoy, LXVIII, 54.
   out, advised, CCLXIII, 158; CCLXVI, 160.
Auction, sale by, advice of, CLXXIV, 110; CLXXV, 110.
   fee for attendance at, CLXXVIII, 111; CLXXXIII, 113.
   conditions of sale insisted on, CCXVI, 130.
   goods recovered, sold by, CCXXXIII, 136.
   account of sale by, CCXXXIV, 137.
   proceeds of sale by, paid over, CCXXXV, 137.
Average, particular, claimed, CLVII, 100.
   recovered, CLVIII, 103.
   account of, required, CLXXV, 110; CLXXX, 112; CXCVII, 120; CC, 122.
   account received, CXC, 115.

Balance, draft for, CXLIV, 91.
   remitted, CLI, 95; CCCVIII, 181.
   direction to remit, CXCI, 116.
Ballast, coals ordered for, CX, 71.
Banker, payment to, LXXVI, 58.
Bill of exchange drawn, LV, 47; LXV, 51.
   remitted, LXXIV, 57.
   firsts for acceptance, *ib.*
   enclosed, LXXV, 57.
   receipt of, LXXX, 59; CXXIV, 81.
   returned, with protest, CXLIX, 94.
   advice of, CLIV, 97; CXCV, 119; CXCIX, 122.
   drawn on account, CLVII, 99.
   enclosed, CLVIII, 101.
   dishonored, CCII, 123; CCIII, 124; CCXCIV, 174.
   costs on, CCVI, 124; CCVIII, 125.
   remitted, CCIX, 126.
Bill of lading, inclosed, LIV, 47; LV, 47; CXVII, 75; CXIX, 77; CXXVII, 82; CXXXIII, 85; CLIII, 97; CCLXIV, 159; CCCV, 179; CCCIX, 182.
   to be made over, CLIII, 97.
   to order, CCVII, 125.
   omission in, CCLXXXIV, 168.
   received, CCCVI, 180.
Bottomry, captain not able to raise money on, CLXVII, 107.
   captain to be called on to sign bond, CLXXX, 111.

Bottomry, captain to be directed to raise money on, CCXCVII, 175.
Broker's remarks enclosed, CCCVII, 181.
Bullion, accumulation of, CXCV, 119; CCXCIX, 176.
Buying, see *Orders*.

Cabinet ware, sales of, CCLXXXIV, 168.
Captain, instructions to, CXV, 74; CCXIII, 128.
    introduction of, CXXXIII, 85.
    complained against, CLXXVI, 111; CLXXXI, 112; CLXXXIII, 113.
    goods to be demanded of, CLXXVII, 111
    refuses to give up cargo, CLXXXV, 114.
    threatened with legal proceedings, CLXXXVI, 114; CLXXXVII, 114.
    to accomodate passenger, CCXIII, 129.
Cargo, condition of, CXX, 77; CXXII, 97.
    disposed of, CLVII, 99.
    landed for repair of ship, CLXVIII, 107.
    part of, to be sold to defray charges, *ib.*
    day of sale of, fixed, CLXIX, 108.
    landed a second time, CLXXVIII, 111.
    delivery of, insisted on, CLXXXII, 113.
    reshipped, CLXXXVIII, 115.
    seized by customs, and recovered, CCXXXII, 136.
Cash payment for wines, with discount, proposed, CCLXIV, 158.
Catalogues enclosed, CCCVII, 180
    Charter of vessel not completed, CXI, 72.
    terms of, CXII, 73.
    claim for loss admitted, CCLXXI, 162.
Coals ordered for ballast, CX, 71.
    drawback on, CXXI, 78; CXXII, 79.
    order for cargo of, CCX, 126; CCXXII, 132.
Commission proposed on sale of wine, LXII, 51.
        on specie, *ib.*
        on insurances, *ib.*
        on orders, CCLXXXVI, 169.
    payment of, *ib.*
    agreement for division of, CCLIV, 154; CCLV, 154; CCLVI, 155.
Consignee, invoice and bill of lading inclosed to, LVII, 48.
    complaint against, CXXXIX, 88.
    vindicated, CXL, 89.
    answer of, to complaint, CXLII; 90.
Consignment of cotton, XLIX, 44; LI, 45.
    of porter, CXIII, 73.
    of specie, *ib.*
    of wine, see *Wine.*
    of hemp, see *Hemp.*
    of quills, CCXLIX, 151.

ANALYTICAL INDEX. 11

Consignement stopped *in transitu*, on account of failure, CCLXXXI, 167.
 of sundries, CCCV, 179.
 of wool CCCVI, 179.
 of sperm oil, *ib.*
Convoy, sailing under advice of, LXIV, 53.
 arrival under, LXVIII, 53.
Copies of correspondence inclosed, CXII, 73; CLV, 98.
Copper, order for, CLIX, 104.
 time required to execute, CLX, 104.
 countermanded, CLXI, 105.
 countermanded too late, CLXII, 105.
 sunk in the lighter, CLXIII, 105.
 got up again and put in order, CLXIV, 106.
Cork, sale of, CCLXIX, 161.
Costs on dishonored bill recovered, CCVIII, 125; CCIX, 126.
Cotton, orders to purchase, XLIX, 44; LI, 45.
 purchased, LIII, 46.
 account-sales of inclosed, LX, 49.
Countermand, see *Orders.*
Credit, letter of, requested, XCVI, 65.
 given, XCVII, 66.
 receipt of, acknowledged, XCVIII, 67.
Cruizers, danger from, LXIX, 54.

Damage of cargo advised, CXX, 77.
Damaged goods condemned, CCXVIII, 130.
Del credere, charge for, LXII, 51; CCLXXVII, 165.
 not to be divided, LXXX, 60.
Departure of ship advised, CLXXXIX, 115; CCCV, 179; CCCVI, 179.
Disbursement on account of ship, CLVIII, 104; CCLXIX, 161.
Dividends received, CCXC, 172.
Draft received, CCCVI, 179.
 enclosed, *ib.*
 protested, *ib.*
 passed to credit of drawing account, *ib.*
 see *Bills of Exchange.*
Dues, town, shippers object to pay, CCLXI, 157.
 objection to pay removed, CCLXII, 158.
Duties at Galatz, CCXLI, 141.

Elephant's teeth, account-sales of, CCXCI, 172.
Exchanges, proposal to speculate in, LXII, 51.
 speculation in, postponed, LXIII, 51.
 terms of speculation in proposed, CXLVII, 93.
 remittance of bills in, CXLVIII, 94; CXCI, 116; CXCIII, 117; CXCVI, 120.

Exchanges, bills sold, CXCIV, 118.
    remittance received, CXCV, 119.
    advice of state of, CCLXIV, 158; CCLXV, 159; CCLXX, 132.
    Lloyd's list, observations on, CCLXXXV, 168.
    advice of endorsement on bills, *ib*.

Failure, advice of, CCLXXXI, 167.
    consignment stopped *in transitu*, in consequence of, *ib*.
Fee for attendance at sale, CLXXVIII, 111.
Freight, payment of, CXXI, 78.
    difficulty of obtaining, CLVII, 99.
    shippers object to pay town dues on, CCLXI, 157.
    procured, CCLXIV, 158.
Fruit, consignment of, CCXCV, 174.

Galatz, peculiarities of trade at, CCXLI, 144.
    charges, *ib*.
    weights, *ib*.
    measures, *ib*.
    assurance, *ib*.
Gauge, short, and deficiency, CCLXXXVIII, 170.
Guarantee of underwriters, CCLXXXVII, 170.

Hare skins, order for, LXVIII, 53.
Hemp, consignment of, CCLI, 152.
                order for, CLII, 95.

Insurances, commission on, LXII, 51.
    orders for, LXIV, 52; LXX, 54; XCIX, 67.
    advised, LXV, 52. LXVII, 53; LXXI, 55; C, 67.
    particulars inclosed, CI, 67.
    value declared on policy, CII, 68.
    account of, transmitted, *ib*.
    policy transmitted, CIX, 70.
    orders for, CXVI, 75; CXXII, 79.
    charges for, CXVII, 75.
    effected, CXII, 73; CXXIV, 81; CXXXV, 86; CCLXVIII, 160; CCCVI, 179.
    account of, CLXVI, 106.
    on specie, CXCII, 117.
    out and home, CCLX, 156.
    cannot be effected at limits, CCLXVII, 160.
    provisional, on ship or ships, CCLXXVI, 164.
    authority to underwrite policy, CCXCII, 173.
Investment in stock ordered, XCII, 64.
    in produce ordered, CLVI, 98; CXCI, 116.

ANALYTICAL INDEX.

Invoice inclosed, LV, 47; LVII, 48; CXIX, 77; CXXVII, 82; CLIII, 97; CLVII, 99; CCCV, 179; CCCVI, 179; CCCIX, 182.
    pro forma, inclosed, CXXV, 81.
    to be made over, CLIII, 97.
    inclosed, CLVIII, 101.
    Irregularity complained of, CV, 69.
    explained, CVIII, 70.
      see *Advice*.
Interest, short, CXCVIII, 121.

Limits of price, XLIX, 44.
    too low, L, 45; LXXXVI, 62; CLXXIV, 110.
    for purchase, LXXXII, 60; CLVII, 99; CCXXX, 134.
    reduced, CLXXIII, 109.
    for freight too low, CCLXXXIX, 170.
Loss anticipated, CXLV, 91.
    of ship, CXCVIII, 121; CCLXX, 162.
    recovered, CXXIX, 121; CLXII, 105.
    settlement of, CC, 122.
    claimed of the assurers, CCLXX, 162.
    claim for, admitted, CCLXXI, 162.

Markets, state of, LVIII, 48; CXXIX, 83; CLII, 95; CLVII, 99; CCXXIV, 132; CCXXXV, 137; CCXXXVII, 138; CCXLI, 144; CCLII, 14; CCXLVIII, 150; CCLXXIV, 163; CCCV, 179; CCCVI, 179; CCCVII, 180.
Memorial to Board of Customs, CCCI, 176.
        to Treasury, CCCII, 177.
            answer to, CCCIII, 178.
Misunderstanding of order, CLVII, 99.

Negligence complained of. CCXLIX, 151.
Non-payment of acceptance, notice of, XCIII, 65.
        threat of legal proceedings, XCIV, 65.
        draft taken up, CXV, 74.
Non-receipt of goods and letters, CCXLIII, 148.
    explanation in consequence of, satisfactory, CCXLIV, 149.
Notary not resident near, CCCLVI, 149.
    indispensable, CCXLVII, 150.

Oranges, proposal to consign, CX, 71.
Orchilla weed, prices of, CCXCI, 172.
Orders for Cotton, XLIX, 44; LI, 45.
    for insurance, LXIV, 52; LXVI, 53; LXX, 64.
    for hare skins, LCVIII, 53.
    to procure a return of premium, LXIV, 52.

Orders for tobacco, LXXXI, 60.
    for investment of stock, XCII, 64.
    for insurance, XCIX, 67; CXXII, 79.
    for sundries, CXXIII, 80.
    for copper. CLIX, 104.
    time required to execute, CLX, 104.
    countermanded, CLXI, 105; CCXI, 127; CCLIII, 153.
    countermanded too late, CLXII, 105.
    to re-purchase part of cargo sold for repair of ship, CLXXI, 109.
    for cargo of coals, CCX, 126; CCXII, 127.
    for empty bottles, *ib.*
    for coals countermanded, CCXI, 127.
    for manufactured goods, CCXXIII, 132; CCXXV, 133.
    for sugar on joint account, CCXXX, 134.
        confirmed, CCXXXI, 135.
    for sundries. CCL, 152.
    for hemp, CCLI, 152.
        countermanded, CCLII, 153.
        advice of, CCLIII, 153.
    for molasses and coffee, CCLXXXII, 167.
    not yet completed, CCCVI, 179.

Partnership, dissolution of, noticed, LII, 45; LXII, 56.
    accounts, balance of, remitted, LXVII, 53.
Payment to banker advised, LXXVI, 58.
    of quarterly pension, CCXXVI, 133; CCXXIX, 134.
    guaranteed, CCXXXI, 135.
    see *Remittance.*
Pension, quarterly, application for payment of, CCXXVI, 133.
    certificates, etc. required to receive, CCXXVII, 133.
        not obtained CCXXVIII, 134.
        must be obtained in future, CCXXIX, 134.
Plague, report of, CCLXXXIV, 168.
Plunderage, deduction for, CCLXIX, 161.
Porter, consignment of, CXIII, 73.
Power of attorney inclosed, CLXXXIV, 113.
    goods claimed under, CCXXXVI, 138; CCXXXIX, 140.
Policy of insurance, refusal to deliver up, CC, 122.
    legal opinion thereon, *ib.*
    surrender of, insisted on. CCI, 123.
Premium, order to procure return of, LXIV, 52.
    return, recovered, LXIX, 54.
    return of, for convoy, CXCVIII, 121; CCLXXXIX, 170.
Presentation of draft advised, CVI, 70.
Price, limits of, XLIX, 44.
    quotations of, CCXXIV, 132; CCXXXIX, 140.

ANALYTICAL INDEX.

Price current inclosed, L, **45**; LVIII. **48**.
Primage and pierage on wines, CVLXX, **162**.
Proceeds, instructions concerning, CXXVII, **82**; CLII, **95**; CLVI, **98**.
    debited to account, CLVII, **99**.
    credited to account, ib.; CCCVI, **179**.
    of sale required, CCXV, **129**.
    will be shortly paid, CCXV, **120**.
    not payable till delivery of goods, CCXVII, **130**.
    of sale by auction, paid over, CCXXXV, **137**; CCCVIII, **181**.
Produce, investment in, ordered, CLVI, **98**.
Protest for non-acceptance of bill transmitted, CCIV, **124**; CCV, **124**;
    CCXVIII, **130**; CCCVI, **179**.
    costs on, CCVI, **124**.
Purchase, see *Orders*.

Quills, consignment of, CCXLIX, **151**.

Recommendation, letter of, CCCIV, **178**.
Relinquishment of speculation in tobacco, LXXXVII, **63**.
Remittance, acknowledged, LXI, **50**; LXXIX, **59**.
    proposal to effect, LXXII, **55**.
    acceptance of proposal to effect, LXXIII, **56**.
    in part, LXXIV, **57**.
    of balance of partnership accounts, LXXVII, **58**.
        expenses on, LXXVIII, **59**; CCCVIII, **181**.
    acknowledged, LXXX, **59**; CXXIV, **81**; CXXXVIII, **88**.
    in specie, XCI, **64**.
    per appoint, and in bills, CXLIV, **91**.
    in produce, CCXXXVIII, **139**.
        bills, CCXLIII, **148**.
        cash, CCL, **152**.
        bullion, CCLXXXIX, **170**.
        deducted, CCCVIII, **181**.

Sale of manufactured goods, CCXL, **140**.
Sales of consignment to be urged, CXXXII, **84**.
    concluded, CCCVIII, **81**.
Security, insurance offered as collateral, XCVI, **65**.
    for non-accepted bill required, CCXVIII, **130**.
        given, CCXIX, **131**.
        acknowledgment of, and engagement to return, CCXX,
        131.
        reasons for requiring, CCXXI, **131**.
Seizure of cargo by customs, CCXXXII, **136**.
Ship detained for repair, CLXVII, **102**.
    captain of, attempting to raise money for repairs, CLXX, **103**.

ANALYTICAL INDEX.

Ship, no unnecessary delay shall take place, CLXXIX, 112.
    cargo of, to be demanded of captain, CLXXXII, 113.
        re-shipped, CLXXXVIII, 115.
    departure of, CLXXXIX, 115; CCCV, 179; CCCVI, 179.
    arrival of, CXC, 115.
    loss of. CXCVIII, 121; CCLXX, 162.
    detained on suspicion of slaves, CCXCIV, 173.
    expected, CCCV, 179.
Shipment, advice of, LIII, 46; LV, 47.
    particulars of, inclosed, CI, 67.
    instructions for, CX, 71.
    advice of, received, CLXV, 106.
    to be made in neutral vessel, CCXXX, 134.
    delayed, reasons for, CCLVIII, 156; CCLIX, 156.
    remarks on, CCIX, 126.
Specie, commission on, LXII,.50.
    consignment of, CXIII, 73.
    insurance on, CXCII, 117.
    terms of sale of, ib.
Specification of goods, CCXXXIII, 136; CCXCVII, 175.
Speculation in tobacco relinquished, LXXXVII, 63.
Stipulation of terms for proposed adventure, XCVI, 65.
Stocks, investment in, XCII, 64.

Time extended for execution of order, XC, 64.
Tobacco, orders for, LXXXI, 60.
    joint speculation in, ib.

Wine, advice of sale of, CXXI, 78.
    shipments of proposed, LXII, 50.
    consignment of, CXXII, 79; CXXIII, 80; CXXV, 81; CXXVI, 82.
    CCLVII, 155.
    unsaleable at quoted prices, CXXX, 84.
    not suited to market, CXXXIV, 85.
    sale of, advised, CXXXVI, 86.
    account-sales of, CXXXVII, 87.
        not yet received, CCCVI, 179.
    re-shipment of, impracticable, CXLI, 89.
    sold by auction, CXLII, 90.
    old preferred to new, CCLXII, 158.
    state of vintage, CCLXIX, 161; CCLXXXIII, 167.
    selected and reserved, CCXCVI, 175.
Wool, consignment of, CCLXXIII, 153; CCLXXV, 154.
    prices of, CCLXXIV, 153; CCCV, 179.
    credit on, CCLXXVII, 165.
    public sale of, CCCV, 179; CCCVII, 180.

COMMERCIAL CORRESPONDENCE

ADVICE TO A PERSON COMMENCING BUSINESS (1).

I.

Mr. (2) Dormeuil, *Havre.*   *Lorent, 3 Jan. 18 —*

My dear Sir, — You ask my advice (3) on the intention you have of establishing yourself in business: and you desire to know what are the best means (4) of ensuring respectability and success in commercial life.

I will give you my sentiments on this subject: — First, aim at (5) acquiring all possible knowledge, and especially such as is connected with business; add to that, irreproachable conduct, which will gain for you both confidence and credit. Do not think of establishing yourself too early in life; for a young man has neither the experience nor the knowledge requisite for such an undertaking (6): nor yet defer (7) it till too advanced an age, when, no longer possessed of the zeal and courage necessary for business, one is led by apathy or dilatoriness to neglect the best opportunities, and when an excess of caution sometimes leads (8) to unforeseen ruin.

Do not commence in times critical or fatal to commerce; consult both political and public events; if there be war going on, watch its progress attentively, especially if it be a naval war.

Be careful (9) not to establish yourself before you possess funds adequate to conduct your affairs, to provide for your personal wants, and the maintenance of your establishment. Always keep some funds in reserve to meet unforeseen demands, such as dishonoured bills (10), etc.

Unless some very advantageous opportunity offer, do not enter into partnership (11); but rather labour and accumulate for yourself alone.

Let the arrangement of your books precede your operations: con-

---

(1) Affare, affari, carriera commerciale. (2) Mr., Signore, *pronunciasi* Mister. (3) Consiglio, consigli. (4) Mezzi. (5) Cercate di. (6) Impresa. (7) Differite, ritardate, rimettete. (8) Conduce (trascina) ad impreveduta. (9) Badate attentamente. (10) Cambiali. (11) Società.

Anderson.   2

tinue always to keep them, or have them kept (1) in the strictest order.

Above all, be studious to acquire a good epistolary style; the art of writing a good letter is very rare and highly valuable in every branch of trade (2), but especially in commerce.

Be prompt in replying (3) to all letters that you receive; it will shew attention to your correspondent's interests, and will gain you many commissions.

Connect yourself with respectable houses in all quarters; those of acknowledged probity, punctuality, and solidity, and whose business is analogous to your own: for such as (4) chiefly import wines, for instance (5), are not always well versed in manufactured goods or corn (6).

Be on your guard against all who are of equivocal character or doubtful stability: your credit will rise in proportion as it is remarked that all your transactions are with houses of unquestionable respectability.

Conduct yourself towards all persons on every occasion with civility, and in a wise and prudent manner; this will render you esteemed, and will prepare for you friendship and support in times of need and embarrassment.

Do not forget yourself in prosperity, be not puffed up (7) with your success; and never despise the unfortunate. Recollect that a reverse of fortune may reduce millions to nothing.

Be exact and punctual in fulfilling (8) your engagements to the utmost. As far as possible, buy and sell for cash (9), or at the shortest credit possible; by adopting this rule you will avoid the chance of being entangled (10) in complicated affairs, which frequently prove (11) ruinous.

Undertake nothing without reflection, but weigh deliberately all your measures: the rash (12) and inconsiderate prosper only by accident, and their prosperity is generally very short-lived.

Lead a regular life, and put a restraint (13) upon your expenditure: this will sustain your credit, and it is more easy to save than to gain.

If you find yourself embarrassed, or in a critical situation, your first step should be to ask advice; but make a judicious choice of your advisers; seek them first among those who have been similarly circumstanced, and then procure the opinion of some other person. From having neglected to ask advice, and from having

---

(1) Farli tenere. (2) Mercatura, affari, mestiere, arte. (3) Rispondere. (4) Coloro che. (5) Per esempio. (6) Grano, cereali. (7) Insuperbito. (8) Adempiere a. (9) Contante. (10) Impacciato, impigliato. (11) Riescono, divengono. (12) Temerari, sventati, sconsiderati. (13) Freno, ritegno.

had too much confidence in themselves, many merchants have been brought to ruin.

Be active, assiduous, honest, and upright (1): but do not imagine that your talents and your virtues will ensure success. No; but by so doing, you will, at all events, have the secret approbation of your own conscience, and the consolation of having acted in accordance with the dictates (2) of prudence and reason: so that whatever be the issue (3) of your affairs, you will enjoy the esteem of sensible (4) men and the approbation of Heaven. I am etc.

II.

Mr. Dormeuil, *Havre*.   *Lorent, 25th Jan. 18—*

I perceive, my dear friend, by your letter of the 20th inst. (5), that you are decided on entering upon the career of commerce. I congratulate you on your resolution. As for (6) myself, I will do all in my power to render our connexion both agreeable and useful.

I notice that you are studying exchanges (7). It is a very essential thing. The profit that a marchant may derive from the fluctuations of exchange is an affair of attention and calculation. The value of moneys known, the par (8) of exchange, and its actual course given, the merchant perceives in a moment on what place it is most advantageous for him to remit or to draw (9), or on what place it is most convenient for him to give orders to be drawn upon (10). But it is not enough to know these combinations; another point essentially necessary is to be able to distinguish good bills (11) from bad or doubtful paper. This is a very difficult and delicate matter; for the greater portion of these bills do not represent funds actually (12) existing, but a constant use of credit; and a bill of exchange, although accepted and indorsed (13), does not always deserve full confidence, because the acceptor relying (14) upon the appearance of solidity in the drawer (15), may have accepted beyond (16) his means: thus, my friend, the merchant ought to endeavour to become acquainted with all good commercial houses, both of his own town and of foreign countries.

It will be no less useful to him in order to judge of the quality of bills, to know the branch of trade in which each house is engaged. He ought to know as much as possible what houses are interested in failures (17); for although a firm (18) be in good credit,

---

(1) Giusto, schietto, probo. (2). Dettami. (3) Esito, riuscita. (4) Assennati, di senno. (5) Inst., *abbreviatura di* instant, corrente. (6) In quanto a. (7) I cambj, il cambio. (8) Il pari. (9) Il rimettere o il tirare. (10) Dar ordini per far tratte. (11) Cambiali. (12) Effettivamente, in effetto. (13) Girata. (14) L'accettante fidandosi. (15) Tiratore, traente. (16) Oltre. (17) Fallimenti, bancarotte. (18) Ditta.

It ought not to enjoy the same confidence if it have sustained losses that may absorb its apparent capital; and its bills may be only a resource to sustain its credit or to support ruinous speculations. A merchant who has been careful to gain this information, refuses to negociate these bills; but he ought not allow (1) anybody to penetrate the motives of his refusal.

One must distinguish, among bills of exchange, those which are drawn or accepted by bankers, from those which are drawn or accepted by merchants not transacting bank-business. Those of a banker have only two objects — the profit of a commission, or the profit of exchange; for the business of banking consists in these two operations. Those of a merchant, who does not transact bank-business, have no object (2) but to make a payment, the profit of exchange, and commission being only mixed up with it as accessories, and as a natural consequence of the operation. In paying more particular attention to this, you will perceive in it the foundation of confidence.

A prudent banker draws no bills except to his own advantage, with the exchange always in his favor; and accepts for no firms not reputed solid, and still to his own advantage. He, then, who draws at a disadvantageous rate (3) of exchange—who, seduced by the attraction of a commission, or bound (4) by previous acceptances which have left him without funds, continues to accept for a house which transacts forced operations, renders his signature suspected; for a merchant never draws at a disadvantageous rate of exchange, unless forced to do so by the necessity for raising (5) money, and by distress (6). This dangerous operation is known by the bills that the banker draws upon the same house, or upon another by direction, for his reimbursement. If in this case we examine this firm with a little attention, we shall find it embarrassed; for rumours of this state of things always transpire, and the third party who puts his name to the return drafts (7) is invariably unstable, or concerned in the embarrassment of the first house; and the reputation of a banker, who has been sufficiently imprudent to lend his signature (8), is seriously compromised. The merchant who perceives this dangerous character in bills presented to him, ought to refuse them, as much from the risk of loss as for his own tranquillity. However, this remark must not be regarded as a general rule (9), and as applicable to all places without exception; for bankers, after having satisfied themselves as to the solidity of a house, often give them credit without regarding the rate

---

(1) Permettere. (2) Obbietto, mira, scopo. (3) Rata, ragione, prezzo, tariffa. (4) Legato, obbligato, limitato, stretto, incagliato, impedito. (5) Levare, riscuotere, trovare. (6) Angustia, scarsezza del numerario. (7) Tratte rimandate, cambiali mandate indietro. (8) Prestare la sua firma. (9) Regola.

of exchange. This is what we call a *blank credit* (1); and the use of this credit may prove necessary to a house in commercial operations, where the profits are far greater than the expense of bills and the loss on the exchanges. In that case the reputation of the merchant, the extent and stability of his business, and the prudence of the banker, ensure the credit of these bills of exchange, and form the basis of public confidence.

With regard to bills of exchange, drawn or accepted by merchants who do a commission business, little attention need be given to the advantage or disadvantage of exchange. As regards bills of exchange accepted by a merchant who sells by commission for the account of the drawer, he is considered to have funds in hand, and these bills are deemed first-rate (2). It matters little (3) if the drawer, proprietor of the goods or the funds which are in the hands of the acceptor, should have been drawn at a disadvantageous rate of exchange, on account (4) of some urgent necessity, if it be for real funds and the acceptor solid.

The bills of a merchant, drawn for his reimbursement upon a house that has given him orders, are also doubly safe, from the solidity of the merchant who draws the bills, and the funds which actually are in the hands of the individual on whom the bills are drawn. But it is rarely that a merchant, who has given orders for goods, makes a reimbursement otherwise than to his own advantage; because he has at home the means of remitting advantageously, or at least at par. If it happen otherwise, either the merchant is straitoned (5), or he acts imprudently. But, in both instances (6), the solidity of the commission merchant who has drawn the bills is the first point for consideration.

The drafts and acceptances (7) of a merchant, given in payment of goods, are of an inferior order, but still generally enjoy good credit; because we see a reason for them in the purchase (8) of the goods, which with an honest merchant is a guarantee of his solvency.

The result of these observations, my friend, is, that a merchant ought to have always at hand a note of the most recent variations in the exchanges, in order to see if the bills, which are presented to him, have been drawn at an advantageous or disadvantageous rate of exchange, or at par.

Nevertheless (9), when in doubt concerning the solvency of the drawer (10), the acceptor, or the first endorser (11), a single good endorsement (12) suffices to remove the apprehension, or even to establish

---

(1) Credito allo scoperto. (2) Stimate eccellenti. (3) Poco importa. (4) A cagione. (5) Nell' imbarazzo, incagliato, impigliato, alle strette. (6) Casi. (7) Tratte e le accettazioni. (8) Compra, acquisto. (9) Nulladimeno, tuttavia, pure. (10) Traente. (11) Giratario. (12) Girata.

confidence. Further (1), we must notice (2), in selecting bills of exchange, if they are conformable, by the date at which they are made due (3), to the custom of the place from whence they are drawn. There are few places from which merchants draw at more than two or three months' date: in this case bills at longer terms do not deserve confidence, unless there exist other reasons for deeming them good.

No doubt, my friend, you will find this letter very long: but I consider it very short for the interesting subject of which it treats. I am, etc.

CIRCULARS.

III.

Messrs. (4) Bell & Co. *Broad-st.* *   London, 1st Jan. 18—

GENTLEMEN. — We beg to acquaint you (5) that we have opened a house of general agency at the Mauritius, under the firm (6) of Young, Forbes & Co. (7); the two senior members of which have been some years established at Port Louis in the same line (8), under the firm of Young & Forbes.

It is our intention to confine ourselves to commission business; and we venture to solicit your countenance (9), assuring you that the strictest attention shall be paid to the management of any affairs which you may think proper to intrust (10) to our care.

We hope it will justify our confidence in addressing you, that we are enabled to refer (11) to the annexed list of commercial friends, comprising houses of the first eminence both in Europe and India, on whose consideration and support we have the advantage of being permitted to rely.

The signature (12) of the only member at present in England is subjoined (13); those of the resident partners (14) will be given in a circular from the Isle of France.   We are, etc.

(Mr. E. Tatham will sign)   YOUNG, FORBES & CO.

---

(1) In oltre. (2) Osservare, badare, rimarcare. (3) Scadere, scadenze. (4) Messrs., *abbrev. di* Messieurs, Signori, i Signori. (5) Ci pregiamo di farvi avvertito. (6) Ditta. (7) Co. *abbrev. di* Company, Compagnia, Socj. (8) Linea, genere. (9) (Volto, viso), buon viso, favore, protezione. (10) Affidare. (11) To refer, riferirci, rimetterceue. (12) Firma. (13) In calce, qui sotto. (14) Socj.

* In all letters of business, it is the practice to write the name and address on the first page; because if the superscription were torn off, or the cover in which the letter was enclosed were lost, it would not appear to whom it had been written. Merchants, bankers, lawyers, etc., usually place the name and address at the top of the page; but in official letters, they are more frequently written at foot. By some persons the latter mode is considered more respectful.

IV.

B. Bassett, Esq. (1) *London.* Calcutta, 10th July, 18—

Sir, — It is with deep regret that we have to apprize you of the death of our Prior*, Mr. John Allsop, which occurred at Cheltenham in December last.

At the same time we have the satisfaction of stating (2) that this melancholy event will in no way interfere with (3) the future conduct of our business, arrangements being now in progress for supplying the place of our deceased partner, which afford (4) us every reason to hope that we shall form a connexion with a London house of the first respectability, on whom the active management of our concerns in that city will devolve.

For the present, no alteration will be made in our firm.

The surviving partner, Mr. James M'Intosh, will conduct the affairs of the house in this presidency, as hitherto (5); and we confidently hope, from the experience you have had of our uniform punctuality and regularity, that you will continue to favor us with your correspondence, resting assured that the same unremitting attention will be paid to the interests of all our commercial friends as heretofore (6). We remain, etc. ALLSOP & M'INTOSH.

V.

B. Bassett, Esq. *London.* Calcutta, Jan. 1st, 18—

Sir, — Referring to our circular of the 10th July last, addressed to you on the demise (7) of Mr. John Allsop, senior partner in our late firm of Allsop & M'Intosh, we have now the pleasure of intimating that articles of copartnership (8), commencing this day, have been entered into between Mr. James M'Intosh, the surviving partner; Mr. John Stephens, of Jeffrey's Square, London, and Mr. Alfred Bowring, a gentleman who has been for many years our confidential clerk (9). Accordingly, the business of the house will henceforth be conducted under the firm of M'Intosh, Stephens & Co. We trust this arrangement will not only meet your approbation, but also ensure your entire confidence.

---

(1) Esq. *abbreviatura di* Esquire, scudiere; *titolo medio tra* Knight, *cavaliere e* Mr. *signore; adoperasi scrivendo (non parlando) ai ricchi possidenti, a' primarj negozianti ed agli esercenti le arti liberali.* (2) *Of stating,* di dire, annunziare, esporre. (3) Non cangerà per nulla. (4) Ci porgono, ci danno. (5) Come per lo passato. (6) Per lo addietro, finora. (7) Trapasso, morte. (8) Società, compartecipazione. (9) Commesso, ragioniere, giovine di studio.

* The terms « PRIOR » « SENIOR » « PRINCIPAL » and « CHIEF » are used indiscriminately to designate the head partner of a Commercial House; the first of these is, however, most in favor at the present moment.

In the name of the old firm, we tender (1) you our best thanks for your past favour and support; and, on behalf of (2) our present establishment, we beg to assure you that our earnest endeavours (3) shall be used, on all occasions, to promote the interests of our constituents, by a faithful execution of their commissions.

Requesting your attention to the signature of the two resident partners, we subscribe ourselves, respectfully, your obedient servants,

          M'INTOSH, STEPHENS & Co.
Mr. M'Intosh will sign,   *M'Intosh, Stephens & Co.*
Mr. Bowring will sign,   M'INTOSH, STEPHENS & Co.

VI.

James Farr, Esq. *Mincing Lane.*   *Mark Lane, July 18th, 18—*

Sir, — I beg to (4) inform you that, under the auspices of the highly respectable house of Messrs. Burtwell Brothers, in whose service I spent thirteen years, I have commenced business as a broker (5) for colonial produce.

In soliciting the favour of your countenance and support, I beg leave to assure you that no exertion (6), no assiduity or attention shall be wanting on my part to justify the good opinion of my abovementioned friends, and to give complete satisfaction to those houses who may entrust me with (7) their orders. I have the honour to be, Gentlemen, your most obedient servant,   CHARLES HOPPE.

VII.

J. Jones, Esq. *London.*   *Pernambuco, June 1st, 18—*

Sir, — We take leave to inform you that, under the auspices of our friends, Messrs. Dawson, Coverdale & Co., of London, we have formed a partnership, and established a house of general agency in this city, under the firm of Sharp and Reynolds.

Our Mr. Sharp having resided in various parts of South America for the last eleven years, and our Mr. Reynolds having spent a great part of his life in Oporto, Lisbon, and other towns of Portugal, we feel confident that our experience and local knowledge will enable us to give you entire satisfaction whenever you may require our services.

We shall make arrangements for keeping ourselves regularly advised of the state of the markets at Bahia and Rio de Janeiro, with the view (8) of availing ourselves (9) of any advantage that they

---

(1) Offriamo, umiliamo. (2) In favore di. (3) Premurosi sforzi. (4) Mi pregio di. (5) Sensale. (6) Sforzo. (7) Mi affideranno. (8) Vista, scopo, intento. (9) Valerci, approfittarci.

may present in forwarding (1) cargoes by vessels directed to call (2) here for orders; and, in such cases, it shall be our constant aim to further (3) the interests of our friends to the best of our ability.

We beg to subjoin references (4), and to assure you of our zeal and attention, if favoured with your correspondence.

We are, etc.,   SHARP & REYNOLDS.
Mr. James Sharp will sign,   *Sharp & Reynolds.*
Mr. John Reynolds will sign,   SHARP & REYNOLDS.

VIII.

R. Smith, Esq. *Liverpool.*   *London, 15th April,* 18—

Sir, — The term of our copartnership with Messrs. Malhiot, Collet and Co., of Oporto, and of Rio de Janeiro, having expired on the 31st December last, it was decided, by consent of all the parties concerned, that the same should not be renewed. Accordingly, both the above houses ceased to exist from that date: and we take the liberty of intimating to you, that we have no interest whatever in the new establishments formed by the respective partners.

The liquidation of the concerns (5) of the Oporto house is intrusted to Mr. James Collet of that city, now trading (6) under the firm of Collet and Larue; while Mr. Langford will undertake (7) the adjustment of the affairs of the house at Rio, and will, for that purpose (8) only, sign *Malhiot, Collet, and Co. in liquidation.*

Our worthy friend and relative (9), Mr. John Langford, continues the business of the Rio house for his sole account, as his circular will have informed you: and we avail ourselves of the present opportunity to recommend his establishment to the patronage of our friends, soliciting, in his behalf (10), a continuance of their confidence and commands. We are, etc.,   LANGFORD & KNAPP.

IX.

J. Peel, Esq. *London.*   *Adra, 1st January,* 18—

Sir, — We have the honor to inform you that we have agreed to unite the two mercantile establishments which have hitherto existed in this city, under the firms of Copinl & Co., and Romecin & Co.

The new firm, which is intrusted with the liquidation of the affairs of both houses, will be styled (11) Copinl, Romecin, & Co.

The capital of both establishments being united, the new firm

---

(1) Spedire, mandare, avanzare. (2) Passare, approdare. (3) Promuovere, vantaggiare. (4) Attestati, commendatizie, indirizzi. (5) Affari. (6) Che negozia, trafficante. (7) Intraprenderà, s'incaricherà di. (8) Scopo, oggetto. (9) Parente, congiunto. (10) Favore. (11) Denominata, chiamata.

will devote its attention principally to commission business, in which the shipping of lead (1) will form an important feature (2); and we assure those friends who may favor us with their orders, that they will have every reason to be satisfied with our zeal, and the faithful discharge of all commissions intrusted to us.

We hope you will grant (3) to the new firm that confidence and preference with which you favored our former establishments; and referring you to our signature at foot, we remain, &.

COPINI, ROMECIN & CO.

X.

John Lamb, Esq. *London.*   *Brussels, May* 10, 18 —

Sir, — Having removed from Boulogne, and established myself in this city, as an English attorney, solicitor, and general agent, I beg leave to tender you my services in either capacity.

Any business which you may have in this city, or at any place within (4) a moderate distance, whether (5) of a professional nature or otherwise, and for the sake of which it may not be worth your while (6) to incur the expense of a journey expressly, I shall be happy to transact (7) as agent; and I beg to assure you that it shall be my endeavour to act with promptitude and efficacy, as well as with a due regard to economy, in all matters intrusted to my care. I have the honor, etc.,   ROBERT ADAIR.

XI.

T. Brook, Esq. *London.*   *Singapore, November,* 18 —

Sir, — It is with the most sincere regret that I have to communicate to you the melancholy intelligence of the death of Mr. Papineau, an event which has deprived the commercial community of this island of one of its most useful and distinguished members, and myself of a most amiable and attached friend.

As managing partner of the house, and executor of my lamented friend, (conjointly with Mr. Edward Forsyth and Mr. James Ewens), the charge (8) of liquidating the affairs of the firm devolves upon me, and I shall, consequently, henceforth sign ·Papineau & Co. in liquidation, · of which be pleased to take notice.

The business of the house will be carried on as heretofore, and my best care and attention shall be given to any affairs with which you may intrust me.

---

(1) Lo spedire piombo (per mare). (2) (Tratto), parte, ramo. (3) Accordare, concedere. (4) Entro. (5) Che sia. (6) Non sia presso dell' opera. (7) Aggiustare, negoziare. (8) Carico, dovere.

The esteem and friendship of my late deeply lamented partner, and the experience of nearly twenty years devoted to commercial pursuits (1), are, I trust, sufficient claims to a continuance of that confidence with which you have hitherto honored our establishment, and which it will be my earnest endeavour to merit at your hands.

I remain, etc., G. SWIFT.

XII.

W. Pell. Esq. *London.* *Bristol, 1st Dec.*, 18 —

Sir, — I beg to acquaint you, that in consequence of my having taken into partnership my nephew, Charles Harrison, the business of my establishment will henceforward be conducted under the firm of T. Harrison and Nephew. Please to note our respective signatures at foot.

Returning you my sincere acknowledgments for the proofs of confidence with which you have favored me during so many years, and which I trust will be continued to our new firm,

I remain, etc. T. HARRISON.
T. Harrison will sign, *T. Harrison & Nephew.*
C. Harrison will sign, T. HARRISON & NEPHEW.

XIII.

Messrs. James Grey & Co. *Liverpool.* *London, 11th August,* 18 —

Gentlemen, — Having formed an establishment in this city, as merchants and general agents, we take the liberty of acquainting you therewith, and solicit the preference of your orders. From our experience in mercantile affairs generally, and our intimate acquaintance with business as conducted in this metropolis in particular, we venture to promise that we shall be enabled to execute any commission with which you may favor us, to your satisfaction, and in the most prompt and economical manner. At least we can safely guarantee, that neither zeal nor attention shall be wanting on our parts, to ensure to our friends every advantage that our markets may afford (2); nor will there, we trust, be any deficiency of ability to fulfil their instructions, and promote their interest.

Possessed of ample funds, not only for the service of our friends, but also for carrying on an extensive export and import trade on our own account, we shall be glad to avail ourselves (3) of any advantage that your market for colonial produce and British products or manufactures may, from time to time, present, by making you consignments. We shall, therefore, thank you to keep us constant-

---

(1) Occupazioni, affari. (2) Offrire, porgere. (3) Approfittare, giovarci.

ly advised of the state of your markets; and as we shall be ready (1) to make advances to the extent (2) of two thirds of the invoice amount (3) of goods consigned to us for sale, on receipt of invoice, bill of lading (4) and orders for Insurance, we shall, on the other hand, expect the same Indulgence from our friends and correspondents.

We are extremely desirous of rendering our correspondence mutually advantageous, as the only means of placing it on a solid and permanent basis; and this, be assured, will be our constant aim.

Requesting your attention to our respective signatures at foot, we subscribe ourselves, with great truth, gentlemen, your faithful servants. HARRISON, WILSON & Co.

Signature of
Benj. Harrison, — *Harrison, Wilson & Co.*
Alex. Wilson, — Harrison, Wilson & Co.
Thos. March, — HARRISON, WILSON & Co.

XIV.

Mincing Lane, London, 11th August, 18 —
Thomas Adams, Esq. *Liverpool.*

Sir, — I take the liberty of apprising you that, under the auspices of several highly respectable and influential houses in this city, I have commenced business as a *Ship and insurance Broker and General Commercial Agent.*

Feeling confident of my ability to conduct any transactions, and to execute any orders committed to my charge in a speedy, economical, and satisfactory manner, I solicit the favor of your commands; to merit a continuance of which I assure you no exertion shall be spared to promote your interest and attain the accomplishment of your wishes.

Referring you to my bankers, *Messrs. Praed & Co.*, for the requisite information as to my stability and character, I have the honor to be, with much respect, Sir, your obedient humble servant,
PETER DUNSTERVILLE.

XV.

Charles Stuart, Esq. *London.* *New York, April 15, 18 —*

Sir, — I take the liberty of transmitting to you the annexed circular, with a respectful request, that, should it meet your concurrence, it may be affixed in your office for the information of whom it may concern; and I beg leave to proffer you my services, with

---

(1) Disposti, preparati, pronti. (2) Estensione, concorrenza. (3) Importare delle fatture. (4) Polizza di carico.

the assurance that whatever claims (1) etc., you may, at any time, be pleased to confide or recommend to my agency, shall be promptly and efficiently attended to. I have the honor to be, very respectfully, Sir, your obedient servant, HENRY BARTON.

Foreign claimants, creditors, assignees (2), heirs, devisees (3), legatees, or fundholders (4) in the American funds, having claims, debts, dues (5), demands, inheritances, or stocks (6), payable or recoverable in any of the states or territories of the United States, or the adjacent British dominions, requiring the intervention of legal proceedings, or otherwise, may have their business promptly and efficiently attended to, on transmitting to the undersigned (7) the suitable legal proofs, testimony, evidence, vouchers (8) or certificates thereof, as the case may be, together with the requisite power of attorney (9), authorising him to act in the premises; the whole properly authenticated under the official attestation of the American Minister, Consul, or Commercial Agent, nearest to the constituent's place of residence. The undersigned has efficient and responsible agents and correspondents in the principal cities and towns of the United States and British America: and he trusts his agency will offer peculiar advantages and facilities to those persons residing abroad (10), who have claims, debts, inheritances, stocks, or dividends, payable or recoverable therein (11).

The undersigned having visited Europe in the years 18 — and 18 — opened a correspondence whith distinguished legal gentlemen in some of the principal capitals thereof, which correspondence he is in progress of extending to all foreign ports and capitals, in commercial relations with the United States, is also prepared to transmit for settlement (12) all claims, etc. of the above description, in behalf of persons residing in the United States or British America, due, payable, or recoverable in any part of Europe, the West Indies or South America, when furnished with the proper proofs, etc. and power of attorney, similarly authenticated by such Foreign Minister, Consul, or Commercial Agent, as the case may require, in the United States. He has made arrangements to enforce (13) with promptitude, the settlement of all business that may be confided to his agency: and will communicate to his principals the earliest information relative to the progress and final adjustment of their concerns, and punctually make over (14) to them whatever sums he may recover in their behalf, either by the usual course of remittance, or in such other mode as they may indicate.

---

(1) Reclami, richiami, pretensioni, diritti. (2) Cessionarj, sostituti, agenti. (3) Eredi, legatarj. (4) Azionisti. (5) Somme dovute, pretensioni, reclami. (6) Fondi, azioni. (7) Sottoscritto. (8) Titoli, prove. (9) Procura. (10) Fuori del paese, all'estero. (11) In quelli. (12) Aggiustamento, liquidazione, saldo. (13) Sforzare, costringere, obbligare, imporre. (14) Rimettere.

In order to insure immediate attention, all applications to his agency, on business strictly professional, or requiring the intervention of legal proceedings, should be accompanied with an appropriate remittance, to defray the fees, expenses, or costs, attendant on such application or procedure; and all letters addressed, postage paid, to • Henry Barton, Counsellor at Law, New York. •

New York, May 12th., 18—   HENRY BARTON.

XVI.

Dowgate Hill, Upper Thames Street.
Wm. Curry., Esq. *Long Acre.*   June, 14—, 18—

Sir, — In announcing the opening of a *Wine, Spirit, and Beer Store* (1), on these premises (2), for the sale of these articles wholesale (3) and retail in casks (4) and bottles, I beg to acquaint you with my determination to select none but the choicest (5) and most approved qualities of the different descriptions of each; by which means I shall, at all times, have it in my power to ensure to my friends and customers (6) such articles as will, I trust, merit their approbation and obtain for me a continuance of their favors.

It is my intention, likewise, to keep a constant supply (7) of *bottled wines, porter, ale* (8) *and cider*, in readiness for exportation; the former direct from the docks (9), to ensure its being genuine as imported.

My terms and prices will be found fair (10) and moderate, being calculated to afford a competent remuneration to the seller, without subjecting the purchaser to imposition.

Relying, for encouragement, on the careful selection of my stock, and the strict attention which I shall uniformly give to the due execution of all orders with which you may be pleased to favor me, I look forward, with confidence, to receiving proofs of your approbation by a repetition of your commands: and I remain, very respectfully, your obedient humble servant,   THOS. WILSON.

P. S. On the other side, I wait upon you with (11) my prices current.

XVII.

Messrs. A. Young and Co. *Bristol.*   *London, 10th May, 18—*

Gentlemen, — It is with deep regret that we have to announce the demise of our respected partner, Mr. Thomas James, on the 8th instant.

---

(1) Magazzini all'ingrosso. (2) Locali, luoghi terreni. (3) All'ingrosso. (4) Barili. (5) Più scelti, più squisiti. (6) Avventori. (7) Assortimento, provvigione. (8) Birrone nero e bianco. (9) Porto, darsena, *docks.* (10) Giusti, equi, ragionevoli. (11) Di contro vi porgo (qui retro vi offro).

We, however, have, at the same time, the consolation of stating that this melancholy event will occasion no alteration in our firm, or diminution of our capital. The business of the house will be conducted as heretofore, and, we trust, with equal satisfaction to our friends, notwithstanding the severe loss we have sustained.

Soliciting a continuance of your valued correspondence, and of the confidence which we have hitherto had the advantage to enjoy, we remain, most truly, Sir, your faithful and obedient servants,

WM. HARRIS & CO.

XVIII.

Change Alley, 10th Sept. 18—

Wm. Cornish, Esq. *High Street, Borough* (1).

Sir, — Having taken the premises lately occupied by Mr. James Harris (deceased), and succeeded to the stationery business (2) carried on therein (3) by him for nearly twenty years, I beg to assure you that, anxious as I am to secure his connections and retain his customers, I shall make it my endeavour to follow, as nearly as possible, his punctuality, and that mode of conducting the business, by which he succeeded in establishing, and whereby (4) I hope to render permanent, this extensive concern.

To this end permit me to solicit the kind continuance of your support, which I shall ever seek by zeal, industry, and integrity, to deserve.

That my means are ample I can satisfactorily prove; and for any informations that you may desire to have on that or any other point regarding me, I beg to refer you to Messrs. Wilson and Wood, bankers, Lombard-street, or to my solicitors (5) Messrs. Newman & Co., Gray's Inn. I am respectfully, Sir, your obedient humble servant,

THOS. FRANCIS.

XIX.

London, 6th July, 18—

Messrs. W. Moon and T. Hooper, *Bristol.*

Gentlemen, — We beg to acquaint you that, in consequence of the lamented death of our late respected friend and partner Mr. James Edgecombe, an alteration will take place in our firm, from and after the 1st. October next.

Our means, however, will undergo no diminution, and our desire to continue our business on the same footing (6) as heretofore, remains unchanged.

---

(1) Borgo. (2) Cartoleria. (3) Esercitato in quelli. (4) Con cui, per mezzo del quale. (5) Procuratori. (6) Piede.

We shall, in due time (1) make you acquainted with our proposed arrangements; and in the interim, we entreat 2) that no interruption may be given to a correspondence which we have cultivated for so many years, and which we shall ever highly prize (3). Believe us to be, most sincerely, Gentlemen, your obliged and faithul servants.
ADAMS, EDGECOMBE & HARRIS.

XX.

London, 16th March, 1856.

Messrs. Young & Andrews, *Hull.*

Gentlemen, — In consequence of the demise (4) of my much valued friend and partner, Mr. Thomas Saunders, our firm of Saunders and Thompson has become virtually extinct, and the name will be continued only so long as may be necessary for the liquidation of its affairs.

I beg to apprize you, however, that I have formed a connection with Mr. John Harris, of this city, a gentleman whose abilities as a merchant, and resources as a capitalist, are well known to you. I cannot doubt that this arrangement will meet your approbation, and secure to our new establishment a full measure of that confidence which the old firm had so long the honor to enjoy; and to merit which, we shall use our most strenuous exertions (5). I remain always, Gentlemen, your obliged and faithful servant.

JAMES THOMPSON.

XXI.

London, 16th March, 18—

Messrs. Young & Andrews, *Hull.*

Gentlemen, — Referring you to the prefixed circular of our Mr. James Thompson, we beg leave to assure you that, in all matters which you may be pleased to intrust to our care, you will find the same attention to your interests, the same promptitude in executing your orders, and the same honourable and liberal conduct in all our dealings (6), as you experienced from the firm of Saunders and Thompson.

We request you to note our respective signatures as given at foot, remaining truly, Gentlemen, your obedient humble servants,

The signature of	THOMPSON & HARRIS.
James Thompson, —	*Thompson & Harris.*
John Harris, —	THOMPSON & HARRIS,
	P

---

(1) A suo tempo. (2) Chiediamo, preghiamo. (3) Pregiare, stimare, apprezzare. (4) Decesso, trapasso, morte. (5) Sforzi. (6) Affari.

XXII.

Joseph Bunfield, Esq. *Birmingham.*   London, 14th April, 18—

Sir, — Permit us to communicate to you an alteration that is to take place in our co-partnership on the 1st of May ensuing. At that period our Mr. John Custance will retire, and the business of the establishment thenceforward (1) will be carried on (2) by the remaining partners, under the firm of *Williams, Wilson & Wood.*

Requesting a continuance of your favor and support, and assuring you that there will neither be a diminution of our means, nor a relaxation in our endeavours to conduct the extensive affairs of the house on the usual scale, we subscribe ourselves, Sir, yours very faithfully,   Custance, Williams, Wood & Co.

XXIII.

Wm. Richards, Jun. Esq. *Glascow.*   London, 1st August, 18—

Sir, — Having determined on taking my son into partnership in the business of *Tea Dealer and Grocer* (3), which I have for so many years carried on in this city, I beg to introduce (4) him to you as my associate in the firm of T. Stephens and Son, requesting your attention to our signature subjoined.

I take this opportunity of soliciting a continuance of your custom (5) and favors; venturing to assert that you will find the same unremitting attention paid to your orders, which first secured to me the advantage of your encouragement and support. With much respect, I remain, Sir, your obliged and very humble servant,

           Thomas Stephens.

T. Stephens, sen. will sign, — *T. Stephens & Co.*
T. Stephens, jun. will sign, — T. Stephens & Co.

XXIV.

Richard Rusden. Esq. *Leeds.*   London, 17th May, 18—

Sir,— We beg to apprize you that, being desirous of rewarding (6) the faithful and valuable services of Mr. Hugh Tredwin, who has been our confidential clerk for many years past, we shall, from and after the 31st instant, admit him to a share in our business, altering our firm to *Wilcox, Strange & Co.*; and we request your attention, accordingly, to the signatures of the respective partners annexed.

Encouraging the hope that, under our new firm, we shall continue

---

(1) D'allora in poi, quindi innanzi. (2) Fatti, condotti. (3) Venditore (negoziante) di tè e drogbiere. (4) Presentare. (5) (Costume, consuetudine, usanza) abitudine di servirsi sempre dallo stesso bottegajo. (6) Ricompensare, rimunerare.

Anderson.

to receive proofs of your confidence and good-will, and with sincere thanks for the many past favors we have received at your hands, we remain, Sir, your very faithful servants,   WILCOX & STRANGE.

Signature of

Wm. Wilcox,	—	*Wilcox, Strange & Co.*
Robt. Strange,	—	Wilcox, Strange & Co.
Hugh Tredwin,	—	WILCOX, STRANGE & Co.

XXV.

John Tresidder, Esq. *Lisbon.*   London, 1st January, 18 —

Sir, — Desirous of establishing in the city of Rio de Janeiro a branch of my London house, I beg to acquaint you that I have committed the management of that department to Mr. John Newman, a gentleman on whose zeal, ability, and integrity I place the utmost reliance (1).

Mr. N., having been managing clerk in my counting house (2) here for several years, is perfectly conversant with every kind of commercial operation, and with all the routine of business.

I shall feel much obliged by any arrangements you may make with him, as he will visit your town prior to (3) his departure for Rio, for the purpose of forming connections; and I undertake to guarantee the due (4) execution of any orders with which you may be pleased to favor him, as he will be furnished with full powers to act in my name, and on my behalf.

Not doubting that you will find Mr. Newman as agreeable in social intercourse as he is intelligent in matters of business, I strongly recommend him to your kind attentions; and remain, very truly, Sir, your faithful servant,   WM. MOON.

XXVI.

John Tresidder, Esq. *Lisbon.*   London, 1st July, 18 —

Sir, — Referring you to my circular of 1st January, I now beg to hand (5) you that of the house of business which I then announced my intention of establishing at Rio de Janeiro.

I shall be greatly obliged by your extending to the new firm of Wm. Moon & Co., the confidence and preference which my establishment in this city has had the honor and advantage of enjoying for so long a period. It will scarcely be necessary to assure you that the same principles of probity and punctuality will regulate the new establishment, as, I trust, you have always recognised in your trad-

---

(1) Massima fiducia. (2) Studio, (ufficio). (3) Prima di. (4) Debito, dovuto, dovere. (5) Porgere, rimettere.

sactions with my London house. I have the honor to remain, Sir, your faithful and obedient servant. WM. MOON.

XXVII.

John Tresidder, Esq. *Lisbon.*   *Rio de Janeiro, 1st March, 18—*

Sir, — The circular addressed to you by our Mr. Moon, under date the 1st January, made you aware (1) of his intention of forming an establishment at this port, as a branch of his London house.

We have now the pleasure of announcing to you the fulfilment of that intention, under the firm of William Moon and Co., consisting of the subscribers, whose respective signatures you will be pleased to note.

With a tender (2) of our best services in this city, whether in the disposal of consignments of European and East Indian products; in the purchase and shipment (3) of the produce of this country; or in attending to your shipping interest; and assuring you that our earnest endeavours will be used to give you satisfaction in every matter intrusted to our care, we remain truly, Sir, your most obedient servants, WM. MOON & CO.

Signature of
Wm. Moon of *London* — *William Moon & Co.*
Geo. Mendez,) resident { — William Moon & Co.
John Newman,) partners, (— WILLIAM MOON & Co.

XXVIII.

John Lanyon, Esq. *Manchester.*   *London, 4th July, 18—*

Sir. — My commercial establishment at Amsterdam having ceased to exist on the 31st. December last, in consequence of my partnership with Mr. Joseph Smith, of that city, being dissolved by mutual consent, I beg to make known my intention to establish two mercantile houses in this country, one in London, and the other in Liverpool.

The partnership in this city will consist of my old and tried (4) friend, Mr. Richard Ellis, and myself, under the firm of Richardson and Ellis. The Liverpool house will comprise myself and my eldest Son, John Richardson, under the firm of Thomas Richardson & Son.

Herewith (5) you will receive the circular of each firm with the signatures of the respective partners, as also that of my second Son, William Richardson, who will sign by procuration for the London house, of which you will be pleased to take due note.

Adding my individual solicitations to those of my commercial establishments, I have the honor to be, Sir, your obedient humble servant,

THOMAS RICHARDSON.

---

(1) Avvertito, avvisato. (2) Offerta, profferta, esibizione. (3) Lo imbarcare, il caricare, lo spedire per mare. (4) Provato, sperimentato. (5) Unitamente a questa, qui annessa.

XXIX.

John Lanyon, Esq. *Manchester.*   *London, 4th July, 18—*

Sir, — We beg reference to the prefixed circular of our Mr. Thomas Richardson, announcing the establishment of our firm in this city.

We shall be proud (1) to be favored with your orders, in the execution of which we will neglect nothing that can contribute towards giving you entire satisfaction.

At foot you will find our respective signatures, to which we request your attention, as likewise to that of Mr. William Richardson (son of our principal), who has authority to sign for us by procuration. With great regard, we subscribe ourselves, Sir, your faithful, humble servants,   RICHARDSON & ELLIS.

Signature of
Thomas Richardson,   —   Richardson & Ellis.
Richard Ellis,   —   RICHARDSON & ELLIS.
William Richardson,   —   p. pro Richardson & Ellis.
                                                      William Richardson.

XXX.

John Lanyon, Esq. *Manchester.*   *Liverpool, 4th July, 18—*

Sir, — We take the liberty of informing you that we have this day commenced business here, in connection with the house of Richardson and Ellis of London.

Permit us, at the same time, to make you a tender of our services at this port, accompanied by an assurance that your interests will be attended to uniformly with the most conscientious zeal, and that our resources are such as to place it always in our power to afford you every facility.

Referring to our respective signatures subjoined, and in expectation of being shortly (2) favoured with your commands, we remain, Sir, your most obedient servants,   THOMAS RICHARDSON & SON.
Mr. T. Richardson will sign,   —   *T. Richardson & Son.*
Mr. J. Richardson will sign,   —   *T. Richardson & Son.*

XXXI.

Alexander Kent, Esq. *Leeds.*   *London, 22nd July, 18—*

Sir, — It is with the deepest regret we inform you, that, on balancing our books on the 1st inst., we found so considerable a deficiency, resulting from engagements (3) which we had entered into with the firm of Rouse, Commins & Co., who became bankrupts

---

(1) Anderemo superbi. (2) Fra breve, fra non molto. (3) Impegni.

last month, that we were induced to submit our affairs to the inspection of our principal creditors.

These gentlemen have, after a full investigation, consented to appoint trustees (1) for the liquidation of our outstanding (2) debts, the sale of our property, and the due distribution of the proceeds (3) amongst our creditors, in proportion to their respective claims on our estate.

We indulge a hope (4) that you will not object to this arrangement, but will immediately furnish the trustees, Messrs. Thomas Jones and William Daniel, with an abstract of your account current, for the purpose of having it compared with our books, in order that the correct balance may be ascertained. We are respectfully, Sir, your obedient humble servants. JAMES THOMSON & Co.

XXXII.

John Rusden, Esq. *New York.* London, 30th June, 18 —

Sir, — We are under the painful necessity of informing you, that, owing to a series of misfortunes during the last six months, we find it is not in our power to meet (5) our engagements, and are consequently compelled this day to suspend our payments.

As soon as our books can be balanced, we purpose (6) calling a meeting (7) of our creditors, when we shall lay before them a balance-sheet, exhibiting our abilities and the means we may possess of meeting them. In the mean time (8), we beg you will suspend your judgment upon us, as we can truly assert that our embarrassments have arisen solely from events which it was impossible to foresee, and over which we had no control. Believe us, under all circumstances, Sir, your obliged and obedient servants,
WILLIAM WELSH & Co.

XXXIII.

Messrs. Purday & Lowe. *Havanna*, 30th June, 18 —

Gentlemen, — We beg leave to inform you that our copartnership is this day dissolved, and that in future, our firm, and that of Messr. Gerardin and Co, our branch in Matanzas, will be used in liquidation only.

Referring you to the annexed circulars of our new establishments, we are, etc. GERARDIN & BURRITT.

---

(1) Fede-commissari, amministratori. (2) Dovuti, non riscossi. (3) Provento, ricavo. (4) Ci lusinghiamo, ci ripromettiamo. (5) Far fronte a, adempire a. (6) Intendiamo, ci proponiamo. (7) Adunanza, convegno. (9) Frattanto.

XXXIV.

To the same. · *Havanna, 30th June, 18 —*

Gentlemen, — Our partnership having ceased by mutual consent, we beg to inform you that both this establishment and that of Matanzas, will forthwith liquidate their pending business, for which purpose alone, our firm will be used hereafter (1).

We beg your reference to the accompanying circulars of our new establishments; and, soliciting a continuance of your confidence, we are, etc. BURRIT & CLARKE.

XXXV.

To the same. *Havanna, 1st July, 18 —*

Gentlemen.— The preceding circulars of Messrs. Gerardin and Burritt, and Messrs. Burritt and Clarke, inform you of the dissolution of their establishments.

Their business will in future be conducted under the firms of Gerardin, Burritt & Co. in Havanna, and Gerardin, Clarke and Co. in Matanzas.

The interest of both establishments being identical, each is responsible for the operations of the other.

We subjoin our respective signatures, and request your attention to them. Trusting that you will frequently have occasion to avail yourselves of our services, which we will endeavour to render at all times valuable to our friends, we are, etc.

GERARDIN BURRITT & Co.

XXXVI.

Gentlemen, *Paris, 19th January, 18 —*

The attention of many persons being particularly directed to the public funds, it may be agreeable to them to see at a glance (2) the rate of interest which they give according to the fluctuations of the market. I subjoin a table shewing the rate of interest upon the 5 per cent. consols (3), from the price of 70 to that of 106 fr. You must be careful to note that 5 francs of Rentes (annuity) or 100 francs Capital give about 1 1/3 centimes per day, or nearly 40 centimes per month. Consequently, you must deduct (4) from the price so many times (5) 1 1/3 centimes as there are days elapsed (6) since the last half year's dividend was paid ; for instance (7), if the Rente be quoted to day at 75. 60, four months having passed since

---

(1) D'ora innanzi, per lo futuro, in avvenire. (2) Colpo d'occhio, occhiata. (3) Consolidati, fondi consolidati. (4) Bisogna diffalcare. (5) Altrettante volte. (6) Scorsi. (7) Per esempio.

* The repetition of the signatures in this case, seems needless, so many examples having already been given.

the 29th September, which makes 1. 60 for the amount of dividend now due, the price will be 74 francs, which, according to the table, gives 6 $^3/_4$ per cent. Interest on the sum invested.

Permit me to tender my services in the purchase or sale of these funds. I have the honor, etc.

Table shewing the rate of interest on the 5 per cent. Consols from the price of 70 francs to 106.

* 70	7 $^{14}/_{100}$	83	6 $^1/_{50}$	95	5 $^{26}/_{100}$
71	7 $^1/_{25}$	84	5 $^{95}/_{100}$	96	5 $^{21}/_{100}$
72	6 $^{94}/_{100}$	85	5 $^{88}/_{100}$	97	5 $^{15}/_{100}$
73	6 $^{85}/_{100}$	86	5 $^8/_{10}$	98	5 $^1/_{10}$
74	6 $^3/_4$	87	5 $^{74}/_{100}$	99	5 $^1/_{20}$
75	6 $^2/_3$	88	5 $^{68}/_{100}$	100	5
76	6 $^{58}/_{100}$	89	5 $^{84}/_{100}$	101	4 $^{95}/_{100}$
77	6 $^1/_2$	90	5 $^{56}/_{100}$	102	4 $^{90}/_{100}$
78	6 $^4/_{100}$	91	5 $^1/_2$	103	4 $^{86}/_{100}$
79	6 $^{34}/_{100}$	92	5 $^{43}/_{100}$	104	4 $^{80}/_{100}$
80	6 $^1/_4$	93	5 $^{38}/_{100}$	105	4 $^{76}/_{100}$
81	6 $^{17}/_{100}$	94	5 $^{32}/_{100}$	106	4 $^{71}/_{100}$
82	6 $^9/_{100}$				

* 70 : 5 :: 100 : X = 7 $^{14}/_{100}$

LETTERS OF INTRODUCTION.

XXXVII.

Charles Holdsworth, Esq. *Bristol*.   *London, 4th May, 18—*

Dear Sir, — The bearer of these few lines is Mr. Edward Watson, of the firm of Watson, Brothers.

In introducing to your acquaintance the nephew of our esteemed friend, Mr. Bryce Watson, of Manchester, so old a connection of your house as well as our own, we feel it to be quite superfluous to claim for him that friendly reception (1) which we know awaits (2) him at your hands.

We doubt not that you will feel the same interest as we do, in the prosperity of the above mentioned firm, and be equally anxious to promote, to the utmost of your ability, the particular objects of Mr. Edward Watson's visit to Bristol. We are always, dear Sir, yours very truly,   THOMAS HOLMES & SON.

---

(1) Ricevimento, accoglienza. (2) Aspetta, attende.

XXXVIII.

London, 4th August, 18—

Messrs. Napier and Son, Bombay.

Gentlemen, — Our highly respectable and esteemed friends, Messrs. Roquet and Favell, of this city, having requested an introduction to a Bombay House, to which they are desirous of intrusting the settlement of some affairs of considerable delicacy and importance, we beg leave to refer them to you, well convinced that we cannot more effectually serve them, than by soliciting your best influence and exertions in their behalf. We are, etc.   REID & CURTIS.

XXXIX.

Edward Smith, Esq. Liverpool.   London, 2nd June, 18—

Sir, — Mr. Charles Burton, the eldest son of our senior, being about to visit your port for the purpose of embarking for Buenos Ayres, we are sensible (1) that we cannot better ensure to him such polite attentions as are calculated to render his short stay (2) agreeable, than by introducing him to you. We need scarcely say that we shall feel personally obliged by any marks of kindness (3) that you may have the goodness to evince (4) towards this young gentleman, and by any assistance that it may be in your power to render him, in making his arrangements for the voyage. We remain, with much esteem, Sir, your very faithful servants,   BURTON, OGLEBY & CO.

XL.

H. Edwards, Esq. London.   Hamburgh, 15th April, 13—

Sir, — We recommend to your particular favor and attention the bearer, Mr. Fred. Schmidt, eldest son of Mr. Augustus Schmidt, of the highly respectable house of Schmidt and Meyer, of this city.

Our esteemed young friend is about to visit France by way of London, on business for the house; we therefore request you, most urgently, to afford him your advice and assistance, and to render his stay in your metropolis as agreeable as possible. He is clever, steady (5) and unassuming, and we are convinced that on a near acquaintance he will prove himself deserving of your esteem and good will.

Command us freely in similar cases, and be assured that we will use our best endeavours to do justice to your introductions. We are, etc.

SCHNEIDER & CO.

---

(1) Persuasi. (2) Dimora, soggiorno. (3) Gentilezza, amorevolezza, amicizia, benignità. (4) Mostrare, esibire. (5) Abile, costumato.

XLI.

A Bergman, Esq. *Hambourgh*. *London, 6th May*, 18 —

My dear Sir, — Permit me to introduce to you my counting-house-colleague and intimate acquaintance, Mr. Robert Fortescue, and to claim for him a very kind and friendly reception.

Mr. Fortescue is a talented young man, who has pricipally, by his own unaided exertions, made himself thoroughly (1) master of several languages. His health having been for some time in a delicate state, owing, probably, to a too close (2) application to his studies, the physicians have recommended him to travel for a few months on the continent; and when his strength is sufficiently recruited to admit of his returning to business, to fix his residence in some sea-port (3) for a couple of years. With this view, my friend intends visiting France, Flanders, and Holland, on his way to Hamburgh, where he is desirous of obtaining a mercantile situation (4).

Well acquainted with Mr. Fortescue's character, I can with justice bear testimony in his favor; and more particularly so knowing that his conduct, during the nine years that he has spent in our counting-house, has been such as to give entire satisfaction to our principals, who regret the circumstances which compel him to quit their employ (5). I therefore most earnestly entreat you to afford him every assistance in your power, in accomplishing his object; and I confess to you, that I expect more from your friendly exertions in his behalf, than from the letters with which the house have furnished him.

Fully persuaded that you will shew Mr. Fortescue every kindness and attention, and will endeavour to make his residence at Hamburgh as agreeable as possible, I beg to assure you that I shall consider myself greatly obliged, and shall be most happy to have an opportunity of serving you in return. Believe me, dear Sir, your's most faithfully.   •   H. WALTHER.

XLII.

London, 15th August, 18.

Messrs. Joseph Phillips & Co. *Liverpool*.

Gentlemen, — I have the pleasure of introducing to your acquaintance the very respectable firm of Messrs. Dugard and Co. of Paris, whose principal, Mr. James Dugard, is at present in this city, and purposes visiting your town. Any civilities or attention that you may be pleased to shew him, I shall consider a favor conferred on myself. These gentlemen occasionally give ordes for cottons and other shipments from your port; and from some conversation which I have

---

(1) A fondo. (2) Stretta, intensa. (3) Porto di mare. (4) Impiego, posto. (5) Servizio (impiego).

had with Mr. D., I am led (1) to hope that the house will give you a preference of their business in future. I shall feel happy should the present introduction lead to transactions mutually advantageous and agreeable. I remain, most truly, Gentlemen, your obedient servant,

JOHN LUKE.

XLIII.

Messrs. George Wallis & Co. *Oporto.*　　London, 31st *July*, 18 —

Gentlemen, — This will be delivered to you by Captain Purkis of the Ceres, whom I beg leave to introduce to your acquaintance. You will greatly oblige me by giving him the preference, should you have any wines for shipment, while his vessel is loading (2) at your port.

The owners (3) of the Ceres are my good friends and valuable correspondents, Messrs. P. Carter and Co. of Hull.

Recommending Captain Purkis likewise to your good offices and attentions in other matters, I am, etc.　　JOHN BIGGAR.

XLIV.

Messrs. Bright & Co. *Bristol.*　　London, 1st *October*, 18 —

Gentlemen, — We beg leave to introduce to you the bearer of this letter, Mr. Richard Templeton, a partner in the highly respectable house of Moore, Templeton and Co., of New York, who is about to visit your city for the purpose of extending the commercial relations of his house with the principal firms of your place. In strongly recommending our friend to your notice, we particularly request that you will not only forward (4) his views by your influence and advice, but that you will also render his stay in your city as agreeable as possible, by shewing him every attention that may be in your power. In case Mr. Templeton should have occasion to take up any money, either for travelling expenses or operations of business, you will please to supply him with funds to the extent of five thousand pounds, taking his drafts (5) upon us at three days' sight* in reimbursement. We beg that upon similar, and all other occasions, you will freely command our services, and we remain, etc.,

G. LYNCH & SON.

XLV.

Messrs. Harvood & Co. *Manchester.*　　London, 5th *April*, 18 —

Gentlemen, — We have much pleasure in introducing to your acquaintance Mr. Frederick Meyer, of the highly respectable firm of Messrs. Gottfried, Meyer and Sons, of Frankfort on the Maine.

---

(1) Led *preterito del verbo* to lead, menare, condurre, indurre : I am led to hope, mi lusingo, mi ripromette. (2) Viene caricato. (3) Padroni, proprietarj. (4) Promuovere, avansare, vantaggiare. (5) Tratte.

* Merchants of respectability prefer having all *English* bills drawn upon

This gentleman is on the point of commencing a tour through our principal manufacturing towns, with a view as well to business as amusement. Should it be in your power to further his objects in any way, we shall be particularly obliged by your so doing; and shall be most happy, should the introduction prove (†) of mutual advantage to yourselves and our young friend.

In the event of Mr. Meyer requiring a supply of cash for his travelling expenses, be so obliging as to accommodate him with any sum to the extent of 200l., taking his draft on us at three days' sight for the amount. We remain, Gentlemen, your very obedient servants,   GEORGE THOMSON & Co.

Mr. Meyer's signature † — *F. Meyer.*

XLVI.

Mr. G. Symons, *Falmouth.*   *London, 28th October, 18—*

Sir, — Permit me to introduce to your acquaintance the bearer of this letter, Mr. John Phillips, who proceeds to Falmouth on his way to Portugal.

Should Mr. Phillips desire to take up cash for payment of his passage, etc., you will please to advance him any sum not exceeding 100l. taking his draft at three days' sight on his house here, Messrs. Richards, Phillips and Co., in reimbursement.

I shall feel greatly obliged by such marks of civility and attention as you may have it in your power to shew my young friend, whom you will find highly deserving of your regard.   I am, etc.

                                               J. CARRUTHERS.

LETTERS OF CREDIT.

XLVII.

Messrs. James Pope and Son, *Plymouth.*   *London, 1st May, 18—*

Gentlemen, — I take the liberty of opening a credit with you in favor of the bearer, Mr. John Ashton. Any sum of money that this

---

them at very short dates; in foreign bills they are not particular, as these are regulated by the customs of the respective places whence they are issued.

† It is usual, and certainly prudent, to affix the signature of the individual in whose favor the credit is given, for this reason: the letter might be lost, and the finder avail himself of it to receive the money, whereas (a) this imposture would be easily detected (b) by a comparison of the signature in the letter, with that to the receipt which the party would be called upon to give.

   (a) Dove che, laddove. (b) Scoperta.
   (1) Riesca, riesce.

gentleman may require, to the extent of fifteen hundred pounds sterling, be pleased to advance on my account, either against his receipt, or his draft on me to your order, as may be most agreeable to yourselves. I am, etc. T. CLARK.

XLVIII.

London, 16th July, 18—
Messrs. Barraud, Frères, bankers, Paris.

Gentlemen, — We request the favor of your furnishing the bearer, Lord George Ryder, with any cash that his lordship may require during his stay in France, to the extent of 3,000l. (say three thousand pounds sterling), taking his lordship's receipt for the sums advanced, and placing the same to our debit.

We refer to our letter of this date, per post, for his lordship's signature*. And remain, etc. HARDY & COX.

XLIX.

Messrs. J. Phillips & Co. *Liverpool*. London, 16th Aug 18—
Gentlemen, — Being without any of your favors to reply to (1) †, my present object is to request that you will purchase on my account, twenty-five bags (2) of Pernambuco cotton, in bond (3), provided you can obtain them, of *superior* quality, at a price not exceeding 9d, per lb. (4); shipping them for Rouen to the address (5) of my friend Monsieur La Roche of that place, and giving me timely (6) advice for insurance.

The bags are to be marked VY, Nos. (8) 1 to 25.

On handing me a bill of lading and invoice (8), you will please to value on me at fifteen days' sight (9) for your reimbursement.

Have the goodness to transmit one bill of lading to the consignee (10) by the vessel. I am, etc., JOHN LUKE.

---

(1) A cui rispondere (privo delle favorite vostre). (2) (Sacchi) balle. (3) Porto franco, dogana. (4) 9d. per *lb.* nove soldi (*inglesi*) la libbra. (5) Indirizzo, direzione. (6) A suo tempo. (7) *Nos.*, abbrev. di numeros o numbers. (8) Fattura. (9) Quindici giorni vista, di vista. (10) Consegnatario.

* The mode here alluded to of giving the signature in a separate letter, which is forwarded immediately per post, is yet more secure than that described in Letter XLV; as it affords no opportunity of imitating the handwriting.

† The original letter commenced thus: « *Deprived of your favors,* I have to request, » etc. This expression, though often used in mercantile correspondence, appears objectionable, since we cannot be deprived of that which we do not possess; and useless, because we have no difficulty in expressing correctly what is really meant.

L.

Mr. John Luke, *London.*   *Liverpool, 18th August, 18 —*

Sir, — We are in receipt of (1) your esteemed letter of the 16th instant, ordering the purchase and shipment of twenty-five bags of Pernambuco cotton for Rouen, provided they could be obtained, of prime quality, at 9d. per lb. We are sorry to say, in reply, that the quality of Pernambuco cotton at market, just now, is very small, and prices, consequently, have advanced, say (2) to 10d. and $10\,^1/_2\,d.$ (*) per lb. It is, therefore, out of our power to execute your order; which we regret the more, as we are about to charter (3) a vessel for Havre, and should have been glad of (4) your parcel (5) of cottons, though small, to help out her freight (6). Should you think of shipping any other quality, it will afford us much pleasure to consign them to our common (**) friend M. La Roche. Annexed is a price-current for your government. And believe us, we are, with esteem, Sir, your very obedient humble sarvants,

Jos. PHILLIPS & Co.

LI.

Messrs. Joseph Phillips & Co.   *London, 20th August, 18 —*

I am favored with your letter of the 18th instant, and observe that you could not execute my order for Pernambuco cottons in bond, at the limit of 9d. per lb.

Being, however, very desirous of opening an account with M. La Roche of Rouen, you may, should you charter a vessel for Havre, ship in her, for my account, and to M. La Roche's consignment (7) thirty bags of cotton, of such description and quality as you may judge most suitable (8) to that market, but not exceeding my former limit as to price.

I hope you will be able to meet with a parcel really cheap (9) at the price, be the latter what it may, so as to ensure me a profit on the sale. Trusting to your good management, I shall shortly (10) look for the invoice and bill of lading, with advice of your draft for the amount of the former. I am, etc.,

JOHN LUKE.

LII.

M. Louis La Roche, *Rouen.*   *London, 20th August, 18 —*

Sir, — From the annexed circular you will observe, that my partnership with Mr. William Thomas was dissolved on the 30th

---

(1) Abbiamo ricevuto. (2) *Say* in vece di *let us say, that is to say,* diciamo, vale a dire. (3) Noleggiare, prender a nolo. (4) Contenti *di avere.* (5) Partita, spedizione. (6) Per ajutarci a completare il (suo) carico. (7) Consegna. (8) Più adattata. (9) A buon mercato. (10) Fra breve.

(*) Ten pence half-penny (pronunciate *hepny*).

(**) The term *mutual*, which I have expunged (*cancellato*) in this place and many others, is incorrect when applied to a third party.

June last, and that I am now established on my own sole account. Being desirous, as Mr. Thomas retires from business altogether, of preserving your correspondence and connection (1), I have requested my friends at Liverpool, Messrs. Joseph Phillips and Co., to ship per first vessel, to your address, thirty bags of cotton, which you will please to dispose of (2) on arrival, on my account, on the most favorable terms your market will permit; furnishing me, in due course, with account-sales thereof (3), and a remittance *per appoint** for the nett proceeds (4). I trust the latter will be such as to encourage me to a continuance of my shipments. Messrs. J. P. and Co. will inclose you a bill of lading by the vessel, and I will hand you an invoice †, as soon as I am in possession of the particulars. Meanwhile, referring you to the inclosed price-current, I am, etc.

JOHN LUKE.

LIII.

John Luke, Esq. *London.*   *Liverpool, 23rd August, 18 —*

Sir, — In consequence of the orders contained in your esteemed favor of the 20th inst., we have purchased for your account, thirty bags of Maranham cotton, of good quality, at 9d. per pound, and shall ship the same on board the Ann, Captain Thomas Ball, a vessel which we have chartered for Havre, and which we expect to sail in ten or twelve days. For your government in insuring the same, the invoice amount will be about 200*l*.: when shipped, we

---

(1) Relazione. (2) Vendere. (3) Conto di vendita di quello. (4) (Provento), ricavo.

* *Per appoint* is another technical term in very general use, both among English and foreign merchants. The word APPOINT signifies *odd money.* « Monnoie qui se do nne pour achever une somme qu'on ne saurait parfaire avec les principales espèces ; » *Dict. de l'Academie.* A remittance *per appoint* is a remittance of the exact sum due.

† There is a difference between an *invoice* and a *bill of parcels*, which is not always regarded. The account of goods sold by one merchant to another, or to a wholesale dealer, as, for instance, sugars to a grocer or sugar baker (*refiner*), is a *bill of parcels.* Again, when a merchant orders of a manufacturer certain goods for shipment, the latter furnishes him with his bill, or account of the qualities and prices of the articles, with the weights, marks, and numbers of the several packages or parcels of which the order consists ; hence (a) the name *bill of parcels.* This account the merchant enters in his invoice book, and adding thereto (b) all the charges incurred in the shipment, with the cost of insurance, his commission, etc., *makes up* (c) (as the commercial phrase is) the invoice. Sometimes a dozen or twenty bills of parcels are comprised in one invoice, especially in the West India and South American trades.

(a) Quindi, da qui. (b) A quello. (c) Compone, fa.

CONSIGNMENT OF COTTON. 47

shall wait on you with (1) invoice, and bill of lading, valuing on you, as requested, for our reimbursement. We are, very truly, etc.
Jos. Phillips & Co.

LIV.

M. La Roche *Rouen*.   *Liverpool, 30th August,* 18—

Sir, — By order, and for account of our common friend, John Luke, Esq. of London, we have shipped to your address, in the Ann, Captain Thomas Ball, for Havre, as per bill of lading inclosed, VY. Nos. 1 to 30, thirty bags of Maranham cotton, which we trust will arrive safe, and in the same good condition in which they are shipped. We hope that you will have in your power to render our above-mentioned friend satisfactory account-sales of this shipment, following his directions as to the disposal of the nett proceeds. We remain, most truly, sir, your very obedient, &. Jos. Phillips & Co.

LV.

John Luke, Esq. *London*.   *Liverpool, 30th August,* 18—

Sir, — Referring you to our letter of the 23rd instant, we have now to advise the shipment of your thirty bags of Maranham cotton in the Ann, Ball, for Havre, to the consignment of M. La Roche at Rouen, agreeably (2) to your directions. Inclosed, you will please to receive bill of lading and invoice thereof; the latter amounts to 205*l.* 8*s.* 6*d.*, for which sum we have valued on you, under this date, at fifteen days' sight, to the order of Jones, Price and Co., which draft we recommend to your protection, thus closing this transaction. We have transmitted a bill of lading to M. La Roche by the vessel. Awaiting (3) the pleasure of your further commands, we remain faithfully, &. Jos. Phillips & Co.

LVI.

London, 2nd September, 18—

Messrs. Joseph Phillips & Co. *Liverpool*.

Gentlemen, — I have to acknowledge the receipt of your esteemed letter of the 30th ult., inclosing bill of lading and invoice of the thirty bags of Maranham cotton, shipped in the Ann, to Havre; for the invoice amount whereof (4), 205*l.* 8*s.* 6*d.*, I have credited your account; and on the other hand debited it with a similar sum, being the amount of your draft at fifteen days' sight, to the order

---

(1) Vi rimetteremo, vi manderemo. (2) Conforme, conformemente. (3) Aspettando, in attesa di. (4) Del quale.

of Jones, Price and Co., which has been duly honored. With many thanks for your attention to my orders in transmitting a bill of lading to the consignee by the vessel, I remain, &.

JOHN LUKE.

LVII.

M. La Roche, *Rouen*.   *London, 2nd September, 18—*

Sir, — In pursuance of (1) the orders given to my friends at Liverpool, as I advised you under date of the 20th ult. (2), they have shipped, to your address, thirty bags of Maranham cotton of excellent quality, by the Ann, Captain Thomas Ball, to Havre. Inclosed I have now the pleasure to wait on you with invoice and duplicate bill of lading of this shipment; the former amounting to $216l. 7s. 10d.$, which sum I hope you will be able to realize, together with a fair (3) profit; and as quick returns are the life of trade, I shall expect that you will, ere long (4), be enabled to remit me the nett proceeds in a good bill on some of your friends in this city. I do not limit you as to price, being well assured that you will effect the best sales your market will allow.   I remain, &.

JOHN LUKE.

LVIII.

Rouen, 7th September, 18—

Messrs. Joseph Phillips & Co., *Liverpool*.

Gentlemen, — I have duly (5) received your valued favor of the 30th ult., accompanied by a bill of lading for thirty bags of Maranham cotton, consigned to me by the Ann, Captain Ball, by order and for account of our esteemed friend, Mr. John Luke of London. The Ann having arrived at Havre, I have ordered them to be landed and forwarded (6) to this place, when I shall do the needful (7) and acquaint our said friend with the result. At present, I have every prospect of rendering him good account-sales, as cottons of all descriptions are in demand, and prices rather on the advance: much will depend, however, on the arrivals from your side of the channel, as there is no great quantity expected, direct, from Brazil or the United States. Referring you to the annexed price-current, I remain, very truly, Sir, your most obedient humble servant,

L. LA ROCHE.

---

(1) In seguito a, conforme a. (2) Ult. *abbrev. di ultimo, scorso.* (3) Giusto, equo, ragionevole. (4) Fra non molto, fra breve. (5) (Debitamente), a suo tempo. (6) Sbarcate ed inoltrate. (7) Farò l'occorrente, procurerò l'usato.

LIX.

John Luke, Esq. *London.*   *Rouen, 7th September, 18—.*

Sir, — I received, in due course, your favor of the 20th ult., apprizing me that you purposed to make me a consignment; to which letter I deferred replying, in expectation of learning that you had carried your kind intention into effect, as I have now the satisfaction to know from your favor of the 2nd instant, as also by advices from our common friends, Messrs. Joseph Phillips & Co. of Liverpool; from whom, by the Ann, arrived at Havre, I have received a bill of lading for thirty bags of Maranham cotton by that vessel. I shall offer this parcel to our buyers as soon as landed; and I have no doubt I shall be able to remit you a very fair percentage (1) on your invoice of £16l. 7s. 10d., since our market for this article is very brisk (2); indeed, all descriptions of cottons are in good demand, with some prospect of an advance in prices, of which circumstance I shall take care to avail myself in the sale of yours. I would not, however, recommend delay, for when the state of our market is known on your side, no doubt we shall have large importations from thence, though, for your government we do not hear of any expected arrivals from North or South America.

As I shall shortly have this pleasure again, I have only now to add that your interests will, at all times, command my best attention, and I beg to assure you that nothing shall be left undone (3) on my part, to extend our correspondence to our mutual advantage. I remain, most sincerely, Sir, your obliged and obedient humble servant,   L. LA ROCHE.

LX.

John Luke, Esq. *London.*   *Rouen, 15th September, 18—.*

Sir, — Herewith you will please to receive account sales of your thirty bags of Maranham cotton, received per Ann, as advised in my letter of the 7th inst. I was enabled to place them at f. 180 per 50 kilogrammes: which I hope will give you satisfaction, as at this price you perceive they nett f. 5996 75. This amount I remit you inclosed, in my own draft at two months' date on my friends Messrs. Bailey and Banfield in your city; convinced it will meet due honour — producing, at the exchange of f. 25 50, 235l., 3s 4d. sterling.

Hoping this small trial (4) will induce you to favor me with more considerable consignments, and begging reference to the annexed price-current, I am happy to say, that our market continues

---

(1) Profitto, utile, guadagno (di un tanto per cento). (2) Animato, attivo. (3) Non fatto, intentato. (4) Saggio, prova, sperimento.

Anderson.   4

encouraging for the importation of all kinds of raw (1) cottons; but, as you will be better informed as to (2) the quantity shipped from Liverpool and your ports, you can best judge to what extent you can go with safety in your speculation in this article. I am truly, Sir, your obliged and obedient humble servant,   L. LA ROCHE.

LXI.

M. L. La Roche, *Rouen.*   *London, 18th September, 18—.*

Sir, — I am in receipt (3) of your favor of the 15th instant, inclosing account sales of my thirty bags of Maranham cotton, per Anna from Liverpool (nett proceeds to your debit f. 5996 75), and at the same time containing your draft on Bailey and Banfield for 235*l.* 3*s.* 4*d.* sterling, making, at the Exchange of 25 50, the same amount of f. 5996 75: thus closing this first transaction, the said draft having been duly honored.

Allow me to thank you for your punctuality and promptitude in this trifling affair, which I shall regard as an earnest (4) of what I may expect in transactions of greater importance. It will ceartainly stimulate me to extend my shipments: and the encouragement you hold out (5) has induced me to give directions already to Messrs. Phillips and Co., to forward 100 bags to your address, per first ship, provided they can effect a purchase at the same prices as the last. On learning the result, I shall address you again. In the interim (6), believe me, Sir, your obliged and obedient servant,   JOHN LUKE.

Second Series.

LXII.

Messrs. Lewis, Drake and Co. *Lisbon.*   *London, 18th August, 18—.*

Gentlemen, — My partnership with Mr. Bull having terminated on the 30th June, I have, since that time, been acting for myself and in my own name only, following, however, the same principles and branch of business as my late firm, namely, the commission line; the wine trade being the chief object to which I intend devoting my attention.

From what your Mr. Drake was kind enough to say, when I had the pleasure of seeing him here, I presume that you will readily ship any wines for which I may get orders, at your fixed prices, allowing me the usual commission of five per cent on all wine shipped to this port; 10*s.* per pipe (7) more when shipped to the outports; and ½ per cent. on remittances; with an allowance of 10*s.* per pipe on all orders above ten pipes, and 1*l.* on all above twenty.

---

(1) Greggi. (2) In quanto a, riguardo a. (3) Vi accuso ricevuta. (4) Arra, saggio. (5) Offrite, porgete. (6) Frattanto, intanto. (7) Botte contenente 477 litri.

It is very difficult, at present, to get orders for wines of any description, particularly Lisbon: but I trust I shall have my share (1) and you may be assured I shall be very careful from whom I take them.

Mr. Drake also spoke of doing something in exchanges. I shall have no objection to make a trial on a small scale, by way of enlivening our correspondence, and in hopes of reaping a better interest, than by having my capital locked up in public securities. For this purpose, I will appropriate a sum not exceeding 1,000*l.*; and if you will come forward with an equal amount, we can work (2) the two thousand on mutual account, each of us charging only our respective disbursements, and allowing interest on advances, at the rate of 5 per cent. per annum: each party to guarantee, or be responsible, for the bills he takes.

The present appearances of the exchange on Portugal indicate a fall, and, in my opinion, a considerable one. I expect to see that on Paris at 26; and on Lisbon 54 $^1/_2$ or 54, as it was in the autumn of 1820. Paris is this day at 24 50, Lisbon 56, and Oporto 56 $^1/_2$.

If, at any time, you wish to make remittances in specie (3) on your own account, I shall charge you only $^1/_2$ per cent., commission on the sales, and nothing on payment of drafts, or on remittances. Should you order insurance to be effected thereon (4), it will of course be free of expense; the premium, I imagine, would not exceed 15*s.* 9*d.* per cent. stamp included. Gold is certain of obtaining the Mint (5) price, or 3*l.* 17 $^1/_2$*d.* per ounce.

I trust you will give me the preference in your orders and consignments to this country. I attend personally at Lloyd's, therefore any insurances you may have to effect I shall be very proud of attending to, and shall make the customary (6) charge of $^1/_2$ per cent. on effecting, and $^1/_2$ per cent. *del credere* * for guarantee of the underwriters, if you wish. It. With great regard, I remain, gentlemen, your obedient humble servant, JAMES CORDELL.

LXIII.

James Cordell, Esq. *London.*   *Lisbon*, 2nd Sept., 18—

Sir, — We have to thank you for your very friendly letter of the 18th ultimo, and beg, in reply, to assure you that we shall have much pleasure in continuing to transact what little business

---

(1) Parte (porzione, azione). (2) (Lavorare), far lavorare, impiegare, utilizzare. (3) Contante. (4) Sopra quello, su di ciò. (5) Della zecca. (6) Solito.

* This is a premium, or commission, charged by merchants for becoming responsible for the buyers of goods, or underwriters; so that in case of the failure of the latter, the owners are secured against loss.

we have in your city, with you, on the same terms as with your late firm of Bull and Cordell. Our present prices for wine are: good dry Lisbon 35*l.*, rich 38*l.*, without discriminating the vintage; Bucellas 38*l.*, and Carcavellos 39*l.* per pipe on board (1). We shall be very glad to receive orders for any quantity, and you may, from the past experience of your late co-partnership, be convinced that all you may transmit us will be faithfully executed.

With regard to the proposed speculation to exchanges, we must decline entering on it for the present, as our capital is at this moment fully employed; but when we have a surplus, we shall gladly avail ourselves of the opportunity of appropriating it in the manner the writer proposed when in your city. Any insurance, or other business we may have to transact, we shall, as a matter of course (2), entrust to your good management; and with an offer of our best services on this side the water, we subscribe ourselves, very truly, your obedient humble servants,   LEWIS DRAKE & Co.

LXIV.

James Cordell, Esq. *London.*   *Oporto, 20th August, 18—.*

Sir, — You will please to effect insurance for my account of 1,500*l.*, on one fifth part or share of the ship Ocean, Captain A. Nogueira, from Pernambuco to this city, against all risk, and at the lowest premium possible, not exceeding, however, 10 per cent. I expect that she will sail under convoy of a ship of war; therefore you will be so good as to stipulate for a return of premium accordingly. It was intended that she should sail within three weeks from the date of my last advices of the 12th June. You may draw on me as usual for the amount of premium and charges. I remain very truly, Sir, your obedient humble servant,   JOHN MATTHEWS.

LXV.

John Matthews, Esq. *Oporto.*   *London, 5th Sept., 18—.*

Sir, — Agreeably to the order contained in your favor of the 20th ultimo, I have effected insurance on your fifth share of the Ocean, Captain A. Nogueira, from Pernambuco to your port, say 1500*l.* as per copy of policy and account annexed, at 8 guineas per cent., to return 4*l.* per cent., if she sails under convoy of a man of war, and arrives. I have taken the liberty of valuing on you, under this date, to my own order for 138*l.* 6*s.* 6*d.*, the cost of this insurance, at the exchange of 57 $^1/_4$ per milrea, and sixty days' sight; which draft I am certain will meet due honour.

---

(1) A bordo, caricato. (2) Ben inteso, naturalmente.

Should you wish me to guarantee the under-writers, I am ready to do so for $^1/_2$ per cent. *del credere*. And in that case you will please to inform my friends in your city, Messrs. A. and F. Rawlings, of your wish and pay them the sum of 7*l*. 10*s*. at the exchange above quoted; when the risk of failure, or non-payment by the underwriters in case of loss, will be mine; otherwise, that risk remains your own.

Always anxious to receive your orders, and determined to execute them in the most punctual and advantageous manner in my power, I remain, faithfully, Sir, your obedient humble servant,

JAMES CORDELL.

LXVI.

James Cordell, Esq. *London.* *Lisbon*, 3rd *Sept.*, 18—.

Sir, — I will thank you to insure 250*l.*, value of twenty five bags of cotton wool (1), marked AI, Nos. 1 to 25, (10*l.* each), shipped at Ceara, for my account, on board the brig General Sampayo, Captain Jose Maria Alves, for this port, against all risks; debiting me with the amount of cost thereof. The brig was to sail about the 15th of last month, without convoy. Relying on your getting the assurance done at five or six guineas per cent., but not limiting you as to premium, I remain, truly, Sir, your obedient humble servant, ANT. ISIDRO.

LXVII.

Don Antonio Isidro, *Lisbon.* *London*, 15*th Sept.*, 18—.

Sir, — In pursuance of (2) your orders, under date of the 3rd instant, I have effected an insurance, as per copy of policy annexed, of 230*l.* on twenty-five bags of cotton valued at 10*l.* each, marked AI, Nos. 1 to 25, by the General Sampayo, Captain Jose Maria Alves, from Ceara, in the Brazils, to your city, from all risks, at six guineas, per cent., amount to your debit as per account at foot, 18*l.* 2*s.* 6*d.*, for which, if found correct, you will please to credit me in account current. Assuring you that I shall always pay the strictest attention to your orders, and soliciting a continuance of them, I remain, very truly, Sir, your obedient servant, JAMES CORDELL.

LXVIII.

James Cordell, Esq. *London.* *Oporto*, 1*st October*, 18—.

Sir, — I received, in due course, your favor of the 5th ultimo, with copy of policy and amount of premium, etc., of 1,5000*l.*, insured

---

(1) Cotone in fiocco. (2) In seguito a, conforme a.

on my one-fifth share of the ship Ocean, from Pernambuco, and advising me of your draft for the amount, 158*l*, 6*s*. 6*d*., which has been duly honored. This vessel having arrived two days since under convoy of the Perola frigate, I wait on you with a certificate to that effect, to enable you to recover the return of premium, which you will please to deduct (1) from your next account.

The present is to request that you will purchase, and ship for my account, by the first regular free trader for this port, ten tousand (10,000) hare skins (2), well packed (3), and in good sound condition, to be marked IM, 1 to 20. Be so good as to effect insurance thereon, so as to cover every expense in case of loss, and take your reimbursement by draft on me at sixty days' sight. Relying on your known zeal, for the proper execution of this small order, I remain, Sir, your faithful humble servant, JOHN MATTHEWS.

LXIX.

John Matthews, Esq. *Oporto.*   *London, 21st October, 18—.*

Sir, — By the Mentor, Captain Bullock, I have shipped the twenty bales of hare skins ordered in your favor of the 1st inst. Inclosed, you will find bill of lading, and annexed, invoice of the same, amount of the latter 46*l*. 13*s*. 7*d*. to your debit. These skins, I am confident, will give you satisfaction, for they are of very superior quality, and are shipped in excellent condition. I hope this will lead to more considerable orders. I have effected insurance on the sum of 500*l*., which will cover all expenses in case of loss, but which, I trust, will not occur.

I have given you credit for 60*l*, return of premium per Ocean, recovered from the underwriters, and I have valued on you, in compliance with (4) your request, for the balance due to me this day, say 404*l*. 13*s*. 7*d*., at sixty days' sight, to the order of Thompson, Croft and Co., value of J. Bulkeley and Co., exchange 55 $^1/_2$ per milrea, to which I request your accustomed protection. Premiums of insurance to and from the Brazils are rising, in consequence of some recent captures by the Buenos Ayrean cruizers (5); but it is to be hoped they will shortly return to the customary level of times of peace. I am, most truly, Sir, your very humble servant,

JAMES CORDELL.

LXX.

John Luke, Esq. *London.*   *Liverpool, 3rd September, 18—.*

Sir, — You will be so good as to cause the following to be insured in London at the lowest premium possible, and not exceeding — the first, six and a half guineas per cent.: the second, 40*s*.; —

---

(1) Diffalcare. (2) Pelli di lepre. (3) Impacchettate, imballate. (4) In adempimento di, conformemente a. (5) Incrociatori, corsali.

ORDER FOR HARE SKINS. — INSURANCE.

at which we could have effected them here; but we have no doubt you will be able to succeed at lower premiums. Say

1st. L. 175 on 100 bags of rice from Maranham to Oporto, by the Senhora da Agonia, Captain Joaquim Da Silva, marked A 1 to 100.
The ship to sail on or about the 10th October.

2nd. Rs. 20,000 ff. 000 at the exchange of 72d. on two fifths of the cargo of the Wellington, Captain Joseph Mandel, from Bahia to Hamburgh, to sail the beginning of the present month. Particulars to be furnished hereafter.

Relying on your executing this order to the best of your ability, and requesting you to carry the amount of both to our debit in account, we remain, as always, Sir, your obedient humble servants,

Jos. PHILIPPS & Co.

LXXI.

Messrs. J. Phillips & Co. *Liverpool.* London, 6th September, 18—.

Gentlemen, — I am favoured with your letter of the 3rd instant, ordering two insurances, viz.

, L. 175 on 100 bags of rice per Senhora da Agonia, Captain J. Da Silva, from Maranham to Oporto, which I have effected at six guineas per cent., with policy (1), commission, etc. . . . per account L. 11 10 6

L. 6,000 equal to Rs. 20,000 ff. 000 at 72d. per millrea on two-fifths of the cargo, per Wellington, Captain J. Mandel, from Bahia to Hamburgh, at 35 shillings per cent., policy and commission per acct. (2) . . . . L. 120 0 0

Total. . L. 131 10 6

to your debit, which you will please note to my credit, accordingly. I hope you will be perfectly satisfied with my exertions on this occasion, since, I assure you, it cost me some pains to get the assurances effected within the limits prescribed. I shall expect you to favour me with the particulars of the Wellington's cargo, for endorsement on the policy, as I always find it best to set a value on each package, for facility of settlement in case of average (3). I remain, your very obedient humble servant, JOHN LUKE.

Third Series.
LXXII.

John Luke, Esq. *London.* Liverpool, 12th September, 18—.

Sir, — We are in receipt of your much esteemed letter of the 6th instant, and beg to assure you that we are much pleased with

---

(1) Polizza di sicurtà, certificato di assicurazione. (2) Acct. *abbrev. di* Account, conto. (3) Average, prezzo, somma o quantità media, avaria.

the premiums of the insurances effected by you, per Wellington and Senhora da Agonia, and have credited you with the amount in the sum of 131l. 10s. 6d.

We have the sum of 4,600l. to remit to our common friends, Messrs. J. Newfield and Co., at Oporto,* which we will do through (1) your agency, provided you consent not to charge us any commission thereon, because, this being more a family transaction than a matter of business, we are anxious to avoid expense as much as possible; brokerage (2) and postage we presume must be incurred. On receiving your answer, if in the affirmative as we anticipate, we shall cause the amount to be paid to your bankers; therefore you must favour us with their firm, and we shall rely on your remitting the same to our above-named friends, in undoubted paper, either on Lisbon or Oporto, as you may be best able to find bills. We are truly, Sir, your obedient humble servants,

Jos. Phillips & Co.

LXXIII.

Jos. Phillips & o. *Liverpool.* London, 15th September, 18—.

Gent., — In reply to your favour of the 12th instant, I beg to assure you, that it will afford me much pleasure to remit the 4,600l. to which you allude, to our Oporto friends, Messrs. J. Newfield and Co., without any charge for commission. You will, therefore, please to order that sum to be paid into my bankers, Messrs. Bosanquet and Co., when I will immediately proceed to execute your order. Lisbon was done to day at 54 to 54 $^1/_2$; Oporto 54 $^1/_4$. To-morrow is post-day, when if any good paper offers, I shall secure it; and to keep the transaction to ourselves, I will have the bills made payable to my order, endorsing them to Messrs. J. N. & Co., of course *without my prejudice*, † since I derive no advantage from the transaction.

Their orders as to remittances on their own wine account, are, that when the rate of exchange on Lisbon is $^1/_4$ below that on Oporto, it makes no difference to them on which place bills remitted to them are drawn; but when it exceeds the $^1/_4$, those on Lisbon are to be preferred. Be so good as to say, whether I am to observe the same rule in the present instance. And believe me truly, Gentlemen, your obedient humble servant,

John Luke.

---

(1) A mezzo di, per mezzo di. (2) Senseria.

* See Letter LXXVII of the same date to J. Newfield and Co.

† This is a reservation frequently made by merchants, and signifies, that it is to be understood they do not, by the act in question, incur any responsibility, and the other parties must « hold them harmless, » or in other words, exonerate them from all consequences.

LXXIV.

Messrs. J. Newfield & Co. *Oporto.*   London, 16th September, 18—.

Gentlemen, — By order of our common friends, Messrs. J. Phillips and Co., of Liverpool, I have to enclose you five bills of exchange, as noted at foot, amounting to 1658*l.* 12*s.* 4*d.*, part of 4,600*l.* which they have paid into my bankers' * for the purpose of being remitted to you, and you may be assured I shall do it with all possible dispatch. No more bills offered to-day of which I could approve. You will observe that these draughts are made payable to me, and I have endorsed them, but this must be understood (as I do not charge commission or *del credere*) to be without my prejudice, my sole object in so doing, being to prevent my prying (1) neighbours from gratifying their curiosity. I shall, notwithstanding, be as careful in the selection of bills, as if the responsibility were entirely my own. By next mail (2), I expect to be able to make you a further remittance. In the mean time, believe me to be, Gentlemen, your assured humble servant,   JOHN LUKE.

Note of Bills inclosed, viz.

1st of	L. 1,000	0 0	at 60 days' date on D. F. Pinto & Co., at 54 1/4.
1st of	214	6 0	at 60 days' sight on D. J. D. Guimanner at 54.
do.	90	8 4	or ff. 1,000, dated Amsterdam, 22nd July, at 1/2 usance on C. and M. Garner, at 54 1/4.
2nd of	253 18	0	at 60 days' date on Widow Moller and Son, at 54 1/4.
do.	100	0 0	at 30 days' sight on A. Follett, Jun. (3) 53 3/4.

(first three: on your city. last two: on Lisbon, firsts with F. and H. Fox.)

L. 1,658 12 4 To the debit of Jos. Phillips and Co., Liverpool.

LXXV.

Messrs. F. and H. Fox, *Lisbon.*   London, 16th September, 18—.

Gent., — I take the liberty of enclosing two firsts of exchange, as per note at foot, which you will be so good as to get accepted (4)

---

(1) Curiosi. (2) Posta, corriere. (3) Juniore. (4) Far accettare.
* This expression, if not strictly grammatical, is truly mercantile; the word « hands » is understood.

and hold at the disposal of the seconds,* remitted this day to our common friends at Oporto, Messrs. J. Newfield and Co. In case of non-acceptance or non payment, be so good as to advise said friends thereof, and cause the bills to be noted, furnishing me with a protest, that I may recover from the drawers; however I feel confident that such will not be needful (1). I remain, most truly, Sir, your obedient humble servant, JOHN LUKE.

Particulars of Bills,
L. 253 18 0 on Widow Moller and Son.
100 0 0 on A. Follett, jun.

LXXVI.**

John Luke, Esq. *London*.   *Liverpool*, 10th Oct. 18—.

Sir, — We have received your esteemed letter of the 7th instant, accompanied by an account of your remittance to Messrs. J. Newfield and Co., of Oporto, of the 4,600l. placed in your hands for that purpose, together with your charges thereon, 4l. 12s. which sum we have ordered to be paid to your bankers, Messrs. Bosanquet and Co. This being a separate transaction, you will please to close it in your books accordingly. With many thanks for your trouble in this affair, we are, &c.   Jos. PHILLIPS & Co.

LXXVII.

Messrs. J. Newfield and Co. *Oporto*.   *Liverpool*, 12th Sept., 18—.

Gent., — Having balanced the books of our late partnership, we find due to your Mr. Thompson, the sum of 4,827l. 13s. 4d. up to (2) 30th June last. But as there are yet some small amounts outstanding (3), and a few claims unsettled, we purpose remitting you 4,600l. (say four thousand six hundred pounds), on account (4), through the medium (5) of our common friend, John Luke, Esq., of London, to whom we have written by to-night's post, apprising him of our intention, and proposing that this being a family affair, he should charge no commission. Persuaded that he will accede to our wishes, we have no doubt that you will by next mail receive a part, if not the whole, of the above sum, in good bills, either on your city or Lisbon, with which you will please to do the needful, and credit Mr. T. accordingly, to whom we defer writing until we can close the partnership accounts altogether. Meanwhile (6) we request him to accept our kind regards, and remain, most truly, &c.
     Jos. PHILLIPS & Co.

---

(1) Necessario. (2) Up to, fino a, a tutto. (3) Non per anco pagate. (4) A conto, in conto. (5) Mezzo. (6) Frattanto, in tanto.
* See « BILLS » in the Appendix.
** The intermediate letters are omitted, as devoid of interest.

REMITTANCE.

LXXVIII.

Messrs. J. Newfield & Co. *Oporto.*   London, *14th October,* 18—.

Gent., — Our worthy friend, Mr. Luke, having advised us that he has completed his remittance of the 4,600*l.* on account of your Mr. Thompson, and moreover (1) furnished us with a note of his charges thereon, amounting, as per mem. (2) at foot, to 4*l.* 17*s.* 6.*d.*, we have placed that sum to Mr. T's debit also; of which you will please to take notice. Expecting to hear shortly of the receipt of this remittance, we remain, &.   Jos. Phillips & Co.

L. 2 17 6 Brokerage (3), 1/16 per cent. on 4,600*l.*
- 2 0 0 Postages to and from Oporto, Lisbon, and Liverpool.

L. 4 17 6

LXXIX.

Messrs. Jos. Phillips & Co. *Liverpool.*   Oporto, *21st October,* 18—.

Gent., — Your much esteemed favour of the 12th ult., informing us of your intention to remit us 4,000*l.* on our Mr. Thompson's late partnership account with you, was duly received; but we deferred answering it until we could advise, as we have now the pleasure of doing, the receipt of the whole of the said sum.

The various bills of which this remittance consisted, having been honoured, and not doubting that they will be discharged at maturity (4), we place the amount to the credit of our Mr. Thompson's private account as desired; and assuring you of the sentiments of esteem with which we are impressed, we are, &.

J. Newfield & Co.

LXXX.

John Luke, Esq. *London.*   Oporto, *21st October,* 18—.

Sir, — Since we last wrote to you on the 15th instant, we have been favored with yours of the 7th of the same month, covering (5) two bills on this city, value 1133*l.* 15*s.* 4*d.*

These drafts have been duly accepted; and the amount, added to your former remittances, completes the sum of 4,600*l.*, on account of Messrs. J. Phillips and Co. of Liverpool, thus closing this transaction.

For your kind attention to this business, we can but request you to accept our best thanks; and hope that on some other occasion your trouble will be better remunerated. With a tender of our best services here, we remain, &.   J. Newfield & Co.

(1) Inoltre, oltracciò. (2) Memorandum, nota, appunto. (3) Senseria. (4) Maturanza, scadenza. (5) (Coprendo), acchiudendo, accludendo.

Fourth Series.

LXXXI.

J. Thompson, Esq. *Liverpool.*   *London, 14th Jan., 18—.*

Sir, — I beg leave to trouble you with duplicate of a letter for Mr. J. M. Da Souza, of Bahia, ordering the shipment of 1000 to 1200 mangoes of tobacco, which you will please to forward by the first opportunity, for that city; I have left it open under a flying seal, for your perusal; the original went per packet (1) on the 14th inst. This tobacco is on joint account, as arranged when you were here, between Messrs. Wm. Thompson and Co. of Hamburgh, your firm, and myself, in thirds.

It is understood and agreed that all commissions charged by the house at Hamburgh, and by me, shall be equally divided between the three parties; consequently, Messrs. W. Thompson and Co. will have to credit you for one third of their commissions, and myself for one third in like manner. But, under these circumstances, all responsibility on my part, in giving the orders, accepting draft, and effecting insurance, must be removed, as well as that of the house at Hamburgh in making sales: so that, in fact, every risk attending this speculation must be borne by all the parties in the proportion in which they are interested; and this will apply to all other transactions of similar nature, in which the three houses may engage. The *del credere* to be charged by the house at Hamburgh, will of course not be divided, because the guarantee of the purchaser (2) is a risk which they take wholly upon themselves.

As soon as I receive Mr. Da Souza's invoice, I shall furnish you with a copy, and you can then remit me the amount of your third share therein. Believe me truly, Sir, your obedient humble servant,

R. JACKSON.

LXXXII.

J. M. Da Souza, Esq. *Bahia.*   *London, 14th Jan., 18—.*

Sir, — At the recommendation of Messrs. W. Thompson and Co. of Hamburgh, I take the liberty of addressing you, and avail myself of the opportunity to make you a tender of my best services in this city.

The object of my present application is, to request that you will have the goodness to purchase, and ship to the consignment of our above-mentioned friends at Hamburgh, from 1000 to 1,200 mangoes of tobacco, of prime quality, if you can. ship them at or under the price of 2 mil. (3) 300 reis, (say two mil. three hundred reis), per

---

(1) Pacchebotto. (2) Compratore. (3) Milreas.

mangote—all charges of shipping, your commission, and freight (1) included. To enable you to ascertain this point, you will please to calculate the mark banco at 300 reis, or the pound sterling equal to 4 mil. 100 reis.

For your reimbursement, you will draw on me at sixty days' sight, and at the most favorable exchange, furnishing me, at the same time, with invoice and bill of lading, and anticipated advice for insurance; when you may rest assured your draft shall be duly honoured. Trusting that this introduction may lead to more important transactions, I remain, most sincerely, Sir, your very obedient humble servant,   ROBERT JACKSON.

P. S. I have ordered the tobacco in Mangotes, because Rolls are not saleable at Hamburgh.

LXXXIII.

Messrs. W. Thompson & Co. *Hamburgh.*   *London, 18th January, 18—.*

Gentlemen, — I beg to inform you that agreeably to an arrangement made with your worthy brother, Mr. James Thompson of Liverpool, when in London, I have ordered from 1,000 to 1,200 mangotes of tobacco, to be shipped for your city, and to your address by Mr. J. M. Da Souza of Bahia, as you will perceive by the annexed copy of my letter under date of the 14th inst. As regards the account and conditions on which this investment is made, I must refer you to the inclosed copy of my letter of the 16th, to your brother, being in conformity with the terms agreed upon with him, and with which I apprehend he made you acquainted, prior to his leaving this place. In full expectation that this little adventure, from its success, will lead to others of greater magnitude, I remain, most sincerely, Gentlemen, your obedient humble servant,

               ROBERT JACKSON.

LXXXIV.

Robert Jackson, Esq. *London.*   *Liverpool, 17 January, 18—.*

Sir, — I have to acknowledge the receipt of your much esteemed favor of the 14th inst., and have noted its contents, wich are perfectly in accordance with the verbal agreement entered into when I was in London. The letter for Mr. Da Souza shall be forwarded by the first vessel for Bahia; there is none, however, at present loading for that city. Hoping this commencement of business on joint account, and in company with my brother's house at Hamburgh, will be the forerunner (2) of more extensive business, and with as-

---

(1) Nolo, Noleggio, (2) Precursore.

surances of my desire to render our correspondence mutually interesting and beneficial, I remain, Sir, your very obedient humble servant,
JAMES THOMPSON.

LXXXV.

Robert Jackson, Esq. *London.* *Hamburgh,* 25th *Jan.* 18—.

Sir, — We are much obliged by the readiness (1) with which you acceded to Mr. J. Thompson's proposition, in regard to trying an adventure or two on joint account, and are glad to observe that, in consequence, you have ordered from 1,000 to 1,200 mangotes of tobacco, to be shipped from Bahia to our address by our friend there, Mr. J. M. Da Souza; which order we have no doubt he will execute within your limit. The demand for this article is slack (2) at the present moment, but by the time we may expect the arrival of the small parcel you have ordered, we doubt not it will be brisker, and we hope to have it in our power to render you satisfactory account-sales, so as to induce you to follow up the operation.

We shall punctually observe the terms on which this, and future transactions, of a similar nature, are to be conducted; and it will, we beg to assure you, afford us much gratification (3) to continue a correspondence, thus, as we consider, auspiciously commenced. We beg you will believe that our best services are always at your disposal, and we remain, your truly obedient humble servants,
WILL. THOMPSON & Co.

LXXXVI.

Messrs. W. Thompson & Co. *Hamburgh.* *Bahia,* 21st *March,* 18—.

Gentlemen, — I am greatly indebted to you for your good intentions in introducing Mr. Robert Jackson of London to my firm, having received a letter from that gentleman, ordering the purchase of 1,000 to 1,200 mangotes of tobacco, to be shipped to your address; limiting me, however, to 2 mil. 300 reis per mangote on board, freight to your place included. I am sorry to say that it is utterly (4) out of my power to execute this order, and I shall be much obliged by your informing Mr. Jackson that tobacco, at our current prices, would stand in (5) nearly 15 per cent. more than his limit, exclusive of freight. I do not write to that gentleman, because I am unwilling to put him to unnecessary expence in postage. Believe me, with great respect, gentlemen, your obedient humble servant,
J. M. DA SOUZA.

---

(1) Prontezza. (2) Poco animato. (3) Piacere, contento. (4) Affatto, del tutto. (5) Costerebbe, verrebbe a costare.

JOINT SPECULATION IN TOBACCO.

LXXXVII.
Robert Jackson, Esq. *London.* *Hamburgh, 4th June 18—.*

Sir, — We have been favored with a letter from our friend, Mr. J. M. Da Souza of Bahia, dated 31st March last, which we transcribe on the other side, and from which you will perceive that he could not execute your small order for tobacco, within your limit: consequently, we must, for the present, forego (1) the pleasure of being interested with you in speculations in this article from the Brazils. It is well that Mr. Da S. resolved on its non-execution, for had he exceeded your limits, it would have occasioned dissatisfaction, since our market would not enable us to realise a profit on the consignment. We, by this post, communicate this result to the writer's brother at Liverpool. On some other occasion, we shall be most happy to join you, when we hope to be more successful. We are, Sir, your obedient humble servants, WILL. THOMPSON & Co.

LXXXVIII.
James Thompson, Esq. *Liverpool.* *Hamburgh, 4th June, 18—.*

Sir, — Having received advices from Mr. J. M. Da Souza of Bahia, that he could not possibly execute our friend Mr. Jackson's order for tobacco, on our joint account in thirds, we beg to apprise you thereof, and to inform you that we have written to Mr. J. to that effect. We expressed to him our regret at this unexpected prevention, or at least suspension of the active correspondence which we anticipated, and assured him that we shall, at all times, be ready to renew the attempt, whenever a more favorable opening occurs. Leaving it, therefore, to you to make such arrangement as you may deem proper, we remain, Sir, your assured obedient humble servants,
WILL. THOMPSON & Co.

LXXXIX.
Messrs. Will. Thompson & Co. *Hamburgh.* *London, 11th June, 18—.*

Gentlemen, — I have been favored with yours of the 4th instant, stating the impracticability of the execution of my order to M. R. Da Souza of Bahia, for the purchase of tobacco. I cannot but regret with you, this disappointment to my hopes of establishing a connection with your respectable house, and your brother's at Liverpool, of an amicable and reciprocally beneficial character. However, we must have patience, and I hope that we shall be more fortunate in a second attempt. In your brothers's next visit to this place, we shall see what can be done; meanwhile, I remain, most sincerely, Gentlemen, your obedient humble servant, ROBERT JACKSON.

P. S. I shall write Mr. Da Souza, that if he can execute the order in the autumn, he may do so.

---

(1) Rinunciare a.

XC.

J. M. Da Souza, Esq. Bahia.   London, 14th June, 18—.

Sir, — Our Hamburgh friends, Messrs. William Thompson and Co., having apprised me of the obstacles you have encountered in the execution of my order of the 14th January last, for the purchase and shipment of 1,000 to 1,200 mangoes of tobacco, I have only to regret this circumstance, and the disappointment consequent upon it.

This is, however, to authorise you to make the shipment at any time before next spring, provided it can be done within the limits already given: therefore you will please to consider my order in full force till March next. Hoping you will, ere (1) then, succeed in effecting the purchase, I remain, most truly, Sir, your obedient humble servant,   ROBERT JACKSON.

XCI.

Messrs. Arthur Collins & Co. Bristol.   London, 11th January, 18—.

Gentlemen, — I received, in due course, your favors of the 3rd and 6th inst. and have credited you 280*l*. 18*s*. 4*d*., being half the account of invoice of flax (2) per William, to Lisbon, on joint account. I have desired Messrs. E. Angove and Co., to whom they are consigned, to remit me the whole of the nett proceeds in specie, to-which I presume you will have no objection, as I deem it better to keep this adventure quite distinct from all other transactions; however, if you would rather those gentlemen should place your moiety (3) of the nett proceeds to your credit in account, you have only to write them to that effect, and I will confirm your letter.

I have taken due note of your acceptance for 450*l*. at two months from 20th ult., payable with me to the order of Castendieck and Co., which shall be punctually discharged at maturity and placed to your debit. Inclosed, I return you four bills received in yours of the 8th inst. for acceptance, the whole being duly honored. Believe me, very truly, Sir, your obedient humble servant,   WILLIAM LUKE.

XCII.

Messrs. H. & F. Vincent, Bell Alley.   London, 11th January, 18—.

Gentlemen, — You will oblige me by investing the sum of 375*l*. 8*s*. 11*d*. (less your brokerage (4) and my commission of $^1/_2$ per cent. on the sum expended), in the three per cent. consols, in the name of Dulz de Merdonza, Esq., of the island of Madeira; handing me an account thereof, when I will send a check (5) for the cost and brokerage. I am truly, gentlemen, yours, etc.   THOMAS ADAMS.

---

(1) Prima. (2) Lino. (3) Metà; parte, porzione. (4) Senseria. (5) Mandato, ordine a vista.

DRAFT DISHONOURED.

Fifth Series.

XCIII.

Joseph Manning, Esq. *Piccadilly.*   *Gt. Winchester St. 10th Jan. 18—.*

Sir, — Your acceptance for 38l., drawn by me on the 6th October last, and payable to my order three months after date, fell due yesterday, and now lies at my bankers, Messrs. Curtis and Co. Lombard street, noted for non payment. I beg, therefore, to call your immediate attention to it, and request you will take up (1) the same with 5s expenses thereon. I remain, Sir, your obedient humble servant,   T. WILLIAMS.

XCIV.

Joseph Manning, Esq. *Piccadilly.*   *Gt. Winchester St. 12th Jan. 18—.*

Sir, — I am very much surprised at your inattention, in a matter of so much importance as a dishonoured draft. Referring you to my note of the day before yesterday, informing you that your acceptance of 38l. had been noted for non-payment: I now beg to say, that if the draft be not immediately taken up, I shall be compelled (2) to have recourse to measures, no less unpleasant to me than disgraceful and disagreeable to yourself. I am, Sir, yours, etc.

T. WILLIAMS.

XCV.

Piccadilly, 14th January, 18—.

Thomas Williams, Esq. *Great Winchester Street.*

Sir, — Having been out of town for the last fortnight, I am truly concerned (3) to find that no provision was made for my acceptance of your draft, due on the 9th inst. for 38l. When on my return to town this morning, your note of the 10th was put into my hands, I immediately took up the bill, which now lies before me, together with your note of this morning. I can only regret having through inadvertency, caused you so much trouble. Believe me, very sincerely, Sir, your obedient humble servant,   JOSEPH MANNING.

Sixth Series.

XCVI.

James Box, Esq. *London.*   *London, 11th August, 18—.*

Sir, — In pursuance of our arrangement, I shall proceed to Paris to-morrow, and from thence to Havre de Grâce, to embark for Fay-

---

(1) (Pigliar su), pagare. (2) Costretto, astretto. (3) (*Interessato*), displacente, afflitto.

Anderson.

al in the Nancy, Captain W. Richards; in which vessel, our friends, Laffite and Co. of Rouen, have shipped goods for my account, to the amount of 650*l*. (say six hundred and fifty pounds sterling). This sum I shall have to pay to their bankers in Paris, Messrs. De la Rue & Fils, and I will, therefore, thank you to furnish me with a letter of credit on those gentlemen, authorizing them to take my draft on you for 700*l*. (seven hundred pounds), at three months' date, and to negotiate the same; all expenses attending the negotiation to be at my charge.

On my arrival at Fayal, I shall ship wines on board the Nancy to a similar amount, one moiety to the consignment of your friends, Messrs. Ross and Co. of Hamburgh, and the other to that of Messrs. W. Williams and Co. at St. Petersburgh, with directions for each of them to remit, or hold the nett proceeds at your disposal. In the meantime, and as collateral security for the 700*l*. draft, you will please to effect insurance on the goods shipped at Havre (of which I shall hand you particulars from thence), in the said sum of 700*l*. (seven hundred pounds). And as soon as you receive advice of the Nancy's safe arrival at Fayal, open a policy (1) for 400*l*. (four hundred pounds) on wines to Hamburgh, and 400*l*. (four hundred pounds) more on ditto to St. Petersburgh, awaiting my further orders to complete the same.

It is understood that you are to charge interest at the rate of 5 per cent. on all sums advanced by you, until reimbursed; also the usual commission of $^1/_2$ per cent. on all drafts drawn on you, and remittances in bills of exchange made by me, or by my orders; the same on all insurances effected, with $^1/_2$ per cent. for *del credere* thereon, as well as on all transactions wherein your correspondence effects sales, etc.

In the hope that this commencement may lead to more extensive transactions, I remain, most truly, Sir, your obliged, obedient humble servant, J. G. SOMMERS.

XCVII.

Messrs. De la Rue & Sons, *Paris*. *London, 11th August, 18—.*

Gentlemen, — I beg leave to introduce to your acquaintance, the bearer, Mr. J. G. Sommers, who is about to visit your capital on business; and I have to request, that, should Mr. S. have occasion to draw on me for 700*l* (say seven hundred pounds sterling), you will be so good as to take his bill of exchange at three months' date, for that amount; relying on the same being duly honoured. It is understood, for your government, that your commission, and all charges attending this transaction on your side of the water, are to

---

(1) Polizza di sicurtà, certificato di assicurazione.

be defrayed (1) by Mr. Sommers, and that the nett amount which I am to pay here, is the before-mentioned sum of 700*l*. I have the honor to remain, Gentlemen, your very obedient humble servant,

JAMES BOX.

XCVIII.

James Box, Esq. *London*.   *Paris, 15th August, 18—.*

Sir, — Mr. J. G. Sommers has delivered to us your letter of the 11th inst., establishing a credit in his favor for 700*l*. (seven hundred pounds sterling), which we shall have much pleasure in supplying him with, taking his draft on you at three months' date for our reimbursement. Requesting you will, at all times, command our best services, we have the honor to remain, Sir, your obedient humble servants,   DE LA RUE & Co.

XCIX.

James Box, Esq. *London*.   *Paris, 2nd September, 18—.*

Sir, — Having nearly completed my business in this city, I shall proceed in a day or two for Havre, to embark for Fayal, and having sent off some more goods for shipment per Lancy, I request you to insure the same for 300*l*. (three hundred pounds sterling). I shall address you from Havre with the further particulars requisite. In the meantime, believe me, Sir, your obedient humble servant,

J. G. SOMMERS.

C.

J. G. Sommers, Esq. *Havre de Grace*.   *London, 5th September, 18—.*

Sir, — I am favored with your letter of the 2nd inst., and have, agreeably to the order it contained, effected insurance on goods, per Nancy, Captain W. Richards, from Havre to Fayal, in the sum of 300*l*, at the same premium as the 700*l*. done previously to your departure from this city, say twenty shillings per cent. I shall expect the promised particulars for endorsement on the policies; and remain truly, Sir, your obedient humble servant,   JAMES BOX.

CI.

James Box, Esq. *London*.   *Havre de Grace, 25th September, 18—.*

Sir, — I have now to wait on you with a specification of the goods shipped on board the Nancy at this port, for my account, and which you will please to have declared on the policies, opened by you for 700*l*. and 300*l*. respectively; retaining the former in your hands, as per agreement, and forwarding the latter (for 300*l*.) to

---

(1) Pa gate.

my friends Messrs. Dugard, Frères, Rue St. Honoré, Paris. It is expected that the Nancy will sail in the beginning of next month. I remain, faithfully, Sir, your obedient humble servant,

J. G. SOMMERS.

CII.

J. G. Sommers, Esq. *Havre de Grace*. London, 2nd. October, 18—.

Sir, — I am in possession of your favor of the 25th ult., and, having endorsed in the policies the necessary declarations of value of the different goods, of which your shipment consisted, I shall transmit that for 300*l.* by this day's post, to Messrs. Dugard, Frères, of Paris. The one for 700*l.* I retain as collateral security for any advances that I may come under for your account. By the bye (1), you have not mentioned whether you made use or not of the credit on Messrs. De la Rue and. Co. — please to inform me in your next.

I shall be looking out for intelligence of the Nancy's arrival at Fayal, in order to effect the insurance on wines to Hamburgh and Petersburgh, 400*l.* each, as ordered in your letter of the 11th August. Inclosed, you will please to receive copies of the respective policies, and an account of the premiums, etc., amounting to 12*l.* 5*s.* to your debit. Wishing you a pleasant passage, and profitable sales, I remain, Sir, your obedient humble servant,   JAMES BOX.

CIII.

Messrs. De la Rue et Co. *Paris*. London, 8th October. 18—.

Gentlemen, — Since the receipt of your letter of the 15th August, respecting the credit for 700*l.* in favor of Mr. J. G. Sommers, nothing has occurred to occasion my troubling you; but this morning, to my surprise, a bill of exchange for 700*l.* has been presented, purporting to be drawn by Mr. Sommers, at three months' date, from the 2nd September, and in favor of Messrs. De la Rue and Co., but indorsed « De la Rue and Co., » apparently in your hand-writing. Mr. Sommers having written to me on the very day (2) on which this bill is dated, and subsequently from Havre, under date of the 25th ult. without mentioning his having drawn such a bill (though of course I expected he would do so), or having given any advice whatever of his having made use of the credit, I have thought it prudent to withhold (3) my acceptance until I hear from you, whether you have negotiated this bill or not, for in these times, when forgeries are so frequent, and fraudulent practices of such common occurrence, the utmost caution is required

(1) Di volo. (2) Lo stesso giorno. (3) Negare, rifiutare.

In transactions of this nature. If Mr. Sommers drew this bill, it is an unpardonable oversight (1), or inexcusable neglect on his part, that he did not give me the necessary advice, in the letters alluded to. I believe he is still at Havre, and I wrote to him on the 2nd inst. respecting this transaction. On receiving his or your answer, I shall of course honor the draft. I remain always, Gentlemen, your obedient humble servant, JAMES BOX.

CIV.

Messrs. De la Rue & Co. *Paris.* *London, 10th October, 18—.*

Gentlemen, — Referring you to my respects of the 8th inst., I have now to inform you that the holders of the draft mentioned therein, would not consent to hold it over until I received your reply; consequently, I have accepted it, under protest for your honor *, as indorsers, in the persuasion that the indorsement is in your handwriting. I hope, in a day or two, to hear from you that all is right respecting this draft, when not only I shall be relieved from the uneasiness which Mr. Sommers's neglect has occasioned me, but you from all responsability; as I shall, in that case, place the draft to the account of that gentleman. I remain, Gentlemen, your most obedient, humble servant, JAMES BOX.

CV.

J. G. Sommers, Esq. *Havre de Grace.* *London, 8th October, 18—.*

Sir, — Confirming the above copy of my respects of the 2nd inst., I am now under the disagreeable necessity of informing you that a bill has been presented for acceptance, which appears to have been drawn by you on the 2nd ult. for 700*l.* at three months' date, to the order of *De Rue & Co.* (without the *la*). Having no advice from you, although you wrote to me on the same day, and again on the 25th ult., from Havre, I have been (however reluctantly) obliged to dishonor it. I hope you will, immediately on receipt of this (should you not have done it before, in answer to my last), do the needful, and put me out of suspense. This neglect on your part (as I have no doubt it will prove to be,) has exposed me to very serious consequences with Messrs. De la Rue & Co., who will perhaps attribute my refusal of your draft to some sinister motive. For Heavens's sake! be more regular and cautious in future. I always considered you a man of business; but these inattentions will shake my confidence in you, which has hitherto been unlimited. Awaiting your explanation with impatience, I remain truly, Sir, your obedient and humble servant, JAMES BOX.

---

(1) Svista, sbaglio.
* See « BILLS » in the Appendix.

CVI.

James Box, Esq. *London.*   *Paris, 11th Oct., 18—.*

Sir, — The bill of exchange for 700*l.* to which you allude in your favor of the 8th inst. was drawn by the gentleman who brought us your letter of credit for that amount; and the signature, « J. G. Sommers, » is his—he having signed the draft in our office. We trust, therefore, that on your receiving this assurance all will be correct, and all responsibility removed from our indorsement. We cannot account for (1) Mr. Sommers' neglect in regard to the advice of his draft, but presume that he will be able to explain this irregularity to your satisfaction. We remain, Sir, your devoted and obedient servants,   DE LA RUE & CO.

CVII.

Messrs. De la Rue & Co. *Paris.*   *London, 14th October, 18—.*

Gentlemen, — The explanation contained in your much valued favor of the 11th inst. is perfectly satisfactory; and, of course, all doubts as to the identity of Mr. Sommers' draft for 700*l.* are removed. Having now accepted this bill in the regular way, you may consider your responsibility at an end. Regretting the trouble you have had in this transaction, I remain, Gent. your obedient humble servant,   JAMES BOX.

CVIII.

James Box, Esq. *London.*   *Havre de Grace, 18th October, 18—.*

Sir, — Your favor of the 2nd inst. has just come to hand, and being on the point of departure, I have only time to say, that I drew on you for the 700*l.* from Paris, at three months' date, in favor of your friends, Messrs. De la Rue & Co., and am surprised that my draft had not made its appearance. I certainly did not mention having drawn it in my letter of the 2nd, because at the time that was written I had not drawn it; and when I did, I considered it unnecessary to advise you of my having done so, as I concluded you would consider it a matter of course (2). Trusting this may yet be in time to prevent any unpleasant consequences, I remain, in haste, but truly, Sir, your obedient humble servant,

     J. G. SOMMERS.

P. S. I find the insurances all right (3).

CIX.

London, 2nd October, 18—.

Messrs. Dugard, Frères, *Rue St. Honoré, Paris.*

Gent., — By desire of Mr. J. G. Sommers, I have the honor to

---

(1) Spiegare, capire. (2) Intesa (da sè). (3) A dovere, in regola, bene.

wait on you with a policy of insurances for 300*l*. effected by me on goods per Nancy, Captain W. Richards, from Havre de Grace to the Island of Fayal. I avail myself of this opportunity to make you an offer of my best services in this city, and to assure you that I am, with great sincerity, Sir, your obedient humble servant,

JAMES BOX.

CX.

James Box, Esq. *London.*   *Fayal,* 15*th November,* 18—.

Sir, — I have the satisfaction to inform you of my safe arrival at this island, in the Nancy, on the 18th inst. after a tolerably pleasant passage. We shall begin discharging in a day or two, and then proceed to ship the wines with as much expedition as possible, before the winter sets in (1).

I have given your address to my friends, Mr. A. J. Martins, and Mr. J. Vicenza of this island, who are both large exporters of fruit (oranges) to your market; and, at my recommendation, will have no objection to send a parcel to your consignment on trial, provided you will permit them to draw on you, on completing the shipment, for one half, or two thirds of the amount of invoice.

I shall likewise be disposed to ship some on my own account, or on joint account with you, if you should have no objection. At all events, you will please to charter a fast-sailing good vessel (a schooner to be preferred) for this port, to bring out coals, shook-pipes, and iron-hoops, as per particulars annexed, and to load fruit and wine for London. The freight for the voyage, out and home (2) must not exceed 500*l*. with five per cent. primage*; the port-charges, etc. to be defrayed by the captain and owners, if you can prevail on them to agree to this. If you succeed in chartering a vessel on these conditions, the sooner she is despatched the better, with sufficient coals for ballast (3), the other articles already named, and the few items (4) comprised in the annexed list, for my own private use.

Should you have an opportunity, you may draw on me for the cost of the coal, etc., together with that of insurance, which you will be so good as to effect on the outward cargo, to its full value, with an addition of five per cent. to cover expences in case of loss. I hope the premium will be moderate.

Time will not allow of the vessel going to Newcastle or Sunderland on the present occasion; but probably, had it been a little earlier in the season, it would have been more advantageous to send her to one or the other of those places to load.

Should you not be able to reimburse yourself by drawing, you

---

(1) Cominci. (2) Fuori e di ritorno. (3) Zavorra. (4) Capi, oggetti.
* See « PRIMAGE » in the Appendix.

will have the goodness to make your purchases at as long credit as may be practicable, to allow for the shipments I shall make being realised, if possible, in time to meet the payments for the outward cargo. I remain, Sir, your obedient humble servant,

J. G. SOMMERS.

CXI.

J. G. Sommers, Esq. *Fayal.*   *London, 30th Nov. 18—.*

Sir, — Prior to entering on the subject of your esteemed favor of the 25th inst. acquainting me with your safe arrival at Fayal, I must acknowledge the receipt of that of the 18th of last month, from Havre de Grace, which sets the transaction of the 700*l.* draft from Paris right; and I immediately did the needful, debiting you for that amount, and my commission, $^1/_2$ per cent. 3*l.* 10*s.*

I have to thank you for your introduction of my firm to your friends at Fayal, and shall be glad to receive any consignments of oranges they may be pleased to send to my address; but it is not usual to make advances on cargoes of so perishable a nature, at least until the vessel is arrived and the state of the cargo ascertained, when, if the latter prove to be in good order and condition, I shall have no objection to come under acceptance for two thirds the estimated nett proceeds; the bills to be drawn at two months' date from the vessel's arrival, or three months from the time of her sailing from your island.

From the perishable quality of the commodity (1), I must likewise decline (2) taking any share or concern in the shipment which you propose making; however, to serve you, I will, in the present instance, ship the goods you order, and await my reimbursement from the sale of such as you may consign to me. But as to purchasing coals, etc. at such credit as to enable me to pay for them out of the proceeds of your shipments, this is wholly out of the question, coal in particular being a ready-money article.

No schooner offering, I have been in treaty for a small brig, the London Packet, Captain Scott, to proceed to your port with the articles ordered in your favor of the 2nd. The broker demands 600*l.* and I have offered him 400*l.* In my next I shall, no doubt, be able to inform you of my having completed the charter, and, you may be assured, on as low terms as possible; but as to port-charges, I fear no captain or owner will consent to defray them.

The coals must be bought here, as there will be no time for the vessel to proceed to Newcastle or Sounderland. Indeed the additional freight which would be demanded, and the premium of insurance

---

(1) Merce, oggetto. (2) Declinare, ricusare.

at this season of the year, would be more than equivalent to the difference in the price of the coals.

When I have concluded the charter, I shall lose no time in despatching the vessel, and hope she will be with you before Christmas. Believe me, Sir, your obedient humble servant, JAMES BOX.

CXII.

J. G. Sommers, Esq. *Fayal.* London, 3rd December, 18—.

Sir, — Referring to the preceeding copy of my last respects (1), I have now to advise you of my having chartered the London Packet to proceed immediately to your island. I have agreed to pay 475*l.* with five per cent. primage. The port-charges you are to defray, as you will perceive by the copy of the charter inclosed. I have purchased the coals, which she will begin to load to-morrow, and finish the next day. The empty pipes (shook) will be put on board the following day, and the iron hoops, which I have agreed for at 17*l.* per ton, will be shipped on Saturday: when the vessel will clear, and, I hope, proceed on her voyage on Sunday next. I feel confident you will approve, not only of the charter, but of the expedition used in getting the cargo on board.

I have effected insurance on 350*l.* the value of the different goods, to be shipped at fifty shilling per cent. which I consider moderate for this season of the year. Premium etc., to your debit, as per account, and copy of the policy inclosed, 13*l.* 10*s.* 10*d.* I have further insured 400*l.* on wines, to Hamburgh, per Nancy, at three gs. (2) per cent; amount 15*l.* 12*s.* to your debit. Also 400*l.* on wines, by the same vessel, to Petersburgh, at five gs. being the lowest I could possibly get it done at, from the circumstance of the Nancy having to winter somewhere in England, for which I have provided, as you will perceive, in the policy. The premium and charges on this assurance are carried to your debit in the sum of 24*l.*

By the chartered vessel, I shall send the articles ordered for your own use, which are in readiness, and for cost of which I have debited you 5*l.* 7*s.* as per note annexed. Believe me, always sincerely, Sir, your obedient humble servant, JAMES BOX.

CXIII.

J. G Sommers, Esq. *Fayal.* London, 7th. December, 18—.

Sir, — The present will be handed to you by Captain Scott, of the London Packet, which vessel sails to-morrow. I inclose a copy of my last respects, of the 3rd inst.; as also invoice and bill of lading of the shipments made by your orders; amount of the former 378*l.* 7*s.*

---

(1) Rispetti, lettera. (2) Gs. *abbrev. di* Guineas.

4d. to your debit. You will also receive herewith, bill of lading and invoice of twenty-five casks, containing 100 dozen, of bottled porter, which I have shipped on my own account, and to assist in filling the vessel. The amount, 42l. I trust you will be able to realise. However, I do not wish to limit you as to sales; but rely on your doing your best to dispose of this small consignment. The nett proceeds you will please to invest in fruit for my account, to be shipped, if possible, in the London Packet. I also send you, by Captain Scott, six gold Portuguese coins, of 6mil. 400 reis each, which I request you to lay out (1) in the same manner, advising me in time for insurance, should an opportunity offer.

The captain has special charge of the few articles for your private use. I will thank you to deliver the inclosed letters to Mr. Martins, and Mr. Vicenza, and I remain most sincerely, Sir, your very obedient humble servant, ——— JAMES BOX.

CXIV.

A. J. Martins, Esq. *Fayal.* London, 8th December, 18—.

Sir, — My friend, Mr. J. G. Sommers, of your island, having informed me of your wish to make me consignments of oranges, from time to time, during the ensuing season, I beg to thank you for this mark of your confidence; but I am fearful my friend, in his anxiety to promote my interest, has overrated (2) my ability, though he cannot my willingness to serve you. I shall be extremely happy to receive such consignments on the usual terms; that is, to advance two thirds of the estimated nett proceeds on the cargo being landed, and the quality, and actual state of the fruit (on which the value of the article so much depends) ascertained. But it is by no means, as you must be aware, the practice to accept bills of exchange, drawn on account of such cargoes in anticipation, on transmission of the bill of lading and invoice.

In the event of your making any shipment, and whising to insure, I shall be ready to effect any insurance you may be pleased to order, deducting (3) the premium, commission, and charges from the proceeds of sales.

Awaiting your commands, and in the hope that this may lead to a permanent correspondence, to our mutual satisfaction, I remain most truly, Sir, your obedient humble servant, JAMES BOX.

CXV.

London, 7th December, 18—.

Captain John Scott, *Brig, London Packet,*
    lying in the Thames.

Sir, — Herewith you will receive a packet, directed to Mr. J. G.

---

(1) Spendere, impiegare. (2) Stimato troppo. (3) Diffalcando.

Sommers at Fayal, to whom your cargo is consigned, and for whose account your vessel has been freighted. You will be so good as to deliver the same immediately on your arrival at Fayal, and follow Mr. Sommers' directions as to all your further proceedings. Mr. Sommers will advance any money that you may need whilst at Fayal, for the use of the vessel under your command, agreeably to the charter-party,*, and you will please to give him duplicate receipts for whatever sums you may receive.

You will avail yourself of the first favorable opportunity to put to sea, and use all possible despatch in the prosecution of your voyage. Wishing you a safe, expeditious and pleasant passage, I remain truly, Sir, your obedient humble servant,   JAMES BOX.

CXVI.

James Box, Esq. *London.*   *Fayal, 28th November, 18—.*

Sir, — Having completed the discharge of the Nancy, and finding it will not answer (1) to attempt sending her to Hamburgh and Petersburgh at this season of the year, I have made an arrangement with Captain Richards, who has consented to annul our agreement, and to proceed to your port with a cargo of fruit, for another house here. As I have no doubt you will have been able to charter a vessel agreeably to my instructions of the 20th inst. (of which I annex a copy), I shall ship the wines, together with some fruit, direct to your port, for you to sell there or trans-ship to the Baltic, as you may deem most to my advantage. Should you have effected the insurance on these wines, per Nancy, please to cancel it, and get it done on the vessel which you have chartered to your port only; also 300*l.* on fruit, say on 300 boxes of oranges, to be marked S, on my account, charging the premium in the account-sales. I remain, Sir, your obedient humble servant,   J. G. SOMMERS.

CXVII.

J. G. Sommers, *Fayal.*   *London, 14th December, 18—.*

Sir, — The foregoing is a copy of my last letter of the 7th inst., since which time I have received your favor of the 28th ult. announcing your having annulled your agreement with Captain Richards of the Nancy, and consequently requesting I would cancel the insurances effected on the wines, intended to be shipped in her for Hamburgh and St. Petersbourgh. This I have accordingly done, and credited your account 14*l.* for premium returned (2) in the former, and 48*l.* for ditto on the latter voyage. The underwriters (3)

---

(1) Non converrà. (2) Restituito. (3) (I soscrittori), gli assicuratori.
* See « CHARTER-PARTY » in the Appendix.

always retain 1/2 per cent. for cancelling a policy, and the stamps are lost.

I have now insured 800l. on the same wines to this port, by the London Packet, at two per cent, and 300l. on 300 boxes of oranges, by the same vessel, at the same rate, making to your debit, as per accounts annexed, 20l. on the one, and 8l. 5s. on the other. I cannot but (1) approve of your determination with regard to the Nancy's intended voyage to the Baltic.

Presuming you will likewise ship some oranges on my account, per London Packet, I have effected a provisional insurance thereon, in 200l. Expecting shortly to hear of her arrival out, I remain, Sir, your obedient humble servant,   JAMES BOX.

CXVIII.

James Box, Esq. *London*.   *Fayal, 21st December, 18—*

Sir, — Referring to the annexed copy of my last respects, I have now the pleasure to inform you that the London Packet, Captain Scott, arrived here safely yesterday, and just in time to get her discharged before the holidays commence. The latter, I fear, will sadly interfere with her loading; however, I shall get her away with all possible expedition. I take due note of the insurances effected, and have credited you in my account accordingly, viz: —

L. 13 10 10 for prem. etc., of L. 350 on goods by her.
15 12   do.   of   400 on wines to Hamburgh.
24   do.   of   400 on do. (2) to St. Petersburgh.
& 5 7   cost of sundries as per your letter of the 7th instant.

I have likewise received your favor of the 30th ult. and have credited you a further sum of 3l. 10s. amount of your commission on my draft from Paris for 700l. in favor of Messrs. De la Rue and Co. The principal I had already carried to your credit, and I beg to apologise (3) for my omission, in regard to the advice of that bill. I am glad to find that all is now right.

The six pieces of 6 mil. 400 reis each, I have received from Captain Scott, and have credited *your* account 38 mil. 400 reis, together with twenty per cent. premium thereon, 7 mil. 680 reis. I shall dispose of your bottled porter, when landed, for the utmost I can obtain for it. In the meantime, for your government in insurance, I intend shipping 200 boxes of oranges, marked B, on board the London Packet, for your account, besides the 300 on my own: and this I think will fill her.

I shall address you again soon after the holidays; meanwhile I remain, ever, Sir, your obedient humble servant, J. G. SUMMERS.

---

(1) Non posso se non. (2) *Do.* abbrev. di *ditto*. (3) Di fare le mie scuse, d'essere scusato.

CONSIGNMENT. — INSTRUCTIONS TO CAPTAIN.

CXIX.

James Box, Esq. *London.*   *Fayal, 15th February, 18—.*

Sir, — The holidays and the weather have combined to defeat my intention and exertions, in regard to despatching the London Packet sooner. However, she is now ready to put to sea, and will, I hope, take her departure to-morrow.

Inclosed, you will find bills of lading for,

40 pipes wine, valued at L. 20 per pipe, L. 800 }
300 bxs oranges, do. at 1 per box, 300 } on my account
200 do. do., do. at 1 per box, 200 on your acct.

The invoice of the latter is likewise inclosed, and I have debited for you the amount, 480 mil. 000 reis in your account, crediting the same, for nett proceeds of your 100 dozen porter, as per sales also inclosed, 400 mil. 000 reis, having, I consider sold them well at 4 mil. 500 reis por dozen. I hope you will approve of this sale; and flattering myself that the sales of the fruit will give you equal satisfaction, it being shipped in prime (1) order, I shall anxiously await the result of this little adventure. Believe me to be, as on all occasions, Sir, your obedient humble servant, J. G. SOMMERS.

CXX.

J. G. Sommers, Esq. *Fayal.*   *London, 15th February, 18—.*

Sir, — Your esteemed favors of the 21st December last and 15th ult. have been duly received; the latter by the London Packet. The wine and fruit have been safely landed, but I am sorry to say that the latter is in very bad condition, and nearly all rotten (2); so much so, indeed, that I was obliged to put it up to auction immediately; and you may form some idea of the loss which will be sustained on this part of the cargo, when I assure you that the nett proceeds will scarcely defray the freight and charges. I attribute the damage to the bad package (3), and bad stowage (4), (there not having been sufficient room (5) left between the boxes for ventilation), and to the length of time the fruit must have been packed before it was shipped. The account-sales of your parcel shall be forwarded in my next letter. I have credited you, in my account, for the cost of my 200 boxes, 480 mil. 000 reis, and debited the same 400 mil. 000 reis for nett proceeds of my 100 dozen bottled porter, and 46 mil. 200 reis, produce of my six gold coins.

I have tasted the wines, as also have several dealers. They are of a better quality than I expected, and I have consequently demanded 25l. per pipe; but I cannot get even 20l. offered for them,

---

(1) Ottimo, eccellente. (2) Fracido, marcio, guasto. (3) Imballaggio.
(4) Stivare, stivamento. (5) Spazio.

although all the parties who have tasted them acknowledge that they are the best they ever knew to come from your island.

I shall put them up to auction; and if I cannot get 25l. bid for them, shall immediately ship them for Hamburgh and Petersburgh, agreeably to your orders. From the pro forma * account-sales and advices I have received from those ports, I think the wines would nett *there* the price I have fixed for selling them at *here*. I remain, etc.
J. Box.

CXXI.

Mr. J. G. Sommers, *Fayal*. London, 8th March, 18—.

Sir, — Without any of your favors since my last respects, of which the preceding is a copy, I have now to wait on you with account-sales of your fruit, the 300 boxes, netting 19l. 2s. 8d. which I have placed to the credit of *your* account, as also 9l. 8s. drawback of duties (1) which I have recovered on the coals per London Packet.

The duty and charges on my 200 boxes of oranges, exceed the gross proceeds (2) by 10l. 18s. 10d. I therefore feel assured that you will not expect me to pay any freight thereon, since it is entirely owing to most culpable neglect, on the part of yourself, or of those whom you employed, that I have sustained this loss. It would certainly be very illiberal, as I entered into the speculation merely to serve you, by helping to fill up the vessel, both out and home, were you to permit me to be an additional sufferer, by paying freight for goods that were evidently not in good order and condition when shipped.

I have settled the freight and primage (3) with Captain Scott, as per account inclosed, and have debited you, in *your* account, 498l. 15s. for balance paid.

Of the wines, four pipes only were sold by auction, at 25l., and I have since disposed of ten pipes at 24l. per pipe, of 110 gallons (4), and four months' credit. The pipes are rather small, and do not run more than 107 gallons upon an average. The remainder, together with the forty pipes and two hogsheads left by you in the docks, I have taken freight for, say thirty-four pipes and two hogsheads (5), per London, Captain John Rumbert, for Hamburgh, and have effected insurance thereon, in the sum of 875l., and 30 pipes per Charles, Captain James Knight, for St. Petersburgh insured for 750l.

Inclosed, you will find the account of the premium, etc., and for

---

(1) Dazio di ritorno, balzello, diritto restituito. (2) Lordo ricavo. (3) Cappa, primaggio (*gratificazione al capitano*). (4) *Gallon*, misura di quattro litri. (5) Hogshead, botte.

* See Appendix.

INSURANCE. 79

which I have debited *your* account, 26*l*. 9*s*. 6*d*. When I am enabled to furnish you account-sales of these wines, I shall deduct the cost of insurance from the respective accounts, and credit you in account current for the same, having entered the amount now to your debit, for regularity's sake (1). I have not charged you *del credere* in the above account, being anxious not to increase expenses; but I have been very careful in selecting the most responsible underwriters.

Inclosed, I wait on you further with your account current, balance carried to your debit this day in a new account, 1743*l*. 6*s*. which I trust you will find correct; and in that case, request you to pass the same in conformity. I remain, Sir, your obedient humble servant, JAMES BOX.

CXXII.

James Box, Esq. *London*. *Fayal, 1st April. 18—*.

Sir, — I have to acknowledge receipt of your favors of the 15th February and 8th ult.; the latter transmitting account-sales of the 300 boxes of fruit, per London Packet, nett proceeds 19*l*. 2*s*. 8*d*. to your debit; also my account current to the 1st ult., shewing a balance in your favor of 1743*l*. 6*s*. This account is under examination, and, if found correct, shall be carried to a new account in conformity. I note that I have to debit you with the sum of 9*s*. 8*l*. received for drawback of the duties on the coal, and that I am to pass to your credit 485*l*. 18*s*. 1*d*., balance of freight per London Packet, and 26*l*. 9*s*. 6*d*. amount of provisional insurance on wines to Hamburgh and St. Petersburgh.

With regard to the fruit, I am astonished, as well as hurt (2), to learn that it has arrived in such bad order, every precaution having, as I considered, been taken to insure its preservation. The fruit was certainly gathered some time before it was shipped; partly on account of the vessel having been expected to arrive much sooner; and partly in order to take advantage of the weather, before the winter set in (3). The loss is deplorable, particularly on your 200 boxes; on which, under the circumstances, I cannot think of charging any freight, although I do not consider that the damage arose from any neglect of mine; and as to the stowage, perhaps the Estivador was too anxious to fill the vessel as completely as he could.

With respect to the wine, I approve of all you have done, it being strictly in conformity with my instructions.

Inclosed, you will receive first of exchange for 250*l*. at sixty

---

(1) Per la buona regola. (2) Offeso, leso. (3) Cominciasse.

days' sight, on George Bury and Co., with which you will please to do the needful, and credit my account accordingly.

I will thank you also to effect insurance on six pipes of wine S t to 6, which I am about to ship on board the Portuguese Schooner, Boa Lembrança, Capt. Dos Santos, from hence to Hamburgh; for which port she will sail in a few days, and will load back various goods that I have ordered from your friends, Messrs. Müller, Son, and Co., of that city. The wines are consigned to that house, as you will perceive by the inclosed letter, which I have left open for your perusal, and which you will be so good as to seal and forward per first mail to Hamburgh.

Our said friends are to account to you for the nett proceeds of the wine, and to remit you the surplus, if any, or otherwhise to value on you for what the articles ordered may cost, over and above the said nett proceeds; in which latter case you will have the goodness to honor their drafts and place them to my debit. I remain, Sir, your obedient humble servant,   J. G. SOMMERS.

CXXIII.

Messrs. Müller, Son & Co. *Hamburgh*.   *Fayal, 1st April, 18—.*

Sirs, -- Our common friend, James Box, Esq., having favored me with your address, when lately in London, and having assured me, that you would gladly receive any consignments of wine or fruit which I might be induced to make to you from hence, as likewise to execute any orders I might transmit, I beg to apprise you that I have chartered the portuguese schooner, Boa Lembrança, from this port to yours, and that I shall ship on board of her six pipes of wine of this island's growth (1), relying on your realising the best price your market will allow. The quality you will find excellent, and fully equal to that of the thirty-four pipes you will probably receive from our London friend.

I shall again address you by the vessel; but in the mean time I must call your attention to the list inclosed, of a still, and sundry articles, which I have to request you to ship by the schooner, for my account, on her return. These you can have prepared forthwith, in order that the vessel may not be detained for them. You will please to furnish me with the account-sales and invoice, advising Mr. Box of the amount of the latter, for his government in effecting insurance thereon. Should the proceeds of the wines leave a surplus, after defraying the amount of the invoice, be so good as to remit such balance to Mr. Box for my account. On the contrary, should there be a deficiency, please to value on him for it. In

---

(1) Prodotto.

INSURANCE. 81

hopes that this small essay (1) may prove the forerunner of transactions of greater magnitude, I remain most truly, Gent. (2) your very obedient humble servant,   J. G. SOMMERS.

CXXIV.

J. G. Sommers, Esq. *Fayal.*   London, *16th April, 18—.*

Sir, — I am favored with your esteemed letter of the 1st inst., inclosing 250*l.* in a bill at sixty days' sight, on George Bury and Co., which, having been duly honored, will appear to your credit at maturity.

I have effected the insurance you order on six pipes of wine, per Portuguese schooner, Boa Lembrança, from your island to Hamburgh, at five guineas per cent. This is, it must be admitted, a high premium, but no more than has been given on the same vessel on a former voyage. The captains of such vessels are, in general, very ignorant and unskilful; and moreover there are reports of pirates being in your seas. Your account is debited 5*l*. 13*s*. 6*d*. for the premium, &c.

I take due note of your letter to Messrs. Müller, Son and Co., and shall transmit it by to morrow's post, confirming your instructions for them to value on me, should the cost of the articles ordered exceed the nett proceeds of the wine sold. I shall duly attend to the insurance you desire to have effected on the return voyage, as soon as I am informed by our above-mentioned friends of the amount to be covered. I remain very sincerely, Sir, your obedient humble servant,   JAMES BOX.

CXXV.

Messrs. Müller, Son & Co. *Hamburgh.*   London, *9th March, 18—.*

Gentlemen, — I hope shortly to receive account sales of the Figueira wines, per Courier. Without waiting, however, for this, I have shipped to your address ten pipes more, by the London, Captain Rumbert.

By the same ship, I have also consigned to you for sale, on account of Mr. J. G. Sommers of Fayal, thirty-four pipes and two hogsheads of Fayal wine. Twenty of them are called Madeira, but they are all, in reality, the produce of the island of Fayal. There is a little difference, you will find, in the other fourteen; but they are far superior to any of the kind hitherto imported. Inclosed, you will receive a bill of lading for these wines, and an invoice, *pro forma,* as you are not limited to price, but must make the most of them your market will allow. As to account sales, you will

---

(1) Saggio, sperimento. (2) Gent. *abbrev. di* Gentlemen.
Anderson.   6

please to furnish distinct accounts for each (Figueira, the thirty-four pipes Fayal, and the two hogsheads being respectively for account of different parties), and remit me *per appoint* for each. I remain, very truly, Gent. your obedient humble servant,

JAMES BOX.

CXXVI.

Messrs. Tollmo and Son, *St. Petersburgh.* *London, 9th March, 18—.*

Gentlemen, — My last respects were under date of the 14th ult., and I have now to wait on you with a bill of lading * for thirty pipes of Fayal wine, marked «M & S 1 to 30,» shipped to your consignment by the Charles, Captain James Knight, for your port. I do not hand you an invoice of these wines, but rely on your obtaining the best possible price for them. For your information, however, they ought to nett above 25*l.* per pipe, your commission, freight, and all duties and charges deducted; but I do not quote (1) this price as a limit.

You will please to guarentee the purchasers, charging *del credere* accordingly; and remit the nett proceeds *per appoint*, as I do not wish this consignment to be mixed up with any other transaction. I have only to add that the sooner you can close the sale, without sacrificing the property, the better. I am most truly, Gent. your obedient humble servant, JAMES BOX.

CXXVII.

Messrs. Müller, Son & Co. *Hamburgh.* *London, 17th April, 18—.*

Gentlemen, — I have, on this occasion, to wait on you with a letter from my friend. Mr. J. G. Sommers of Fayal, inclosing bill of lading and invoice of six pipes of Fayal wine (such as I consigned to you per London) which he has shipped to your address by the Portuguese schooner, Boa Lembrança, Captain J. Dos Santos, and which I have insured here.

Mr. S. has also ordered sundry articles to be purchased for his account, and shipped by the Boa Lembrança, which he has directed me likewise to insure; therefore you will be so good as to apprise me, in due time, of the probable amount, that I may be enabled to attend to his wishes. For any balance arising from the sale of the wines and purchase of the goods, you will please to account with me.

You will also find inclosed a bill of lading for twenty-two chests (2) of Bahia sugars, shipped at Lisbon, on board the Hoffnung, Captain

---

(1) Citare, dare, addurre. (2) Casse.
* When the bill of lading is signed, the goods are shipped.

Peter Peterson, and consigned to you by my agent Mr. Da Silva, on my account, for which you will, I trust, be enabled to find a good market. Mr. Da Silva mentions his having obtained for you likewise from one of his friends, the consignment of twenty more chests of sugar, and thirty-three bags of tapioca. Believe me very truly, Gent. your obedient humble servant, JAMES BOX.

CXXVIII.

James Box, Esq. *London.* *Hamburgh, 23rd March, 18—.*

Sir, — Your highly valued favor of the 9th inst. has been received, and its contents noted. The London is not yet arrived, but as soon as she does, we shall take charge of the ten pipes of Figueira, and thirty-four pipes two hogsheads of Fayal wine, and dispose of them to the best advantage; observing your directions as to the account sales and remittances for proceeds.

It is impossible to say what the Fayal will fetch (1) in our market. You say the quality is good, but not equal to madeira; however, you may rely on our best exertions. For the Figueiras now with us, we have not yet had an eligible offer, but when the others arrive, we shall endeavour to close the sale of the whole. In the mean time we remain, Sir, your obedient humble servants,

MÜLLER, SON & CO.

CXXIX.

James Box, Esq. *London.* *Hamburgh, 6th April, 18—.*

Sir, — Our last respects were under date of the 23rd ult. We have now the pleasure of replying to yours of the 17th inst. which inclosed a letter from J. G. Sommers, Esq. of Fayal, informing us of his having shipped six pipes of wine in the schooner Boa Lembrança to our address, and ordering sundry articles to be got ready for shipment by the said schooner on her return voyage. We shall pay strict attention to his orders, and have already bespoke (2) the still, which it will take three weeks to complete.

We feel extremely obliged to you, and also to Mr. Da Silva, for the consignments of sugar and tapioca, by the Hoffnung, from Lisbon and you may be well assured we shall exert ourselves to the utmost, to prove ourselves deserving of your recommendation. Sugars have been rather flat this spring; but the demand appears to be getting brisker, and we hope will go on improving, when of course prices will rise. Referring you to the quotations below, we remain, most truly, Sir, your obliged and obedient humble servants,

MÜLLER, SON & CO.

P. S. The London has arrived and delivered her cargo, but we have not yet tasted the wines.

---

(1) Recare, produrre, dare, fruttare. (2) Ordinato.

CXXX.

James Box, Esq. *London.*   *Hamburgh, 21st May,* 18—.

Sir, — We have delayed writing until we could inform you of the probable value of the articles ordered by Mr. J. G. Sommers to be shipped in the Boa Lembrança, which vessel only made her appearance about a week since. You will please to insure 150*l.* (say one hundred and fifty pounds) for Mr. Sommers' account, and we shall, in due time, hand you the necessary particulars.

The six pipes of wine we find nearly of a quality with those you sent us from your city; but are sorry to add, that neither for those, nor for the Figueiras, can we find purchasers at anything like the prices you quote as current with you. We do not like to submit to a great sacrifice, and no sales could be made at present without; therefore we are apprehensive we shall have them on hand for some time. The Boa Lembrança we shall despatch with as much expedition as possible. We remain, truly, Sir, your obedient humble servants,   MÜLLER, SON & Co.

CXXXI.

James Box, Esq. *London.*   *Hamburgh, 1st June,* 18—.

Sir, — We have to announce the departure of the Boa Lembrança for Fayal, this morning; and to hand you inclosed, a copy of the invoice furnished Mr. Sommers, for your government in effecting insurance; it amounts to 148*l.* 7*s.* 6*d.* As the wines are not yet disposed of, or likely to be for some time, we cannot obey Mr. S.'s orders, as to drawing on you or remitting you the balance at present; therefore, we presume we must remain this sum in advance, debiting Mr. Sommers therewith in account current, which we have done and advised him to that effect. Believe us, very truly, Sir, your obedient humble servants,   MÜLLER, SON & Co.

CXXXII.

Messrs. Müller, Son & Co., *Hamburgh.*   *London, 9th June,* 18—.

Gentlemen, — I have received, since the date of my last, your esteemed favors of the 26th April, 21st May, and 1st inst. and have noted their respective contents. I have effected an insurance of 150*l.* on goods, per schooner, Boa Lembrança, from your port to Fayal, for account of Mr. Sommers; and I conceive you have done quite right to debit him in account for the amount of the invoice transmitted him; since under the circumstances of the case, you cannot close the transaction in the mode prescribed. It is with great regret that I observe the difficulties you experience in disposing of the wines, and the delay that is likely to occur; particularly, as being rather heavily in advance for Mr. S., I am anxious to be reimbursed, which I can only be from the sale of these and other winesof his, which I have shipped to St. Petersburgh. Therefore, although I would not wish you to sacrifice his property, yet I must earnestly recommend that you will neglect no opportunity that may offer, of disposing of both parcels. Believe me, truly, Gent. your obedient humble servant, JAMES BOX.

CXXXIII.

Messrs. Müller, Son & Co. *Hamburgh.* *Fayal,* 10*th April,* 18—.

Gentlemen, — Referring you to the foregoing copy of what I took the liberty of writing to you on the 1st inst., I beg to confirm the tenor of that latter, and to wait on you with the inclosed bill of lading for the six pipes of wine therein mentioned. I do not trouble you with an invoice, as I rely entirely on your doing the best you can with the wines, and am persuaded that you will dispose of them as if they were your own. Should you not be able to close the sale in time for this vessel's return, please to correspond with our common friend, Mr. Box, respecting their sales, etc., as opportunities, I presume, do not offer frequently from your port to these islands.

This letter will be delivered to you by Captain Dos Sanctos, of the Boa Lambrança, whom I beg leave to recommend to your kind attentions. Although he now goes addressed to one of your neighbours, perhaps on a future occasion, I may prevail on him to consign his vessel to your respectable house. Assured that you will execute the little order, as per duplicate list annexed, to my satisfaction, I subscribe myself, with esteem, Gentlemen, your obedient humble servant, J. G. SOMMERS.

CXXXIV.

J. G. Sommers, Esq. *Fayal.* *Hamburgh,* 31*st May,* 18—.

Sir, — We were duly favored with your much esteemed letters of the 1st and 10th April, the latter by the schooner Boa Lembrança, and the former through the medium of our common friend, Mr. James Box of Loudon, to whom we feel greatly obliged for his introduction to your correspondence. No opportunity having offered for your island, since the receipt of these letters, we have deferred replying thereto, till the Boa Lembrança's return. This will, therefore, be delivered to you by Captain Dos Sanctos, to whom we have paid every attention, in honor of your recommendation.

Inclosed, you will please to receive bill of lading and invoice of the sundry articles ordered to be shipped in the Boa Lembrança for your account, amounting to 148*l.* 7*s.* 6*d.* independent of premium of insurance, which has been effected, conformably with your directions, by Mr. Box.

We are sorry to have to inform you that the wines proving, though of good quality, not well calculated for our market, being too slight and not full-flavored, we have not been able to effect a sale of the six pipes consigned us by the Boa Lembrança, and consequently have not been able to close this transaction, by arranging with our London friend for the balance. We have, therefore, debited you, for the present, with the amount above stated, and when the wines are sold, shall draw for, or remit the balance, as the case may be. Trusting that our execution of your orders will prove satisfactory, and entertaining hopes of having frequent opportunities of evincing (1) our zeal, we remain most sincerely, your obedient humble servants,   Müller, Son & Co.

CXXXV.

J. G. Sommers, Esq. *Fayal*.   *London, 4th June, 18—.*

Sir, — The above is a copy of my last letter, under date of the 16th April, since which time I am without any of your favors: I have, therefore, on the present occasion, merely to advise you that I have insured 150*l.* on goods per Boa Lembrança, Dos Santos, from Hamburgh to your island, to cover the invoice thereof; amounting to 1481. 7*s.* 6*d.* as appears by a duplicate received from our friends, Messrs. Müller, Son and Co. From them I learn that the vessel sailed from Hamburgh on the 31st ult. For the cost of insurance, I have debited your account, 4*l.* 10*s.*; having effected it at the low premium of thirty shillings per cent. as per copy of policy and account annexed.

Messrs Müller have neither valued on me, nor remitted me anything on account of this transaction, as they have not been able to sell your six pipes of wine, nor indeed any of those that I have consigned to them from hence. In fact, I am fearful the wine will prove almost as disastrous a speculation as the fruit, since the prospect of sale appears very dubious and distant.

From St. Petersburgh, I have not as yet had any tidings (2) respecting the fate of those sent thither; but I hope soon to hear a more favorable report from thence, which I will not fail to communicate immediately. Believe me to remain, Sir, your very obedient humble servant,   James Box.

CXXXVI.

            St. Petersburgh, 30th May 11th June, 18—.
James Box, Esq. *London*.

Sir, — We received your favor of the 9th March, in due course, but awaited the arrival of the Charles, and a sight of the thirty

---

(1) Mostrare, dimostrare, far vedere. (2) Nuovo, notizie, avvisi.

pipes of Fayal wine you were so good as to ship on board her to
our consignment, before we put you to the expense of postage. We
have now the satisfaction of announcing both the arrival here of
the Charles, and delivery of the wine: but are sorry to add, that
though the quality may be superior for this description of wine, it
is not well adapted to this market; for, with the exception of French
and Rhenish white wines, our buyers look for those fullbodied, and
high-flavored, such as Madeira and sherry; therefore we were glad
to avail ourselves of an offer on the quays for half the quantity, at
700 roubles per pipe, and should have been equally happy to dispose of the other moiety at the same price, being convinced that
we shall not advance your friend's interest by warehousing it (1).
However, this we shall, we fear, be compelled to do. You may rest
assured that we shall do our best with this small consignment. We
are, Sir, your obedient humble servants,   TOLLMO & SON.

CXXXVII.

St. Petersburgh, 31st July-12th August, 18—.
James Box, Esq. *London.*

Sir, — Confirming our respects of the 30th May, of which we
transmitted a duplicate, we have now to advise the sale of the remainder of your consignment of Fayal wines, which we were glad
to effect at 650 roubles per pipe; and inclosed we beg leave to
wait on you with the account-sales, nett proceeds 14,120 roubles,
to your credit; and per contra, we debit you with our remittance,
this day at three months' date, for 592$l.$ 0$s.$ 2$d.$ at 10 $^1/_{16}d.$ per
rouble, on E. Austin and Co., making the like sum of 14,120
roubles, with which you will please to do the needful, and close
this transaction in conformity with us.

Although you or your friend may be disappointed with the result
of this adventure, we assure you no better could be done, and are
persuaded that had we kept the wines longer, the proceeds would
have been still farther from the sum of 25$l.$ per pipe which you
expected them to realize. Begging that you will freely command
us on all occasions, we are, Sir, your obedient humble servants,
    TOLLMO & SON.

CXXXVIII.

London, 4th July-24th August, 18—.
Messrs. Tollmo & Son, *St. Petersburgh.*

Gentlemen, — I was favored, in due course, with your esteemed
letters of the 30th May, and 31st ult. old style; the former advising

---

(1) Col metterlo in magazzino.

the arrival, and the latter transmitting account-sales of the thirty pipes of wine per Charles, which I am truly concerned to find were so little adapted to your market, and the proceeds consequently so far short of my anticipation. The bill on £. Austin and Co. for 59*2l.* 0*s.* 2*d.* which accompanied the account, has been duly honored; making, at the exchange of 10 ¹/₁₆*d.* per rouble, the nett proceeds 14,120 roubles, thus closing the transaction.

With many thanks for your punctuality and attention to my wishes, I remain, Gentlemen, your obedient humble servant,

JAMES BOX.

CXXXIX.

James Box, Esq. *London.*   *Fayal, 21st June,* 18—.

Sir, — I am in receipt of your favors of the 16th April, and 4th inst., and also of Messrs. Müller, Son and Co.'s letter of the 31st ult. by the Boa Lembrança, which vessel arrived here on the 10th inst. and has discharged her cargo in good order. I observe that Messrs. Müller, Son and Co., not having sold the wines, have debited me, provisionally, for the cost of the articles shipped for my account, in the sum of 148*l.* 7*s.* 6*d.* and I have noted the same accordingly. I have also credited you for premium of insurance 4*l.* 10*s.* the account thereof having been found correct.

It is matter of great disappointement to me, that so much delay has taken place in the sale of the wines; and I am fearful your friends at Hamburgh, having business of so much greater importance to attend to, or being out of their routine, have not paid that attention to this small consignment which I could have wished, and had a right to expect. I hope Messrs. Tolimo and Co. will be more successful at St. Petersburgh, otherwise I shall be awkwardly situated, having arranged for another shipment, as soon as the wines of the present vintage are ready. I had calculated on drawing on you for another 1000*l.* in the expectation that you would have been reimbursed in full, by this time, for your advances last autumn. Under the circumstances, and considering that you are fully covered for any balance that may be owing when you receive this, I trust you will allow me to value on you for that sum. The wines and some fruit (in better condition), shall be shipped as before, direct to your address, as I do not doubt but you will be able to obtain in London the same price of 25*l.* per pipe, which you obtained for the last; and that was a remunerating price. Anxiously awaiting your reply, I remain, etc.   J. G. SOMMERS.

CXL.

J. G. Sommers, Esq. *Fayal.*   *London, 10th July,* 18—.

Sir, — Your letter of the 21st ult. has just come to hand, and I confess that I feel very much hurt at your insinuations respecting the conduct of my Hamburgh friends, as I cannot but consider your observations equally applicable to myself, for having confided your property to their care. Allow me, however, in my own and their vindication, to say, that I am confidently persuaded no other house in Hamburgh would have done better than they have: it is impossible to force a sale when the market is flat, without sacrificing the property in such a manner as vould be quite unjustifiable; and then you would have real cause for complaint, whereas now you have only imaginary grounds. It is to be regretted that the wines were sent to Hamburgh at all, but now they are there, the expense of re-shipping them would only increase the loss. Had I kept them here, I might have disposed of them ere this, but not at 25*l*. as all descriptions of wines have since declined in price; and although the quality of your Fayal has given satisfaction, still it would have felt the general depression of the market. I have written to Messrs. Müller and urged them to close the sales as speedily as possible, even at a small sacrifice; and should that be the case, no blame will attach to them or me.

I am anxious as yourself to close this transaction previously to embarking in another; and as I am very apprehensive that I shall not be reimbursed the whole of my advances from the proceeds of the wines, you will, I hope, excuse me from coming under any further engagements until those now pending are wound up. I shall regret exceedingly should my refusal in any manner interfere with your proposed speculation, or defeat your ulterior object; but, having occasion for all the capital I possess, I cannot afford to have any part of it locked up, as is the case at present, to accommodate my friends, however desirous I may be of promoting their interests.

Messrs. Tollmo and Co. have been more successful than our Hamburgh friends, as you will observe by the account-sales, which I hand you herewith and the copy of their letter to me inclosing it, together with a remittance of 592*l*. 0*s*. 2*d*. sterling for the nett proceeds. The draft, having been duly honored, is placed to your credit. Though the wines do not nett more than 16*l*. per pipe, perhaps you will be better pleased than if they had been longer kept on hand. Sincerely wishing you better success in your future operations, I remain, etc.
JAMES BOX.

CXLI.

Messrs. Müller, Son & Co., *Hamburg*.   *London, 12th July, 18—.*

Gentlemen, — Having none of your favors to reply to, I beg to wait on you with the inclosed copies of rather an unpleasant correspondence which has just taken place between Mr. J. G. Sommers and myself, respecting the sale of his wines consigned to you per London and Boa Lembrança. I beg your reference to these letters, and have only to add that the wines sent to St. Petersburgh, fetched 16*l.* per pipe, and if you can realise this price or more, pray do it at once and close this unfortunate transaction. Unfortunate I am fearful it will prove to me as well as to Mr. S., since it is to be apprehended that the nett proceeds will not cover my advances on account. The wines might have fetched more here, but it was Mr. S.'s particular desire to make trial of your market, and that of St. Petersburgh. They cannot be re-shipped to this port, no wines being allowed to be imported but from the place of their growth, the islands of Guernsey and Jersey only excepted.

Claiming your particular and immediate attention to this troublesome though trifling affair, I am ever, Gentlemen, your obedient humble servant, JAMES BOX.

CXLII.

James Box, Esq. *London.* Hamburgh, 19th July, 18—.

Sir, — We were extremely surprised at the contents of your favor of the 12th inst. and utterly at a loss to account for the construction which Mr. Sommers has put on our conduct with regard to his wines. We were actuated solely by a wish to serve him. This description of wines, as we before remarked to you, and stated to him, is nearly unsaleable here; and had we forced them on the market, they would have fetched little or nothing. We have tried every means of putting them in a way of disposal, but hitherto without success, for we have had no offer whatever for them, and if we put them up to auction, and they are not sold, no person will look at them afterwards. We are now determined, however, to accept any offer that may be made equal to what the other parcel netted at St. Petersburgh, and hope, in a few days, to announce that the sale is accomplished.

We beg, at the same time, to remark, that this is such a falling-off from their supposed value of 25*l.* that we should never have thought of accepting it, had it not been for Mr. Sommers' illiberal insinuations and the urgency with which you press for a winding-up of this, as you justly term it, "troublesome, though trifling affair." We regret to find that you are likely to be a sufferer through your desire to serve Mr. Sommers, but yet hope that your fears may prove groundless. We are, &c. MÜLLER, SON & CO.

CXLIII.

James Box, Esq. *London.* Hamburgh, 26th July, 18—.

Sir, — Referring to, and confirming our respects of the 19th inst.,

PROPOSAL TO DRAW IN ANTICIPATION.

we have now to advise the sale of Mr. Sommers' wine, per London and Boa Lembrança, having put them up to auction, as a *dernier ressort*. We shall by next post furnish you with account-sales; in the meantime, suffice it to inform you that they fetched from 265 to 300 marks current; and will average, we should imagine, about 15*l*. per pipe. We considered it better to let them go at these prices, than be compelled to sell them afterwards, at ten to twenty per cent. lower. We are, &c.   MÜLLER, SON & Co.

CXLIV.

James Box, Esq. *London*.   *Hamburgh, 2nd August, 18—.*

Sir, We beg your reference to our last respects of the 26th Instant, and have now the pleasure to wait on you with account-sales of Mr. J. G. Sommers' wines, viz. —

34 pipes per London, producing nett, Mks. Bco.	6,355	12
2 hhds. per do.	158	2
6 do. per Boa Lembrança	1,120	0
	7,633	14

The first two sums we have remitted *per appoint* agreeably to your instructions, viz: In two bills of exchange on your city, as noted ad foot, for Mks. Bco. 6,513, 12, exchange 12 $^1/_2$ and 12, producing 521*l*. 14*s*. 7*d*.; with which you will please to do the needful, and credit us accordingly.

The nett proceeds of the six pipes per Boa Lembrança, we have carried to account in Mks. Bco. 1,120, which sum, deducted from the invoice of the sundry articles shipped for Mr. S.'s account by that vessel, on her return voyage, amounting, as advised at the time, to Mks. Bco. 2,171 4, leaves a balance in our favor of Mks. Bco. 1,051 4. For this sum we have drawn on you, at two months' date exchange 12, making 87*l*. 12*s*. 1*d*. with which you will please to debit Mr. S. and credit us in your account.

Although we expect Mr. Sommers will loudly exclaim against this conclusion of his unfortunate adventure, yet we can safely acquit ourselves of any, even the slightest inattention to his interest; much less can the charge of culpable neglect be brought against us. Wishing him better success in his future speculations, but which we doubt, unless he acts with greater prudence and more judgment, we remain, etc.   MÜLLER, SON, & Co.

CXLV.

Messrs. Müller, Son & Co. *Hamburgh*.   *London. 9th August, 18—,*

Gentlemen, — I have to thank you for your favors of the 19th and 26th ult. and 2nd instant. Passing by the contents of the two

first, I proceed to reply to the last, which inclosed the account-
sales of Mr. Sommers' wines, say: — 34 pipes of Fayal, per London,
nett proceeds

Mk. Bco.		6,355 12
2 hhds. of do. per do. do.		158 2
6 pipes of do. per Boa Lembrança do.		1,120 0

Total, to your debit. Mks. Bco. 7,633 14

And, per contra I have credited you for your remittances of the first two sums, *per appoint*, the two bills for 521l. 14s. 7d. on sundries having been duly honored.

For the small sum of Mks. Bco. 1,051 4 drawn on me, I have credited you in my account, at the exchange of 12, 87l. 12s. 1d. and debited Mr. Sommers. I am very glad that this unfortunate transaction has been at length brought to a conclusion, although I should have been much better pleased had the result been more favorable. I fear Mr. Sommers will be loud in his complaints, but he certainly has no cause to be displeased, either with you or myself. As I feel confident you have done the best that lay in your power for his interest, and am conscious that I have done the same, I shall await the ebullition of his anger with perfect indifference. The loss I suppose will be divided between us, for I much fear he will take advantage of the ill success of his speculation, and leave me minus a balance of about 250l. now due, independent of 53l. that I lost by a fruit speculation. Under all circumstances, believe me, etc., —— JAMES BOX.

CXLVI.

G. J. Sommers, Esq. *Fayal.* London, 10th August, 18—.

Sir, — At length I am enabled to transmit you the final accounts of your shipments last autumn, per London Packet, and Boa Lembrança, although the result of these speculations is not such as to afford subject for congratulation to yourself on learning, or gratification to me in communicating it.

Messrs. Müller and Co. have, as you will perceive, by copies of their correspondence annexed, been obliged to force a sale by putting your wines up to public auction.

34 pipes consigned per London, netted Mks. Bco.				6,355 12
2 hhds.	do.	do.	do.	158 2
6 pipes	do.	do.	do.	1,120 0

for which they have remitted me on *your* account, Mks. Bco. 6,355 12, at the exchange of 12 1/2 . . . . L. 508 8 9

And on account of Serjeant and Delaine, for proceeds of the two hogsheads at 12 } 13 5 10

L. 521 14 7

COMPLAINTS AGAINST THE CONSIGNEES.   93

the whole at two months' date, for which I have credited you without my prejudice, should the two bills remitted not be discharged at maturity.

I have debited you in the same account, 87*l.* 12*s.* 1*d.* being the amount in sterling drawn on me by said friends for the excess of the amount of goods shipped per Boa Lembrança, over the nett proceeds of the wines by the same vessel.

I am thus enabled to inclose your account current, balance in my favor, 251*l.* 10*s.* 8*d.* which you can remit me at your convenience, after debiting me with the balance of *my* account, 26*l.* 10*s.* 1*d.* as per accompanying statement, being the equivalent of 126 mil. 080 reis, difference between your invoice of fruit per London Packet, 400 mil. 000 reis, and the produce of porter and gold coins consigned to you by that vessel, 526 mil. 080 reis. Exchange 60*d.* per milrei.

It would have given me much pleasure had the result of this transaction been totally different; but I am conscious of having done my duty, and feel equally assured that my friends did theirs. I remain, &c. JAMES BOX.

Seventh Series.

CXLVII.

Henry Holland, Esq. *Paris.*   *London, 27th Feb.* 18—.

Sir, — I have before me your very acceptable letter of the 22nd instant, and feel very much flattered by the friendly sentiments which it contains. You may be assured that I shall, at all times, endeavour to prove myself deserving your good opinion, and not unworthy of your correspondence. Whatever may have been my determination with regard to entering into extensive speculations, I cannot but yield to your solicitations to commence Exchange Operations on joint account with your respectable house, persuaded that commercial relations, based on such solid foundations, cannot but prove advantageous and gratifying to both parties. I am, therefore, ready to adopt the conditions you propose, namely:

1 — To charge no commission on either side.
2 — Each party to guarantee the bills he takes.
3 — Postages of letters to be reciprocally charged.
4 — As, also, stamps and brokerages, according to the custom of the two places.
5 — Interest to be calculated on each account current, at the rate of 5 per cent. per annum.

At first I should wish our operations to be conducted on a limited scale, and afterwards extended as circumstances may permit: with this restriction, I am willing to make a commencement whenever you may feel so disposed. Awaiting your determination, I remain, most sincerely, Sir, your obedient humble servant,

JOHN LAPIDGE.

CXLVIII.

Henry Holland, Esq. *Paris.*   *London, 16th March, 18—.*

Sir, — I have to thank you for your much-esteemed favor of the 12th instant, and as you desire me to state to what amount I would wish to limit our exchange operations monthly, I beg to say that I think 5000*l.* per month, for the first three months, and, for the next three, 10,000*l.*, may be considered appropriate limits, and the utmost extent to which I should wish our transactions on each side to reach. After the experience of six months we shall be enabled to govern ourselves by circumstances; and should the result come up to our anticipations, of course I shall have no objection to enlarge our limitation.

As a commencement of our operations, you have inclosed, for my negotiation, ten bills of exchange on Madrid, for Pesos 1756,3 30, as per note, which, at 15 55 and 15 62 $^1/_2$, cost you frs. 27,526 40. These bills I negotiated, immediately on receipt, at 63 $^3/_4$*d.*, making 1075*l.* 12*s.* 6*d.* cash 19th instant, which sums are respectively placed to your credit, the one in your column in francs, and the other in mine in sterling.

I at the same time received your remittance of 700*l.* direct on this city, at 25,47 $^1/_2$ — frs. 17,832 50, for which, the bill having been duly honored, the respective columns have been credited, cash 3rd February.

Per contra, your account is debited with the amount of cost of the enclosed three drafts on Genoa, and one on Leghorn, as per note at foot, *viz.:*

Ps. 4011 0 7, on Genoa, at 43 $^1/_4$ . . . . . L. 739 13 9
» 1269 16 10, on Leghorn, at 47 $^1/_4$ . . . . . » 250 0 0
                                                  ─────────────
                                                  L. 989 13 9

(cash 19th instant), all of which I hope will turn to good account. Referring you to the quotation of our exchanges noted below, I remain truly, Sir, your obedient humble servant,   JOHN LAPIDGE.

CXLIX.

Henry Holland, Esq. *Paris.*   *London, 15th June, 18—.*

Sir, — The draft for 23*l.* which, as I advised you on the 1st instant, had not been accepted, having since become due and not

---

* Several letters of this series are omitted, as deficient in interest.

being discharged, I have now to return it to you with a protest for non-payment, together with an account of my commission and charges, amounting to 23*l.* 0*s.* 4*d.*, for which I have drawn on you at sight, and *per appoint*, to the order of Robert Collins, who has endorsed my bill to you. I debit you in your column frs. 646 70, for the same, at the exchange of 23 85, and trust you will experience no difficulty in recovering that amount from your endorser. I am, with great regard, Sir, your obedient humble servant,

JOHN LAPIDGE.

CL.

Henry Holland, Esq. *Paris.*   *London, 10th July, 18—.*

Sir, — Herewith you will please to receive *my* account current of our transaction to the 30th ultimo, with interest account to the same date. The balance, 3,935*l.* 11*s.* 3*d.* in sterling, is reduced to cash that day: and I shall be glad to be furnished with your account made out in the same manner, that I may be enabled to ascertain and remit your moiety of the profit, and to draw on you *per appoint*, for the nett balance, with interest to the date of my draft, in order to close our transactions up to that period. Believe me, &c.

JOHN LAPIDGE.

CLI.

Henry Holland, Esq. *Paris.*   *London, 6th August, 18—.*

Sir, — I am favored with your very acceptable letter of the 2nd instant, accompanied by *your* account current in francs. The balance due by you being in conformity with my account rendered you to the 30th June, 3,953*l.* 11*s.* 3*d.* sterling, I have carried the same to a new account, instead of valuing on you for it; but, in order to close our transactions to that date, I inclose you my draft on Daquenois & Co. of your city, for frs. 1,623 46, being the amount of your moiety of profit on the negotiations of the last three months. I wish it had been more considerable, and hoping in the present quarter to be more successful, I remain, Sir, your very obedient humble servant,

JOHN LAPIDGE.

Eighth Series.

CLII.

P. F. de Oliveira, Esq. *Lisbon.*   *Riga, 4-16th* June, 18—.*

Sir, — We have the pleasure of transmitting you, inclosed, a bill of lading for —

---

* The 4th old style and 16th new style. In the Russian dominions, where the old style is still in use, merchants generally mark both as above. If in a letter or bill of exchange only one date be given, it is taken as old style, and twelve days are added to make up the real date.

G. & C. 102 bundles of Outshot Hemp, weighing nett 149 shipponds, 14 lbs.
Z. 44 ditto ditto, nett weight 64 shipponds, 17 lbs.
shipped in the Danish vessel, Fortuna, Capt. N, J. Wickman, to your consignment.

The freight, as per charter-party, is 8 rbls. silver per ton, with 15 per cent primage and port-charges; 12 days are allowed for discharging the cargo, and the captain is to address the vessel to you.

We also inclose two invoices of this shipment—one of the 44 bundles, marked Z, amounting to 6,261 roubles 82 copecks, which are for account of our common friend, Mr. Joseph Vancouver, of London—and the other for the 109 bundles, marked G & C, which are for our own account, amounting to rs. 15,134 67 cop. You will please, however, to observe that both of these parcels are shipped with the understanding that it shall be at the option of Mr. A. J. Morreira, of your city, to take them for his own account; and should he decide upon so doing, the bills of lading and invoices are to be mader over to him. Should he decline them, you will be so good as to follow the directions of Mr. Vancouver, as to the disposal of his portion, and to sell ours when you think it advisable for our interest so to do, holding the proceeds at the disposal of our friends, Messrs. Coutts and Gammon of London, and corresponding with them on the subject.

The exchange on London last post was 10 $^1/_2$d. We hope, at the worst, to clear the invoice price, but leave our interest entirely in your hands.

The remainder of the Fortuna's cargo consists of A. I. 76 bundles of outshot hemp, weighing nett 103 shipponds, 3 lbs. shipped by order and for account of Mr. Morreira.

We forward this letter by the vessel, and shall write to-morrow per mail. Annexed is a price-current, to which we beg reference.

The prices of hemp are steady, although the demand is slack. Polish hemp is much in request this season: it is softer and more pliant than the Ukraine; fitter for twine and finer purposes, and serves as a substitute for Douana hemp. That we have shipped is Ukraine, as is always understood when no particular description is given.

Flax is not likely to decline, the stock being much reduced. Potash is in no demand, although there is very little in the market; tallow is dear and scarce; corn very dull. No imports of any kind sell very currently at present. The consumption of ports is very limited at this place, and we are overstocked with almost all descriptions of wine. It is a heavy article, and generally lies long on hand.

Havannah and Martinique sugars are the most current here; Brazils, though less in favor, are saleable; salt dull, and a dangerous article.

We are extremely obliged to you for the assistance which you kindly gave Mr. Villapol in the attainment of his object, the procuring commissions for our firm; and we assure you that we shall at all times be happy to reciprocate good offices with you, or any of your friends who may visit this city.

We remain respectfully, Sir, your obedient humble servants,

GAMMON & COUTTS.

CLIII.

A. I. Morreira, Esq. *Lisbon.*   *Riga, 5-17th June, 18—.*

Sir, — We refer you to our respects of the 22nd ultimo and 6th instant, and have now the pleasure of handing you the invoice and bill of lading of—

A. I. } 76 bundles of Outshot Hemp, weighing 103 shipponds,
O. H. } 3 lbs.

shipped for your account, and to your port, on board the Fortuna, Capt. I. Wickman. Invoice amount 10,429 rbls. 16 copecks, to the debit of your account.

We shall draw for this sum to-morrow on our common friend, Mr. Joseph Vancouver of London, and advise you what we have done per post; the present goes by the Fortuna.

We have in accordance with Mr. Vancouver's desire, sent the invoices and bills of lading for the remainder of the cargo, consisting of 153 bundles of outshot hemp, weighing 210 shpds. 31 lbs. to Mr. P. F. de Oliveira, of your city; the invoice for forty-four bundles shipped in Mr. Vancouver's name, is 6,261 roubles, 82 copecks; and of the 109 bundles in our name, 15,134 roubles, 676 copecks. Should you think proper to accept of the whole, these documents will be handed over to you by Mr. de Oliveira, and you will please to remit the cost of the same to Mr. Vancouver, calculating the rouble at 10 $^1/_8$d. sterling.

There is not the least alteration in trade. Believe us, most truly, Sir, your obedient humble servants,   GAMMON & COUTTS.

CLIV.

A. J. Morreira, Esq. *Lisbon.*   *Riga, 5-17th June, 18—.*

Sir, — We confirm the foregoing copy of our respects of yesterday's date by Captain Wickman of the Fortuna, and inclose duplicates of the documents therein mentioned. The present will be forwarded through the medium of our friend Mr. Joseph Vancouver of London, on whom we have this day drawn at three months' date, for your account, the invoice amount of the hemp by the above vessel, in one draft for 439*l.* 19*s.* 7*d.* to our own order; being at the exchange of 10 $^1/_8$d. per rouble, 10,429 rs. 16 cops. to your credit.

Anderson.

Hoping to have frequent opportunities of being useful to you at this place, we are, with regard, Sir, your obliged humble servants,

GAMMON & COUTTS.

CLV.

P. F. de Oliveira, Esq. *Lisbon*. *London, 27th July, 18—.*

Sir,— Herewith I hand you extracts of my correspondence with Messrs. Gammon and Coutts, of Riga, and also two letters from them, one for Mr. A. J. Morreira, the other addressed to yourself. I refer you to their contents, and leave it with you to make an arrangement with Mr. Morreira, for the sale of my forty-four bales of hemp per Fortuna, at the invoice price, if he will accept them; or otherwise to dispose of them in the best manner you can for my interest, crediting me in my account for the nett proceeds. I think the price very reasonable. Here the same quality is selling for 33*l*. to 34*l*. per ton; but as I wish to conciliate Mr. Morreira, and to induce him to enlarge his orders to my Riga friends next spring, I shall be glad if he will take my parcel and Messrs. Gammon's too. I am truly, Sir, your obedient humble servant, Jos. VANCOUVER.

CLVI.

P. F. de Oliveira, Esq. *Lisbon*. *London, 27th Sept., 18—.*

Sir,— I am in receipt of your much-esteemed letter of the 19th instant, transmitting account-sales of my forty four bundles of hemp per Fortuna, nett proceeds, 1402 mil. 283 reis, which, if found correct, shall be placed in conformity to your debit on my account.

Messrs. Gammon and Coutts, as well as myself, feel extremely well pleased with the result of your exertions in this affair; and I have no doubt their house at Riga will make you further consignments. Your letter for those gentlemen having been duly delivered to them, together with the account-sale of their 107 bundles, nett proceeds 3,504 mil. 566 reis, this amount, you will perceive by their order inclosed, is to be remitted to me. You will, therefore, please to invest the whole produce of the hemp, 4,906 mil. 849 reis, in sugars, to be shipped for Hamburgh, to the consignment of my friends there, Messrs. Sillem and Co., giving me timely advice for insurance. As to the quality of the sugars, I leave that entirely to your judgment; but I must request that the browns may exceed the whites in the number of chests; and I also recommend that you will be very careful to select a good vessel, or the average.* will absorb very much of the profit. Should there be a small balance left on this transaction, either one way or the other, you will have the goodness to draw for or remit the same *per appoint,* Messrs. Gam-

---

* See Appendix.

mon and Co. being interested with me in this speculation. I remain, very truly, Sir, your obedient humble servant,

Jos. Vancouver.

Ninth Series.
CLVII.

Messrs. J. Horrocks & Co. *Bahia*.   London, 16th Aug., 18—.

Gentlemen, — My last letter to you was under-date of the 10th instant, as per copy annexed; the contents of which I now confirm, and have, on the present occasion, to acknowledge receipt, by the Racket and Camden packets, of your favors of the 1st, 4th, and 8th of June, which I proceed to answer:

Your three drafts on me at sixty days' sight for your account, viz.
L. 272 18 11 order of J. H. Harrison.
  31 11 3   do.   M. J. Jago.
 800 0 0   do.   Newman and Co.

L. 1,104 10 2 shall be duly honored, and placed to your debit at the exchange of 49, say 5,409 mil. 837 reis.

Your three drafts on Martin and Co., to my order, have been accepted by Smith and Co. for honor of Messrs. Pauls, Jorge and Co. These gentlemen have also effected insurance on the sugars; all is therefore now in order, and your account duly credited for the amount of 4,935 mil. 000 reis, exchange 49 $^{1}/_{4}$, 1000*l*.

I have debited you in my account for the nett proceeds of the following parcels of goods, viz.

100 boxes soap ex Aurora . . . . 457 mil. 182 reis
 30 cases cheese ex Jane . . . . 161 • 449 •
Ironware and packthread ex Lucretius . . . 725 • 670 •

        1,344 mil. 301 reis

all which have been found correct.

Inclosed you will find invoices of the several consignments to you on my account, by this vessel, the Famo; viz.

50   pipes of Catalunha wines . . . . . . L. 325 1 8
 6 $^{1}/_{2}$ tons copper in sheets . . . . • 786 11 0
 3   do.   do.   in cases . . . . • 361 16 0

        L. 1,473 8 8

the disposal of which I recommend to your accustomed attention.

I intended to ship some saltpetre by this vessel, but it could not be got ready in time; it will go by the next ship, which will be put on the *berth* * shortly.

---

* A ship is said to be put on the berth, when notice is given of her intended voyage and time of sailing.

Messrs. I. Lange and Co. of Antwerp, have sold the sugars by the Vrow Cecilia, and have sent me the account-sales, a copy of which I inclose; but I cannot credit you for the nett proceeds, as they have not yet remitted me the whole amount.

I credit you, however, for the following, as per statement annexed.

Proceeds of 100 cases by the Caroline, your ¹/₄th cash
23rd July . . . . L. 265 0 1
Do. of 50 do. ex Brodhoe, do. 7th May . 722 3 5
_____
L. 987 3 6

which I have no doubt you will find correct.

On the former of these, and the parcel per Asoph, I have claimed a particular average from the underwriters, and will credit you for your share when recovered.

Of the sugars, per Commerce, to Trieste, I have not yet received the account-sales; on these there will likewise be an average.

Part of the cargoes of the Lucretius and Henrietta to Hamburgh are disposed of, and at tolerably fair prices; as per note at foot. Both of these shipments are, however, partially damaged.

By the last account from Petersburgh, the Mary had just arrived there, but had not discharged her cargo. The state of that market was represented as very bad.

J. L. Anderson's widow, of Genoa, has sent me account-sales of the parcels per Johanna and Emilia, of which the inclosed are copies; but she has not yet remitted the balance.

I have letters from Mr. Barnett, dated the 4th August, from Sinigaglia, where he had met most of the Ancona merchants at the fair: but he says nothing can be done with them, as none of the manufacturers will make consignments on their own account: the only house likely to give an order is that of _____ who have an establishment also at Trieste; they are the only _____ in the papal dominions, and are people of considerable property; but our friend recommends great caution in any transactions with them.

He says we have misunderstood his order regarding the shipment for Genoa. They are to consist of two cargoes; one of 300 cases for Messrs. de la Rue and Co., and another of 500 cases, to the consignment of Mr. Canleuf, comprising 200 cases for him, 200 for D. Elena, and 100 for Bernese; or, if more convenient, you may send two of 400 cases each. Mr. Canleuf's limit of two months is for the purchase, and not for the shipment.

I am likewise in receipt of a letter from Mr. D. Elena of Genoa, dated the 5th August, of which I hand you a copy for your government. You will observe that he allows you to send a regular assortment, not to exceed, however, his limits of 20 soldi per 100 lb., and choose the time you think most advantageous for the purchase. As to his proposal of your drawing only for a part of the amount of invoice, leaving the remainder as security for the punctual execution of his order, I have written to him to say that it is quite out of the question.

On account of sixty pipes of wine consigned to you by the Hiram from Oporto, U. I. Da Lima has drawn on me 480l. at ninety days' date; against which he will send me his draft on you to negotiate here. You must therefore take care to reserve sufficient from the proceeds to cover it. Mr. N. J. Da Precia informs me, that the Hiram sailed on the 25th July with the goods stated at foot to your consignment. The Fiel Portuense was put up at Oporto for your city, and will go to your address.

Mr. John Gomez writes me from Lisbon, under date the 5th August, that there were very few goods offering for your place, insomuch that the small brig Paquete de Ceara could scarcely find a cargo. He talks of chartering a small vessel, to take out the remainder of his Figueira wines, and of filling her up with salt. The Coquilhos (cocoa nuts) that you sent him by the Frederica Louisa, and which cost 1 mil. 640 reis, sold for nine milreis.

I understand that Messrs. Harman and Co. of Trieste, have sent you an order for a cargo of sugar, to be shipped on their account and to their address, which I am glad to hear. They are a house of the first respectability, therefore you will do well to cultivate their good opinion.

I inclose an invoice of forty-seven packages, containing sundry Portuguese manufactures, which I have caused to be shipped to your consignment on my account, by the Hiram from Oporto: it amounts to 841l. 11s. 9d. and I recommend the sale to your best care. Remaining, most truly, Gentlemen, your obedient humble servant,

JOHN HORROCKS.

CLVIII.

Messrs. J. Horrocks & Co. Bahia.   *London, 8th May,* 18—.

Gentlemen, — I wrote you last on the 5th instant, by way of Liverpool, as per copy enclosed. I have since received your letters of the 18th, 19th, 20th, 23rd and 25th February, by the Eagle, the Sceptre, and the Sunberg.

Due note has been taken of your several drafts, for 32,134 mil. 465 reis, on the 16th, in fourteen bills at 49 $^1/_2$ per milrei; viz.—

5000 mil. 000 reis, or 1031l. 5s. on account of P. H. Mohrinam.

3,379 mil. 976 reis, or 697l. 2s. 5d. on account of Viventi and Constantini.

4000 mil. 000 reis, or 825l. on your account.

19,754 mil. 189 reis, on my account.

And further 6,571 mil. 288 reis; viz. —
48 mil. 488 reis, or 10*l*. at 49 ¹/₂ on the 18th, on my account.
521 mil. 800 reis, or 107*l*. 16*s*. 7*d*, at 49 ¹/₂ on the 21st, on my account.
6,000 mil. 000 reis, or 1225*l*. at 49 ¹/₂ on the 25th, on account of P. H. Mohrinam.

All of which will be accepted, and the different accounts debited as you desire.

For the amount of the different invoices transmitted in your letter, I shall credit you in my account; viz. per Magnanimous and Hamburgh.

602 mil	826 reis,	cost of sixteen bales of leaf tobacco.
262 •	673 •	do. eleven do. do.
1,147 •	599 •	do. 150 mangotes do.
2,028 •	338 •	do. twenty-four cases of sugar, per Charlotte to Trieste.
2,196 •	679 •	cost of 211 cases of sugar.
2,759 •	883 •	do. twenty-six do. per Laura to Genoa.
1,097 •	003 •	cost of 116 mangotes of tobacco.
1,787 •	434 •	do. twenty cases of sugar.
1,328 •	129 •	do. seventeen do.
1,104 •	175 •	do. sixteen do.
1,027 •	398 •	do. thirteen do.

15.342 mil. 132 reis.

The bills of lading were all found to be in order; and I shall expect the particulars of the shipment per Henrietta.

For your disbursements for the Laura, as well on my account as on that of the captain, I have credited you 1113 mil. 759 reis, and have taken due note of the arrangement made as to the freight. I am glad to find that you have consigned this vessel to Messrs. Davison and Co.

Your remittance of 4,261 milreis on Lisbon, I shall negotiate as soon as a good opportunity occurs; to-day the Exchange was very flat; I would have taken 50*d*. but was offered only 49 ³/₄.

The bills of lading of the two parcels of sugar for Constantini and Co., and Ernest Mordaunt and Co., I have forwarded to the parties. The insurance on both I have effected here.

Mr. Mohrinam will make his own insurance on the goods per Henrietta at Hamburgh.

I observe that you have shipped my 270 sheets of copper sheathing to Rio de Janeiro, by the Gallana. Fortunately I have saved the insurance thereon, having received advice of its arrival there on the same day that your letter reached me. I could not have done it under five guineas per cent.

I notice your objection to allow me the 6l. 1s. 9d. for difference in quality of a case of sugar by the Laurentius. You will do as you think proper; but you may be assured of this, that the claim is perfectly just; and any other correspondent who might receive a chest of brown instead of white, would insist, without doubt, on an allowance in consequence.

I always endeavour to take as little concern or share as possible in all orders sent you; but, in most instances, the procuring of the order itself depends on my taking an interest in its execution. To the house of my relative at Hamburgh, for instance, I am pledged to take a moiety of any orders they may give; but I generally contrive to prevail on some house here to take half of my interest, so that I retain only one quarter.

In regard to Mr. _____ of Oporto, he continues to act as your agent; and will, probably, for some time, since I find it would be impolitic on our part to break with him.

I take this opportunity of inclosing the insurance accounts of the Laurentius and the Mary, amount to your debit 74l. 7s. 6d.; and at the same time wait on you with a statement of the several averages I have recovered on sugars in which you were interested, having credited your account with the sundry sums therein quoted, amounting to 320l. 0s. 1d. I remain, very sincerely, Sir, your obedient humble servant,   JOHN HORROCKS.

Particular average on sugars per Laurentius —
Amount recovered from the underwriters . . . . L. 31 2 0
        Statement . . . . L. 4 4 0
        Translation . . . . . . » 1 0 0
        Postage . . . . » 0 7 6
        Brokerage ½ per cent . . » 0 3 1
        Commission 2 ½ per cent. » 0 15 6
                                                                       6 10 0

                                                                         L. 24 12 0

Cash 28th April, 18—, ½ to the credit of J. Horrocks and Co. . . . . L. 12 6 0

Ditto on ditto per Henrietta —
Amount recovered from the underwriters on 12,800l. L. 31 3 0
        Charges for recovering . . . . » 3 4 4
                                                          L. 27 18 8

¼ to the credit of J. H. and Co, cash 28th April, 18— . . . . L. 6 19 8

Particular average on sugars per Asoph —
Recovered of the underwriters on 3,300l. Insurance L. 623 6 6
Charge for recovering . . . . » 21 17 8
                                                    ─────────────
                                                    L. 601 8 10

⁴⁄₈ to the credit of J. H. and Co., cash 3rd May,
18—. . . . . L. 300 14 8
                                                    ─────────────
                       Total . . L. 320 0 4

P.S. — I further debit you 61l. 16s. 6d. as follows: —
Account of insurance against fire on goods at
Bahia, valued at 5,000l. Insured with the Phoenix
Fire Assurance Company, from 20th January, 18—,
to 25th March, 18—, at 10s. 6d. per cent. per annum L. 30 16 6
Policy . . . . » 0 3 6
                                                    ─────────────
                                                    L. 31 0 0

5,000l. Insured in the Protector Insurance Company . . . . » 30 16 6
                                                    ─────────────
                    Paid the 22nd March . . . L. 61 16 6

Tenth Series.
CLIX.
Broad Street, 25th January, 18—.
Messrs. W. Green, Fell and Co. *London.*
Gentlemen, — Have the goodness to ship on board the Tenterden, Captain Benjamin Russell, for Lisbon, 150 sheets of copper sheathing; the whole to be 48 Portuguese inches in length; one half to weigh 18 lbs. and the other 19 lbs. each sheet; each box to contain an equal number of sheets. Likewise one box of copper nails, proper for the said sheathing, not to exceed 500 lbs. weight.

When the goods are shipped, you will, of course, send me the invoice and bill of lading. I am, &c. EDWARD ODGER.

CLX.
Edward Odger, Esq. *Broad Street.* *London, 26th January,* 18—.
Sir, — Thanking you for your kind order of yesterday, for 150 sheets of copper sheathing, we beg to say that we shall immediately attend to its execution; but, as we verbally informed you on 'Change, the length being unusual, we shall be obliged to have the sheets

made expressly, and, consequently, some little delay will unavoidably occur. We trust, however, they will be ready in time for the Tenterden, which vessel, we are informed, will not sail for a fortnight. We are, etc.   Wm. Green, Fell & Co.

CLXI.
London, 9th February, 18—.
Messrs. William Green, Fell & Co. *London.*

Gent. — I am sorry to inform you that my friend, for whose account, and at whose desire I ordered the 150 sheets of copper on the 25th ultimo, having determined, as he has since informed me, to defer the repairs of the ship for which they were intended, wishes the order not to be executed, at least for the present. If, therefore, the copper be not already entered for shipment, and can be kept back, I shall be much obliged by your giving directions for it to remain till further orders. Of course, I shall consider myself liable for any expense you may incur, or loss you may sustain in consequence, or, indeed, for the ultimate completion of the transaction, should you not consent to cancel my order. I remain truly, Gent, your obedient humble servant,   Edward Odger.

CLXII.
Edward Odger, Esq. *London.*   *London, 9th February, 18—.*

Messrs. W. Green & Co. present their compliments to Mr. Odger, and are sorry they cannot comply with the request contained in his letter of this morning, with regard to suspending the order for the 150 sheets copper sheathing, as they are now actually on board a barge in the river, and have been entered out at the Custom-House for the Tenterden. Besides, having been cut expressly for Mr. O.'s order, they are unsaleable for any other purpose.

CLXIII.
Messrs. W. Green, Fell & Co. *London.*   *London, 12th February, 18—.*

Mr. Odger presents his compliments to Messrs. W. Green and Co., and begs to state that, as he understands the copper sheathing, intended to be shipped on board the Tenterden, has been sunk in the lighter that was conveying it alongside, he cannot consent to its shipment until put into a proper state, so as to insure its arrival in perfect order. Mr. O. will, consequently, thank Messrs. Green and Co. to inform him when the sheathing has been scoured, that he may send a competent person to inspect it, prior to its being taken on board.

CLXIV.

Edvard Odger, Esq. *London.* London, 13th February, 18—.

Messrs. W. Green and Co return their compliments to Mr. Odger, and, in reply to his note of yesterday, beg to say that they will not fail to inform him when the copper sheathing, which was unfortunately sunk in going alongside the Tenterden, is again put in order for shipment, that he may send some person whom he may deem competent to inspect it. At the same time, they cannot but assure Mr. O. that they would naturally, for their own credit's sake, take every necessary precaution to prevent injury to the goods from the accident alluded to.

Eleventh Series.

CLXV.

J. F. Wizeu, Esq. *Oporto.* London, 26th September, 18—.

Sir,— I had the pleasure of addressing you on the 5th instant, as per copy annexed, and have now that of advising you that I have received a letter from Mr. P. I. Darros, of St. Petersburgh, dated the 1st (13th) July last, informing me that he had shipped, by your orders, for your account, and to your address, in the Swedish ship Sophia, Capt. Jorgan Barker,

       8 bales, containing 4000 Hare Skins;
       6   .   .   60 pieces Canvas; and
      30   .   .   80 bundles of Hemp;

and ordering me to open a policy thereon for 14,000 rs. which I have done, at eight guineas per cent.

The apprehensions I expressed in my last have been too truly verified in regard to insurances from Russia, for it was with the utmost difficulty I could effect yours even at the above premium. I offered five, six, and seven guineas without success. Many of our underwriters would not take the risk at any premium whatever, on account of the season being so far advanced, and dreading the heavy averages to which they are exposed on Baltic voyages in winter, so that I was glad to close even at these terms.

I shall expect from Mr. Darros the requisite particulars, that I may make the declaration on the policy, and furnish you with the account of cost. I remain, Sir, your obedient humble servant,

                                  JAMES BYRNE.

CLXVI.

J. F. Vizeu, Esq. *Oporto.* London, 13th October, 18—.

Sir, — Confirming the preceding copy of my last respects, and being since without any of your favors, I have now to wait on you with an account of the insurance effected by order of Mr. Barros of Petersburgh on goods, per Sophia, valued at 800*l.* equivalent to 17,176 rbls. 53 cops. and charges in case of loss, as per copy of policy annexed.

For the amount 76*l.* 14*s.* 10*d.* I have debited you in account current.

Mr. Barros at the same time, under date of 31st August (12th September), inclosed to me for acceptance, a first of exchange for 67*l.* 6*s.* 1*d.* payable to your order, on Mr. M. I. Silva. I beg to inform you that this bill has been duly honored, and that I shall hold it at the disposal of the second or third. Having nothing further to communicate at the present moment, I remain, Sir, your obedient humble servant, JAMES BYRNE.

CLXVII.

George Payne, Esq. *East Cowes.*   London, 30th May, 18—.

Sir, — I have been informed that the Sophia, Captain Barker, from St. Petersburgh to Oporto, was compelled to put into your port, where she has undergone a very heavy repair, and is still detained, the captain not being able to defray his expenses, or to raise money on bottomry*; and that he will, in consequence, be obliged to sell a part of his cargo. Having effected insurance on some of the goods, I shall be obliged to you for all the information it may be in your power to give me, respecting the actual state of the affair; and particularly as to what part of the cargo is likely to be sold for the purpose in question, for should any portion of the goods I have insured be put up, it is my wish to attend the sale personally, or to send some one on my behalf. In that case, the purchases would be made through you, and the goods left in your charge for re-shipment; but as my intention of coming down to the sale might operate unfavourably to my friend's interest, you will please to consider this communication as confidential, and not let it be known even to the captain. From the introduction to you, with which my friend, Mr. Thompson, favored me, I am led to hope that you will promptly furnish me with the information required. Assuring you of my respect, I remain, Sir, your obedient humble servant,   JAMES BYRNE.

CLXVIII.

East Cowes, Isle of Wight, 5th June, 18—.

James Byrne, Esq. *London.*

Sir, — In reply to your esteemed favor of the 30th ultimo, I beg to inform you that the cargo of the Sophia has been landed and

---

* See Appendix.

warehoused here, and the vessel is undergoing the necessary repairs. Her damage, I find, is not very great, and may be made good in a fortnight or three weeks. The captain has, however, no letter of credit on any house in England, and will proceed to your city in a few days to endeavour to raise money on a bottomry bond, when he will call on you and the other houses concerned.

Should he be compelled to sell any part of his cargo, I will duly apprise you, and I shall be happy to see you here when the sale takes place; but I presume you are aware, that in cases of goods being sold to defray the expenses of vessels under average, or for account of the underwriters, it is usual for the commissioners of the customs to allow them to be disposed of duty-free, for home consumption; consequently, in the present instance, the articles, no doubt, would fetch their full market price, the same as if the duty had been paid on them, and, as no drawback could be obtained, they would not be worth purchasing for exportation. At all events you may rely on receiving the earliest intimation when a sale is appointed.

Mr. Knight, of West Cowes, has the menagement of the vessel and cargo, and they could not be in better hands. Believe me, truly, Sir, your obedient humble servant, GEO. PAYNE.

CLXIX.

James Byrne, Esq. *London.* *East Cowes, 4th July, 18—.*

Sir, — Since I last wrote to you, on the 5th ultimo, I have not had the pleasure of receiving any of your favors; but I now beg to apprise you that the sale of a part of the Sophia's cargo is fixed for the 11th instant, and that I await your presence or orders. The hemp and flax are the only articles to be disposed of, which I mention for your government. Believe me, truly, Sir, your obedient humble servant, GEO. PAYNE.

CLXX.

J. F. Vizeu, Esq. *Oporto.* *London, 13th June, 18—.*

Sir, — I have received your favor of the 8th ultimo, and, in reply, I beg to say that you were rightly informed as to the ship Sophia having put into Cowes leaky, and having been obliged to discharge her cargo. Captain Barker has been with me this morning, having come to town for the purpose of raising money to defray the expenses of repairing his vessel, and likewise those attending the cargo: but hitherto he has been unsuccessful, as no person is willing to advance the cash he requires, even on bottomry, so I fear he will be under the necessity of selling part of his cargo, to enable him to get away.

PART OF THE CARGO TO BE SOLD.

Should any part of your property on board be brought to the hammer, I shall do my best to purchase and re-ship it. I am of opinion, however, that it will be sold for home consumption, and will therefore fetch too high a price to admit of its being re-exported; for, being sold without payment of the import duty (such indulgence being generally granted in cases of average), of course there can be no drawback allowed on the re-shipment.

As, however, the duties on the exportation of hemp and flax are trifling, I have ordered my correspondent at Cowes to purchase those articles, if sold within your limits, which I much doubt. Believe me, truly, Sir, your obedient humble servant. JAMES BYRNE.

CLXXI.

Geo. Payne, Esq. *East Cowes.* London, 6th July, 18—.

Sir, — Permit me to thank you for the information conveyed in your favors of the 5th ult. and 6th inst.

If the hemp proves to be clean and of first quality, and the flax 12 head, and both in good condition, I authorise you to purchase, for my account, the whole or any part thereof, at such prices that, when re-shipped for Portugal, on board another vessel, they may not stand in more than the following prices, viz.: — the hemp 19*l.* and the flax 31*l.* per ton, on board (shipping charges, and your commission included, but not the freight). I shall send a vessel round to take them in, should you succeed in purchasing to any extent; at all events, I hope you will secure twenty tons, or upwards, and please to say how I am to reimburse you.

If the hemp or flax proves to be of inferior quality, or damaged, I should not desire to have any thing to do with it. I am, etc.

JAMES BYRNE.

CLXXII.

James Byrne, Esq. *London.* East Cowes, 9th July, 18—.

Sir, — I am in receipt of your favour of the 6th inst., with your orders to purchase the hemp and flax, ex Sophia, provided the former can be obtained at 19*l.* and the latter at 31*l.* per ton, all charges included. I regret to say, in reply, that the hemp is rather damaged, and, notwithstanding, will, I should think, fetch much more than your limits. The flax is in good condition, and of the description you mention. I shall do the best in my power for your interest — no less than if you were on the spot. I remain, Sir, your obedient humble servant, GEO. PAYNE.

CLXXIII.

Geo. Payne, Esq. *East Cowes.* London, 10th July, 18—.

Sir, — I am favored with your letter of yesterday's date, and from the circumstances under which I understand the hemp, ex Sophia, is to be disposed of, it will not answer my purpose to become a purchaser.

But, should the flax be sold at my former limits, including the duty of 13s. 4d. per ton, and if also, it can be admitted to an entry for exportation (which is my only object) without any additional expense, I will, in that case, thank you to purchase the whole of it for my account, and your drafts on me at one month, for the cost, shall be duly honored.

Finding, since the above was written, that it may be difficult to procure a vessel to call at your port for the flax, if purchased, without some additional freight, I must reduce my limits to 30l. say thirty pounds, instead of 31l. I remain, Sir, yours, &c.

JAMES BYRNE.

CLXXIV.

James Byrne, Esq. *London*.   *East Cowes*, 12th July, 18—.

Sir, — I have to inform you that at the sale yesterday of the hemp and flax, ex Sophia, the former went at 22l. 10s. and 25l. 10s. per ton, and the latter at 39l. 10s., consequently I could not effect any purchase thereof for your account. On some other occasion I hope I shall be more fortunate, being very desirous of keeping up our correspondence. I am sincerely, Sir, your obedient humble servant,

GEO. PAYNE.

CLXXV.

J. F. Vizeu, Esq. *Oporto*.   *London*, 13th July, 18—.

Sir, — My last respects were under date of the 13th ultimo, and I have now to inform you that, of the Sophia's cargo, nothing more than a part of the hemp and flax has been sold—the former as high as 23l. 10s. per ton, and the latter at 39l. 10s., consequently none has been bought for your account, your limits precluding such purchase.

I would advise you to look sharp after Capt. Barker, and as soon as he arrives with you to get all the documents, protests, surveys, &c. from him, and forward them to me, that I may lay your claim before the underwriters. In my opinion it would be preferable to have the average accounts submitted to arbitration here, where these things are better understood than with you. I am apprehensive this will prove a troublesome business. I remain truly, Sir, your obedient humble servant,

JAMES BYRNE.

CLXXVI.

James Byrne, Esq. *London*.   *Oporto*, 2nd September, 18—.

Sir, — I received, in due course, your favors of the 13th June, and 13th July, respecting the Sophia and her cargo; and I perceive that part of the latter has been sold at Cowes to defray the expenses of her repairs, &c. On Captain Barker's arrival I will attend to your suggestions. I am sorry to say, that he is not only not arrived here, but I learn that the vessel has sustained further damage, and that it was supposed the cargo would have to be landed a second time. I do not like these delays, and I am apprehensive there may be some collusion between the captain and the people at Cowes. Be so good as to make enquiry, and let me know the result. The proprietors of the cargo are not only sufferers by having to pay for the goods before they arrive; but the season for disposing of them is nearly gone by—so that they will have to keep them on hand till next spring. Believe me, very sincerely, Sir, your obedient humble servant,   J. F. Vizeu.

CLXXVII.

George Payne, Esq. *East Cowes.*   London, 1st *October*, 18—.

Sir, — Being informed that the Sophia has again put back to your port, that the cargo has been damaged, and, in consequence, again landed at your place, I have to request, that you will be so good as to claim the goods mentioned at foot, stating, in reply, what commission you will consider yourself entitled to, for taking them under your charge and shipping them for Portugal on board of some other vessel. Believe me, truly, Sir, your obedient humble servant,
            James Byrne.

CLXXVIII.

James Byrne, Esq. *London.*   East *Cowes*, 2nd *October*, 18—.

Sir, — In answer to your letter of yesterday, I have to state, that the Sophia's cargo is again landed, that vessel having met with an accident in getting under way; but I am informed the captain intends re-loading in a day or two, and will immediately proceed on his voyage. I applied to him and to Mr. Knight respecting the goods mentioned in your note; but as the vessel will proceed shortly, I declined pressing their delivery to me, so I need say nothing about my commission on re-shipment thereof; but there is the sum of ten guineas due to me for my attendance at the sale by your desire, although no purchases were effected. You will find this is in perfect accordance with the customs of this port.

I shall be in town shortly, when I will do myself the pleasure to call on you, and this little affair can be settled. In the mean time, I am, with great truth, Sir, your obedient humble servant,
            George Payne.

CLXXIX.

J. F. Vizeu, Esq. *Oporto.* — London, 11th October, 18—.

Sir,— Referring to the annexed copy of a letter received this morning from Cowes, in answer to the enquiries which I made in consequence of your letter of the 2nd. ult. respecting the Sophia and her cargo, I have nothing to add to the information therein contained, except that I understand Mr. Knight, under whose care Captain Barker has placed his vessel, to be a very honorable fair-dealing person. Hitherto I have no reason to believe any unnecessary delay has occurred; but should proper steps not be taken to enable the vessel to proceed immediately on her voyage, I shall, you may be assured, interfere in the most effective manner for the interests of the parties concerned in her cargo. I remain, with great esteem, Sir, your obedient humble servant, JAMES BYRNE.

CLXXX.

George Payne, Esq. *East Cowes.* London, 29th November, 18—.

Sir. — Understanding, when last I had the pleasure of meeting you in town, that you proposed returning to Cowes in a few days, I have been in daily expectation of hearing from you on the subject of Captain Barker's intentions with respect to his ship and cargo. It has since occurred to me, that it would be for the interest of my friends concerned in her cargo, to obtain from the captain copies of the following documents; viz. —

The protest* — the surveys held on the ship and her cargo — disbursements at Cowes — and account-sales of such part of the cargo as may have been sold, specifying to whom it belonged.

These documents should be signed by Captain Barker's agent, and countersigned by himself.

As soon as these papers are procured, it may be advisable to call upon Captain Barker to sign a bottomry bond, as security for the goods sold, belonging to the party for whom I am interested. You will please, however, not to hint at such an intention until you are in possession of the documents; otherwise Captain Barker might refuse to furnish them. Believe me, very truly, Sir, your obedient humble servant, JAMES BYRNE.

CLXXXI.

James Byrne, Esq. *London.* East Cowes, 30th November, 18—.

Sir,— In reply to your esteemed letter of yesterday, I beg to inform you, that I have called on Captain Barker, but can only get from him an assurance that he will proceed as fast as possible to take in his cargo, the vessel being now nearly ready to receive it.

---

* See Appendix.

Respecting the accounts and documents, he says, they are not yet in his possession; when they are, he will give me an answer. I do not like his proceedings, I must confess, and think him rather indifferent about prosecuting his voyage. Indeed, I believe that he would gladly winter here, if he could find an excuse for so doing. I am, faithfully, Sir, your obedient humble servant, GEORGE PAYNE.

CLXXXII.

George Payne, Esq. *East Cowes.* *London, 11th December, 18—.*

Sir, — I have duly received your esteemed favor of the 30th ult., and with many thanks for the trouble you have already taken with Captain Barker, must entreat that you will again call on him, and insist on his proceeding on his voyage, or delivering up that part of his cargo for which I am authorised to act. You will please, at the same time, to assure him, that unless he does one or the other, I will immediately take such steps as shall compel him to do justice to the proprietors of his cargo.

Messrs. Bunster and Co. and Messrs. Martin and Alger, of this city, who are likewise interested in Captain Barker's proceeding on his voyage without further delay, will act in concert with me. I remain, Sir, your obedient humble servant, JAMES BYRNE.

CLXXXIII.

J. F. Vizeu, Esq. *Oporto.* *London, 2nd December, 18—.*

Sir, — I regret to have to inform you, that Captain Barker is still at Cowes, and that there is little or no appearance of his proceeding on his voyage, since he has not yet begun to take in his cargo. This is very vexatious, and I would recommend that the proprietors of the cargo should, without loss of time, furnish me, through your medium, with a power of attorney and other necessary documents, to act for them in case of need. The bills of lading, specially endorsed to me, will be particularly requisite. I shall then be enabled to call on him effectually and legally, either to proceed or to deliver up to me what remains of his cargo.

I have already paid my agent at Cowes 5*l*. 5*s*. for his attendance at the sale as requested, although he made no purchases on my account; this being the usual practice at the Isle of Wight. He at first demanded ten guineas: but I resisted, and it was submitted to the decision of a gentleman well versed in these matters, who awarded him half the sum, which I paid him to your debit. I remain, truly, Sir, your obedient humble servant, JAMES BYRNE.

CLXXXIV.

James Byrne, Esq. *London.* *Oporto, 11th December, 18—.*

Sir, — I am in receipt of your favor of the 2nd instant, and, in
Anderson.

compliance with your wish, I inclose you my power of attorney and bills of lading, endorsed to your order, for such part of the cargo of the Sophia as belongs to me. I shall endeavour to prevail on the rest of the proprietors to follow my example; and I hope this will have the desired effect, and drive Captain Barker from his winter quarters. I have credited you the 5*l*. 5*s*. paid your agent. Really this is a truly unfortunate speculation and troublesome affair. I am, always, Sir, your obedient humble servant, J. F. VIZEU.

CLXXXV.

James Byrne, Esq. *London.*   *East Cowes, 15th December, 18—.*

Sir, — Agreeably to the wish expressed in your favor of the 11th inst. I have insisted on Captain Barker's immediately proceeding on his voyage, or delivering up to me the goods of which you have the bills of lading; but I regret to say that he still procrastinates, and evades all expostulation by asserting that he intends to sail as soon as the weather will permit, which is certainly not very favorable just now: in my opinion he purposes eating his Christmas dinner here.

Mr. Knight promises me the documents you require, or copies as soon as the ship departs. Believe me, truly, Sir, your obedient humble servant, ——— GEORGE PAYNE.

CLXXXVI.

George Payne, Esq. *East Cowes.*   *London, 21st December. 18—.*

Sir — In acknowledging the receipt of your letter of the 15th instant, I beg to assure you that I feel very much obliged by your prompt attention to my request relative to the vexatious business of the Sophia. I must now further trouble you to deliver to Captain Barker the inclosed letter (which is left open for your perusal); and I hope you will not relax in your endeavours to prevail on him to do justice to the parties whose property has been placed under his care.

I am in possession of a power of attorney from my friend at Oporto, and shall act upon it, if Captain Barker does not, without further procrastination, either proceed on his voyage, or deliver up the goods for which I hold bills of lading.

I hope Mr. Knight will furnish you with copies of the documents required, in accordance with his promise.

Be so good as to state in your next, whether the cargo is still on shore, or whether the Sophia has begun to reload. And believe me, truly, Sir, your obedient humble servant, JAMES BYRNE.

CLXXXVII.

London, 21st December, 18—.

Captain J. Barker, Ship Sophia, *Cowes.*

Sir, — Being informed that you refuse to deliver up the remainder of the goods for which I hold a bill of lading, and still delay the prosecution of your voyage to Oporto, I take the liberty of addressing you on the subject, and of intimating that, unless you do the one or the other, without further procrastination or excuse, it will be my duty to take the necessary legal measures to compel you to do justice to my friends, who have entrusted their property to your care.

I hope, however, that an alternative so disagreeable to me, and so troublesome and expensive to yourself, will be rendered unnecessary by your immediate departure for your port of destination. I am, &c.

JAMES BYRNE.

CLXXXVIII.

James Byrne, Esq. *London.*   *East Cowes, 24th December,* 18—.

Sir, — Your esteemed letter of the 21st is before me, and I have, in compliance with its contents, again waited on Captain Barker, who has got the major part of his cargo on board; therefore there are some hopes that he will now soon get under way. I delivered to him your letter, and it appeared to have some little effect. The fact is, I believe, that he has been waiting all this while for money from his owners, M. Knight having been averse to disposing of any more of the cargo. In haste, but sincerely, I remain, Sir, your obedient humble servant,   GEORGE PAYNE.

CLXXXIX.

James Byrne, Esq. *London.*   *East Cowes, 7th January,* 18—.

Sir, — At length I have the satisfaction of announcing the departure of the Sophia; Captain Barker having set sail yesterday for Oporto.

Mr. Knight assures me he will do the needful, and forward you the papers as soon as possible. I am, always, and most truly, Sir, your obedient humble servant,   GEORGE PAYNE.

CXC.

G. Payne, Esq. *East Cowes.*   *London, 26th April,* 18—.

Sir, — I received in due course of post your much esteemed letters of the 24th December, last year, and 7th January of the present; as also one from Mr. Knight dated 13th of the latter month, handing me the valuation of the Sophia, taken at Cowes, previous to her repairs; to all which I deferred replying at the time, to avoid postage. Be so good as to mention this to Mr. K.

I cannot refrain from repeating how much I feel indebted for your kind attention, and for the information with which you furnished me relative to the Sophia and her cargo. That vessel has at length arrived at Oporto, and delivered what remained of the goods shipped on board her at St. Petersburgh. The papers and documents relating to her unfortunate average have been transmitted to me, and are now in the hands of an accountant at Lloyd's for adjustment. If, therefore, you will be so good as to favour me with the particulars of any expense you may have incurred, or charge you may have to make, in regard to this transaction, your demand shall be promptly satisfied. An early answer will oblige, Sir, your obedient humble servant, JAMES BYRNE.

Twelfth Series.

CXCI.

Messrs. Daniel Brothers and Co. *Lisbon*. *London*, 20th June, 18—.

Gentlemen, — Although I am well aware of the causes which prevent our correspondence from being as active as I could wish, yet resolved on my part to leave nothing untried that can tend to enliven it, I have determined on remitting you inclosed on my account, 2nd of a bill of exchange for 1000*l*. (one thousand pounds) on B. Hogg at sixty days' sight, exchange 58 $1/_8d$. 4,788 mil. 030 reis. The first has been sent via Paris to Mr. F. P. De Silvestre, of your city, for acceptance, to whom you will please to apply for it.

Against the above remittance, I have taken the liberty of drawing on you this day for 500*l*. at 50 $1/_4d$. 2,398 mil. 060 reis at sixty days' date, to the order of J. Mineret, which draft I recommend to your protection, debiting me for it at maturity.

You will please, when in cash, to make me returns for the balance in Spanish dollars, provided they will give an exchange of 52 $1/_2$ (without my commission). The insurance is already effected at 10*s*. per cent., policy stamp included.

Should this operation not be practicable, you will be so good as to invest the cash as follows: —

First, in sugars for Hamburgh, if an exchange of 12 $1/_4$ from thence on London can be realised, calculating the insurance at 2, and a profit of 10 per cent.

Secondly, in coffee for the same place, provided the same exchange (calculating the profit at 20 per cent.) can be obtained.

Thirdly, in cotton for this port or Liverpool, whenever a profit of 5 per cent. can be reckoned on, insurance 1 per cent.

Should neither of these objects be attainable, you will then remit me the balance in question in good bills on this place, when your course of exchange shall be at or above 52 $1/_2$ per milrea.

In case of an investment taking place in goods, you will please to give me timely advice for insurance; consigning your shipment, if to Hamburgh, to Messrs. Müller and Co.; if to Liverpool, to Mr. John Williams.

I am very desirous of extending our commercial relations, and should be most happy to find you disposed to join me in this or any other speculation. I remain, with the greatest sincerity, Gentlemen, your obedient humble servant, WM. WILLIAMS.

CXCII.

Messrs. Daniel Brothers & Co. *Lisbon.* *London, 12th July, 18—.*

Gentlemen, — I am in receipt of your much valued favor of the 30th of last month, and rejoice to find that you have no objection to embark with me in a speculation in bullion and bills of exchange, on a small scale, by way of enlivening our correspondence. I have accordingly effected an insurance for 5000*l.* on gold and silver, both or either, by packet from your port to Falmouth; and thence, by waggon to the Bank of England at 10*s.* per cent., policy-duty, etc. included.

In compliance with your request, I hand you inclosed *pro-forma* account-sales of both gold and silver. The former is now at the mint price of 3*l.* 17*s.* 10 $^1/_3$d. per oz. in bars, which is equal to about 3*l.* 17*s.* 6d. for ports* (Joannes), expense of smelting, etc. deducted. Dollars are 4*s.* 10 $^1/_2$d. per oz., and there is every appearance of these prices remaining firm.

If sold to the Bank of England, there is no charge for brokerage on bullion, as they purchase without the intervention of a broker; but when sold to individuals, a broker is constantly employed, and of course $^1/_8$ per cent. brokerage paid. I observe your purchase of fifty bags of Pernambuco cotton on my account; and expecting further particulars, I remain, Gentlemen, your obliged and obedient humble servant, WM. WILLIAMS.

CXCIII.

London, 23nd December, 18—.

Messrs. Daniel Brothers & Co. *Lisbon.*

Gentlemen, — I addressed a few lines to you yesterday, via Franco, of which I do not send you a copy, as they were merely to confirm my respects of the 19th instant, duplicate of which was annexed.

I am still without any of your esteemed favors; but as the wind continues in the same quarter, directly against the packet's sailing, I send this to Falmouth in the expectation of its being in time to go with Wednesday's mail; my object being to inclose you the first of the four following drafts on joint account, viz.

---

* Portuguese gold coins worth 1*l.* 16*s.* sterling, at par.

L. 100 0 0 on J. A. Mendes at 60
              days' date, ex. 49 3/4, 482 mil. 412 reis.
   100 0 0 on M. A.   Metto do.   482 » 412 »
   100 0 0 on L. J. de Britto do.   482 » 412 »
   284 5 3 on R.   Ardisson do. 1,371 » 317 »
   ─────────   ─────────────────
L. 584 5 3   cash 24th Inst. 2,818 mil. 553 reis.
                     to your debit.

I have further to remit you, on my own account, the six following drafts, for which you will be so good as to make me returns in the most advantageous manner you can, without waiting for their falling due (although they will have but a few days to run), for I hold them on joint account, and am desirous of closing my connexion with the party concerned, as speedily as possible.

The returns must, of course, be *per appoint.*

8,482 mil. 534 reis on W. Carruthers at 60 days' date, from 23rd ult.
 478 » 803 » on L. J. de Britto at 60 days' date, from 20th ult.
 800 » 000 » on F. and H. Vanzeller at three months' date,
                   from 15th October.
1,200 » 000 » on   do.   do.
 340 » 000 » on F. A. Driscol at 1 1/2 usance*, from 22nd
                   October,
 420 » 762 » on J. J. Alves at 1 1/2 usance, from 25th October.
─────────────────
11,722 mil. 099 reis.

Inclosed, I also beg leave to trouble you with firsts of two drafts on your city, to which I shall be obliged by your procuring acceptance, and holding them at the disposal of the seconds; viz.

   L. 1000 at 30 days' sight on James Ashforth.
      500 at 60   do.   on   do.

As there are regular traders or packets intended to sail from Liverpool for your port on the 1st and 15th of every month, and as they will, no doubt, make their return voyage at stated periods likewise, it may be well to avail ourselves of that channel of correspondence occasionally. Believe me, very sincerely, Gentlemen, your obedient humble servant,   WM. WILLIAMS.

CXCIV.

Messrs. Daniel Brothers & Co.   *London, 24th Dec.* 18—.

Gentlemen, — Referring to, and confirming the foregoing copy of my respects of the 22nd instant, I now hand you seconds of the drafts therein mentioned for 584l. 5s. 3d., on joint account, and 11,722 mil. 099 reis, on my own account.

---

* See Appendix.

I have this day negotiated the two drafts on Paris for 15,000 frs, at 25 15, producing 582*l.* 10*s.* 6*d.* to your credit in joint account, cash the 28th instant. I was induced to negotiate them, having some others to dispose of at the same time, and, moreover, because an opportunity presented itself of making you returns at 49 $^1/_2$d. in the three drafts mentioned at foot, amounting to 656*l.* 13*s.* 11*d.* cash, likewise the 28th instant.

Wishing you every enjoyment this convivial season generally brings with it, I remain, Gentlemen, yours most truly,

WM. WILLIAMS.

CXCV.

Messrs. Daniel Brothers & Co. *Lisbon.* *London, 2nd January,* 18—.

Gentlemen, — The above is a copy of my last letter of the 28th ult. via France. This morning I have had the pleasure of receiving yours of the 12th of that month through the same channel, inclosing thirds of your remittance of the 8th instant on Hamburgh and Genoa, which are in order.

I further received your remittance of 4,000 fl. on Amsterdam at 43 $^3/_4$, 1,497 mil. 676 reis, which is noted in conformity.

Your remittance for 150*l.* on M. Fletcher, and 200*l.* on R. Brander and Co. are out for acceptance; and not doubting that they will be honored, they will duly appear to your credit, at 51*d.* in 2,117 mil. 646 reis, the same having been found correct.

I am glad to observe you were picking up some more ports; the parcel E, by the Kent, is arrived at the Bank, but owing to the holidays could not be disposed of till to-day. I hope to hand you account-sales of this parcel, and that per Arabella by next mail. Inclosed you will find those of

1,943 ports and 725 dollars, per Marlborough,
netting . . . . L. 4,068 9 11
And 2,885 ports, per Stanmer, netting 5,099 15 10

To your credit, cash the 26th ult. . . . L. 9,168 5 9

I have this day valued on you a small *appoint* 59*l.* 13*s.* 3*d.* at sixty days' date, exchange 50*d.* per milrea, to the order of A. and J. H. Schneider and Co., which I recommend to your protection, being 286 mil. 380 reis to your credit, cash the 4th instant.

The 1,500*l.* of which I sent you the firsts for acceptance, I negotiated yesterday at 49 $^3/_4$d.; something considerable having been previously done at 49 $^1/_2$, so that you will perceive our exchange is looking up, and I shall therefore be enabled to make you some handsome and profitable remittances shortly. I remain, most truly, Gentlemen, your obedient humble servant,   WM. WILLIAMS.

CXCVI.

Messrs. Daniel Brothers & Co. *Lisbon*. London, 9th January, 18—.

Gentlemen, — Since I last wrote to you * on the 2nd inst. I have received your esteemed favors of the 12th and 19th ult., via Paris, by which I perceive that the Packet, Duke of Kent had arrived out on the 17th, and was to sail on the 22nd. She has not, however, yet made her appearance.

The first-mentioned letter contained three drafts on Genoa, for p. 5,000 fuori di banco, taken at 870 reis, for which I credit you 4,350 mil. 000 reis in the milreis column, and 923*l*. 3*s*. 6*d*. In that for sterling, having succeeded in negotiating them at 44 ⁵/₁₆, cash the 11th instant.

I have also negotiated your remittance on Amsterdam of fl. 4.000, at 12 florins 7 ¹/₂ stivers per pound sterling, and for which I credit you 323*l*. 4*s*. 8*d*., cash the 8th instant.

Inclosed, I wait on you with account-sales of 1515 ports, and 180 dollars, per Lady Arabella, and for the nett proceeds have credited you 2,828*l*. 12*s*. 11*d*., cash the 31st. ult.

Inclosed, you will also find the seven firsts of exchange noted at foot, amounting to 2.302*l*. 9*s*. 11*d*. which having been taken, as there stated, at 49 ⁵/₈ to 49 ³/₄, make 11,114 mil. 000 reis to your debit, all which, if found correct, please to note accordingly. Further, I have entered to your credit in milreis, 22,945 mil. 192 reis, account of invoice of bullion, per Duke of Kent 2nd, the letters by her having reached me since the commencement of this letter, Believe me, very truly, Gentlemen, your obedient humble servant,

WM. WILLIAMS.

Thirteenth Series.

CXCVII.

Messrs. Vanhausen and Co. *Hamburgh*. London, 10th October, 18—.

Gentlemen, — With reference to the general average per Gustave, and in answer to your enquiry what documents will be necessary to settle with our underwriters, I beg to say that an attested copy of the captain's protest will be indispensable, with such other papers and accounts as may have been laid before your insurers; and the statement on which they have settled the loss. If the average be not of large amount, the general statement and protest only may satisfy our underwriters, and they will, probably, be governed

---

* *Since my last* is a common phrase, but an ungrammatical one. *Since*, being an adverb of time, cannot have direct reference to a letter, as it has to a day, an hour, a week, a date; and *my last* can never be used without an antecedent, which in this case must be the word *letter*; as for instance, « I have written several letters to him, and in my last I stated » etc.

by the latter; but, should it be a general average of any magnitude, they will require all the accounts connected with the repairs, etc. In the first instance, to save expense, you had better transmit me the general statement and protest only, and I can inform you if any other documents will be demanded. Believe me, truly, etc. JAS. NICHOLS.

CXCVIII.

Jacob Rawlings, Esq. *Hamburgh*. *London, 2nd January,* 18—.

Sir, — I have been favored with your letter of the 24th ult. Inclosing copy of one that you had received from Mr. Warde of Heligoland, announcing the loss of the Veränderung on the coast of Jutland. This event was, however, previously known here, and I had taken the preliminary steps for recovering the amount of your loss by that vessel, which I hope to accomplish in a few days; when I shall wait on you with the account thereof.

I shall likewise furnish you with a sketch of your account current for the last six months.

The underwriters on the Felicidade would not consent to make any return for convoy of armed ships. The return for *convoy* can only be claimed when the vessel convoying is a ship of war, unless it be stipulated otherwise in the policy. You will please likewise to take note, that when goods are valued in a policy, there can be no demand made of a return of premium for short interest; but in the instance of the cottons, per Mercurio, the underwriters, on perusing your letter, allowed me a return in conformity with your statement, for which I have credited you 4*l*. 5*s*., as per memorandum at foot.

The documents relative to the average per Three Sisters from Oporto, are received; and I shall do what is necessary with them, crediting our friends in that city with the amount I may recover, and yourselves for cost of these papers 23 mks. bco., 6*s*. exchange 36-8 1*l*. 14*s*. 3*d*. in your account. Believe me, etc.   JAS NICHOLS.

CXCIX.

Jacob Rawlings, Esq. *Hamburgh*. *London, 11th January,* 18—.

Sir, — My last respects were under date of the 4th inst. since which time I have received your letter of the 31st ult. with a statement of *my* account current to that date, which shall be examined, and the balance, banco mks. 25,792, 4 carried to a new account, if found correct.

Inclosed, I now wait on you with *your* account current, leaving a balance, at the same period, of 2.897*l*. 12*s*. 6*d* in my favor, which if found free from error, you will be so good as to pass to a new account in conformity. Subjoined thereto, you will find a note of the sundry transactions now pending, relative to the shipments and losses per sundry vessels, of which, when finally settled, you will be furnished with a detailed account.

GENERAL CORRESPONDENCE.

Inclosed, you will also find a statement of the various sums I have accepted for account of the cargo per Veränderung; amount to the debit of yourselves and Mr. Carvalho of Bahia, 2,051*l*. 18*s*., independent of the insurances effected thereon, the account of which has been already furnished.

Further, an account of the loss, as settled with underwriters, for the 150 chests of sugars by that vessel, the charges for recovering the same deducted, leaving 2,484*l*. nett to your credit, cash the 11th of March next.

Further, an account of the loss of 120 chests sugar by the same vessel, insured for account of Mr. Manvel. I dos Reys, by order of Mr. Carvalho, amount to your credit 2,289*l*., cash also the 11th of March.

As I debited you with the premiums I have credited you with the above loss provisionally; but, as I must pay the drafts which I have accepted on account of these sugars, perhaps it would be as well for me to open an account with Mr. Carvalho, and close it by carrying the balance to your debit or credit. Please to say how it is to be. If those entries are to remain, I must debit you with his drafts as they fall due, and with my commission on them.

Agreeably to what I suggested in my last, I have this day taken the liberty of valuing on you for marks banco 6,968 12*s*. at three months' date, exchange 13-5 to the order of Benjamin Hearne (which draft I recommend to your protection), and have credited you in your account 500*l*. It is probable I shall draw on you for 1500*l*. more by next post, to complete the 2000*l*. which I shall be in advance on account of Mr. Carvalho's drafts for your 1/2 of the sugars per Marion and Thames. Our exchange appears to be nearly stationary, and I am rather short of cash. I remain, Sir, etc. JAS NICHOLS.

CC.

I. I. Manvel, Esq. *Fayal.*   London, 15th August, 18—.

Sir, — I am favored with your valued letter of the 11th ult. together with a power of attorney to claim and recover the sum of 543*l*. insured on twenty-eight pipes one hogshead of wine, shipped on board the brig, Duke of Victoria, for account of, and consigned to, Mr. J. J. Da Cunha of your city; that vessel having been taken by pirates on her voyage from your Island to Rio de Janeiro.

On receipt of your letters, I called on two of the underwriters on your policy, who informed me they were ready to settle the loss as soon as they were put in possession of the requisite documents respecting the capture.

I then waited on Mr. J. Ferguson, and demanded the policy, but he refused to deliver it up; alleging, I am sorry to say, that he had made the insurance by order of Mr. Charles Le Roy, with whom he had an open account, and who was indebted to him in several sums of money. I immediately consulted my attorney, who informed me that Mr. Ferguson had no right to retain the policy, or set off any thing except the premium. I have accordingly written to him to demand the policy; and if he does not give it up, I shall take legal measures to obtain it, advising you of the result in due course.

I shall be expecting shortly to receive the bill of lading for these wines, and the captain's protest, without which nothing can be done. An invoice too would be serviceable.

As soon as I recover the loss from the underwriters, I will remit the amount, less 85 mil. 000 reis due to you, and the charges which may be incurred here, to Mr. Da Cunha, unless I receive, in the mean time, orders from him to the contrary. Be so good as to inform me at what exchange I am to calculate the 85 mil. 000 reis, there being no course established between your island and this city. Believe me always, etc. WM. MATTHEWS.

CCI.

J. Ferguson, Esq. *London, 25th Nov., 18—.*

Sir, — Some time having elapsed since you were requested to give up the policy of the wines, insured by you for account of Mr. J. J. Da Cunha of Fayal, and having recently called at your counting house for your determination, without being able to see you, I take this method of informing you, that if the policy be not immediately given up on payment of the premium and charges, which I have already tendered to you, I must, however reluctantly, place the business in the hands of my attorney. My instructions on this point, from both Mr. Manvel and Mr. Da Cunha, are peremptory.

Hoping that you will not put me to the trouble and expense consequent upon such a step, I am, WM. MATTHEWS.

Fourteenth Series.

CCII.

Rio de Janeiro, 24th December, 18—.

Messrs. Thomson & Sons, *Liverpool.*

Gentlemen, — We are favored with your letter of the 30th August last, as also with one from your friend in London, Mr. Wm. Mitchell, inclosing us the sum of 392l. 10s. mentioned in yours, in a bill of exchange at ninety days' sight, drawn by A. Spencer and Co. on Rowden and Fletcher of this city; but which draft, we are sorry to say, has been refused acceptance. We avail ourselves of the departure of the Montezuma for your port, to give you the earliest possible intelligence of this circumstance, and by packet shall send Mr. Mitchell the protest for non-acceptance. In haste, we remain, very truly, Gentlemen, your obedient humble servants. J. V. GOMES & Co.

CCIII.

Wm. Mitchell, Esq. *London.*   *Liverpool, 31st March, 18—.*

Sir, — Subjoined you will receive a copy of a letter just received from our common friends, Messrs. J. V. Gomes and Co., dated Rio de Janeiro, the 24th December last, advising me that R. Spencer and Co.'s draft for 392l. 11s., on Bowden and Co., remitted them by you in September last, on our account, has been noted for non-acceptance. We lose no time in transmitting you this unpleasant information, in order that you may give your indorsers the necessary notice. We are, etc.   ———   Thomson & Sons.

CCIV.

Wm. Mitchell, Esq. *London.*   *Rio de Janeiro, 2nd January, 18—.*

Sir, — We were in due time favored with your letter of the 2nd September last, transmitting us R. Spencer and Co.'s draft on Bowden and Fletcher for 392l. 10s. at ninety days' sight, on account of our Liverpool friends, Messrs. Thomson and Sons. By the inclosed protest, you will perceive that this bill has been refused acceptance, for reasons advised the drawers; if not paid at maturity, as we have cause to apprehend, the goods for which it is drawn not having been taken by Messrs. B. and F. to account, we shall wait on you with the protest for non-payment also. We remain, etc.   J. V. Gomes & Co.

CCV.

Messrs. Wood, Willis & Co. *London.*   *London, 4th March, 18—.*

Gentlemen, — Having received this morning, from Rio de Janeiro, the protest for non-acceptance of B. Spencer and Co.'s draft on Bowden and Co. of that city, for 392l. 10s., I beg to inclose it to you, and to inform you for your government, that I am led to think the bill is not likely to be paid when due. On receipt of the protest for non-payment, I shall of course wait on you with it. I remain, with esteem, etc.   ———   Wm. Mitchell.

CCVI.

Wm. Mitchell, Esq. *London.*   *Rio de Janeiro, 20th March, 18—.*

Sir, — Referring you to the above copy of your respects under date of the 2nd January, we have now to hand you the protest for non payment of the draft, therein mentioned, on Bowden and Co. for 392l. 10s., with which you will please do the needful, and recover the amount from your indorsers, or from the drawers. At foot you have a note of the expenses attending this disgraceful transaction. We do not re-draw for the amount, but beg you to remit it to us *per appoint*, that we may have no claim on, or correspondence with, Messrs. Thomson and Sons on the subject. You can communicate to them the result. Hoping you will be more fortunate in your next selection, we subscribe ourselves, Sir, your obedient humble servants,

                             J. V. Gomes & Co.

BILL DISHONORED.

L. 392 10 0 at 58 ¹/₂ per milrea,
Cost of protest, 2 mil. 240 reis,
Postages, 3 » 160 »
Comm. ¹/₂ per ct. 8 » 051 »
Brokerage ¹/₂ do. 8 » 051 »
at 60 ⁴/₂ per milrea, = L. 407 18 9.

1,610 mil. 256 reis
21 mil. 502 reis
―――――――――
1,631 mil. 758 reis

CCVII.

Messrs. Wood, Wills & Co. *London.*   *London, 1st June,* 18—.

Gentlemen. — Messrs. B. Spencer and Co.'s draft on Bowden and Fletcher, of Rio de Janeiro, for 392*l.* 10*s.* having been returned to me under protest for non-payment, the bearer will deliver it to you, together with an account of the re-exchange and charges, amounting to 408*l.* 16*s.* 1*d.*, which I claim from you, as indorsers to me of the said bill of exchange, and which amount you will please to pay the bearer, who is authorised to give you an acquittance for the same. I am truly, Sir, your obedient humble servant, Wm. MITCHELL.

Re-draft, 1,631 mill. 758 reis, at 60 ¹/₂ per milrea   L. 407 18 9
Deduct sixty-three days' interest 3 10 3
                                                                                                  L. 404 8 6

Postages in London, L. 1 19 0 . . . .)
Commission ¹/₂ per ct. 2 0 7 . . . . }   L. 4 7 7
Brokerage, ¹/₂ do.   0 8 0 . . . .)

                                                                                                  L. 408 15 1

CCVIII.

Messrs. Thomson & Sons, *Liverpool.*   *London, 4th June,* 18—.

Gentlemen, — Having recovered on the 1st inst., from Messrs. Wood, Willis and Co., indorser, the amount of B. Spencer and Co.'s draft for 392*l.* 10*s.* on Bowden and Co. Rio de Janeiro, which had been protested for non-payment, I yesterday remitted Messrs. J. V. Gomes and Co. the proceeds, in J. Nunes and Co.'s first of exchange for 404*l.* 5*s.* 6*d.*, at sixty days' sight, as you will learn more fully from a perusal of the inclosed duplicate, which you will be so good as to close and forward to Messrs. Gomes.

I have credited you 1*l.* 0*s.* 3*d.*, your moiety of the commission, which I am fairly entitled to charge on the remittance of the above sum. Your friend receives his commission at Rio, on the 404*l.* 8*s.* 6*d.*, and having benefited by not *redrawing,* inasmuch as he will now receive 1,751 mill. 020 reis, instead of 1,610 mill. 256 reis, he is amply remunerated for the interest which he would have derived from the use of the latter sum, from the 28th March to the present period when the present remittance will fall due, say about the 4th October next. If I had charged interest, it could only have been from the date on which I paid for the bill, the 27th September last, to the day I received the amount of the protested bill, the 1st instant: consequently, even in that case, Messrs. Gomes would not have been benefited so much. The holder of a bill returned under protest, where the amount is not redrawn, has the option of charging the drawer or indorser either interest or re-exchange (but not both), with one commission of $1/_2$ per cent. and one brokerage: that usually paid at the place on which the bill was drawn. I state this for your future guidance. I remain, etc. WM. MITCHELL.

CCIX.

Messrs. J. V. Gomes & Co. Rio de Janeiro. *London, 3rd June, 18—.*

Gentlemen, — Your esteemed favors of the 2nd January and 29th March have been duly received, the first covering protest for non-acceptance, and the latter that for non payment of S. Spencer and Co.'s draft on Bowden and Fletcher, of your city, for 392l. 10s. remitted you the 2nd September last, by order and for account of Messrs. Thomson and Sons, of Liverpool. I have however, the satisfaction to inform you, that I have recovered the amount of this bill from the indorser, with re-exchange and charges, say 407l. 18s. 6d. less interest for sixty-three days, which the draft would have had to run if re-drawn, being, nett, ... L. 404 8 6
Less my commission for remitting 401l.
5s. 6d. $1/_2$ per cent. 2 0 6
Brokerage on do. $1/_2$ do. 0 10 0
Postages on do. to and from Brazil and
Liverpool 0 12 6
                                       ─────
                                       3 3 0
                                       ─────
                                       L. 401 5 6

This sum I now remit you in J. Nunes and Co.'s draft on J. P. De Amorrim at sixty days' sight, exchange 54 $3/_4$ per milrea, making 7,751 mil, 020 reis, with which you will please do the needful, and when discharged, as I have no doubt it will be at maturity, close this transaction, as I have done in my books. Always at your service, I remain, etc. WM. MITCHELL.

Fifteenth Series.
CCX.

Messrs. Wm. Cook & Son, *Newcastle*. *London, 18th December, 18—.*

Gentlemen, — I have not recently had occasion to trouble you; but I now request your attention to an order which I have received from Lisbon, for a cargo of coals, to be shipped from your place;

and should it be executed to the satisfaction of my friend there, it is probable he may be induced to continue his orders monthly.

This cargo must consist of from 10 to 15 (say from ten to fifteen) keels of coals of good quality, and proper for the use of smiths. Of course you will endeavour to ship them at as low a freight as possible; and as vessels are now constantly going out for cargoes of fruit, I should think you would have no difficulty in getting one to take the above quantity at a very low freight, since the coals would answer the purpose of ballast, and save the expense of heaving the latter in and out. I rely not only on the coals being of the description, and the quality recommended, but also that you will put them in at the lowest shipping price.

You will be so good as to give me timely advice of the shipment, stating the probable cost for my government in effecting the insurance: and on my being furnished with invoice and bill of lading, your draft for the amount of the former will be duly honored.

The bills of lading you will be pleased to fill up to order, and inclose one to Mr. F. P. da Rochos at Lisbon. You will stipulate in the charter-party, that the captain is to consign his vessel to my above-named friend, who will, I am confident, do every thing in his power to procure him a return-cargo.

Should there be any spare room in the vessel, you may ship a few empty bottles on my account, unless you prefer doing so on your own, by way of trying the market. I remain, very truly, Gentlemen, your obedient humble servant, WM. MATTHEWS.

CCXI.

Messrs. W. Cook & Son, *Newcastle.*   London, 23rd January, 18—.

Gentlemen, — I had the pleasure yesterday of urging you to charter a vessel to take coals for Lisbon without further delay. I have now however to countermand that order, in consequence of the receipt of letters this morning, per mail, bringing me instructions to that effect. You will therefore, if not already executed, please to consider the order for charging such a vessel as null and void. I am extremely sorry to have given you so much trouble to no purpose, but hope, on another occasion, to have it in my power to make you amends. Believe me, most truly, Gentlemen, your obedient humble servant, WM. MATTHEWS.

CCXII.

Messrs. W. Cook & Son, *Newcastle.*   London, 11th March, 18—.

Gentlemen, — This letter will be delivered to you by Capt. Benjamin Britten, of the Brig Eliza, which vessel I have chartered to proceed to your port to take in a cargo of coals, for the island of Fayal. She is 103 tons burthen per register. I have to request that you will lose no time in putting on board of said vessel a full and sufficient loading of coals, to consist of Pelau *small*, or Townly Maine *small*, being intended for the purpose of heating furnaces. You will be very particular in letting them he of good quality and riddled, so that they may be subject to the *low duty* on exportation. Relying on your best attention to this small order, I beg to assure you that your draft for the amount, on furnishing me invoice and bill of lading, shall be punctually discharged.

The bill of lading is to be made out to order, and deliverable at Fayal or Lisbon; one to be inclosed in a blank cover, addressed « To the Consignee of the Cargo, per Eliza, at Fayal or Lisbon; » and given in charge to Captain Britten. With great esteem, believe me, Gentlemen, your obedient humble servant, Wm. MATTHEWS.

CCXIII.

Captain Benjamin Britten, *Brig Eliza*.   *London, 11th March, 18—.*

Sir, — You will avail yourself of the first opportunity, after the receipt of this, to proceed, agreeably to the charter-party, to Newcastle-upon-Tyne, and on arrival there deliver the inclosed letter to Messrs. W. Cook and Son, at Bell Quay Bottle Works. These Gentlemen will put on board the Eliza, with all possible dispatch, a full and sufficient cargo of coals, for which you will, when loaded, sign proper bills of lading, as filled up by Messrs. Cook and Sons.

As soon as you have cleared out from the Custom House, you will immediately proceed with your cargo to the Island of Fayal, and on your arrival off that island, hoist as a signal, at your foretop-gallant-mast head, the Spanish Ensign, with which you will be provided. Which signal, together with your cargo and the inclosed letter, you will deliver to Mr. J. Maciel, merchant of that island; and follow his directions with respect to unloading your cargo of coals.

But in case the said Mr. J. T. Maciel should have unfortunately died, quitted the said island, become bankrupt, or be otherwise incapacitated from receiving the cargo, you will please to get certificate of such death, removal or incapacity, drawn up by the British Consul or Vice Consul at Fayal, and signed by two or three respectable British merchants at that island; and instead of delivering the coals there, proceed with them to Lisbon, with as little delay as possible, and deliver the said cargo to Mr. P. A. Da Silveira, who will have my authority to receive the same. And in such case you will also deliver to Mr. Silveira the letter directed to • The Consignee of the Cargo, per Eliza, at Fayal or Lisbon. •

You have received on board here, two puncheons of brandy, which are likewise to be delivered to Mr. Maciel at Fayal, if there; but if not, or he be rendered incapable of receiving them, you will deliver them to the British Consul, or Vice Consul, requesting him to sell them for my account, and deliver over to you the nett proceeds; out of which you can defray the expenses of your vessel during your stay at the island, and account with Mr. Silveira at Lisbon for the balance.

Whether you discharge your cargo at Fayal or Lisbon, you will take in another for Petersburgh, which M. Maciel or Mr. Silveira will put on board; furnishing you with the necessary instructions for the further prosecution of your voyage, and the delivery of your said return-cargo on reaching your destination. You will also accommodate a cabin passenger. Such cash as you may require for the ship's use, will be advanced by Mr. Maciel, at Fayal, or by Mr. Silveira, at Lisbon, or by their correspondents at St. Petersburgh, on your endorsing at each place on your charter-party, the sums received respectively.

On your return to this port you will, without loss of time, wait on me at my counting-house with such letters and documents as may be intrusted to your care by the party to whom you will be consigned at St. Petersburgh.

Wishing you a successful voyage, and quick return, I remain, very truly, Sir, your friend and humble servant, WM. MATTHEWS.

Sixteenth Series.
CCXIV.

Messrs. Martin and Son, *London.*   *London, 11th March, 18—.*

Gentlemen, — The fruit, ex (1) Jane, sold by you by auction, having become due yesterday, I fully expected you would send me the amount. When I gave you orders to sell, you assured me that I might rely on being in cash in a month. Confiding in that assurance, I have remitted a bill for the nett proceeds to the party who made me the consignment, calculating that I should receive the same from you, in time to take up that bill. I must, therefore, request you will have the goodness to send me a check for the proceeds of the sale without delay. I am, etc,   THOMAS JAMES.

CCXV.

T. James, Esq. *London.*   *London, 11th March, 18—.*

Sir, — In reply to your letter of yesterday, we beg to inform you that several of the purchasers have not yet cleared their oranges, ex Jane, and that notwithstanding we furnished you with an anticipated account-sales at your earnest request, we cannot close the transaction until the fruit is all taken off our hands. This we expect will be the case in the course of two or three days, as we have

---

(1) *Ex lat.* fuori di, sbarcato da, scaricato da, per. *Anderson.*

given the parties notice of re-sale, if the goods be not taken away this day, or to morrow. We remain, etc. MARTIN & SON.

CCXVI.

Messrs. Martin & Son, *London.* *London, 13th March, 18—.*

Mr. James presents his compliments, and begs to inform Messrs. Martin and Son, that the reason stated in their note of yesterday for not paying the proceeds of fruit per Jane, is by no means satisfactory. If the purchasers have not taken away their lots, it is no concern of his, as Messrs. Martin should have enforced the conditions of the sale, which took place under their guarantee. Consequently Mr. James looks to them for the proceeds, agreeably to the account rendered, and expects a check for the amount, 344*l*. 3*s*. 3*d*. without further correspondence on the subject, or loss of time and interest.

CCXVII.

T. James, Esq. *London.* *London, 13th March, 18—.*

Sir, — In reply to your note of this date, we wait on you with a check on our bankers for the proceeds of fruit per Jane, being 344*l*. 3*s*. 3*d*. which the bearer will hand you, and to whom you will please to deliver a receipt for that amount. We cannot conclude without observing, that we shall not, on any future occasion, furnish sales until the whole of the fruit is *delivered.* In the present instance we did it prematurely, to oblige you, at your earnest solicitation. Although we guarantee the purchasers, after delivery, we do not take upon ourselves to make good the amount of the biddings; for it is a circumstance of almost daily occurrence, that allowances are made to purchasers, even at auctions, where there is any very great falling-off in the quality of the article sold. We are, etc.

MARTIN & SON.

Seventeenth Series.
CCXVIII.

Messrs. Cumming & Co. *London.* *London, 5th July, 18—.*

Gentlemen, — I am under the necessity of waiting on you with a protest for non-acceptance of A. L. Pastor's draft, dated Lisbon, the 22nd December last, on P. J. Fernandez, of Pernambuco, at forty days' sight, for 2,000 mil. 000 reis, which I took of you the 12th Jan. last, at the exchange of 55*d*. per milrea, 458*l*. 6*s*. 8*d*. I must request that you will be so good as to furnish me with security to that amount, till the ultimate fate of this bill of exchange be decided. My correspondent observes, that in the event of a certain vessel arriving at Pernambuco prior to its falling due, the above draft may still be paid; but this is a contingency that I cannot await. I remain, truly, Gentlemen, your obedient humble servant,

THOMAS ATKINS.

CCXIX.

Thomas Atkins, Esq. *London.*   *London, 5th July, 18—.*

Sir, — In reply to your letter of this date, acquainting us with the dishonor shewn to A. L. Pastor's draft on P. J. Fernandez, of Pernambuco, for 2,000 mil. 000 reis, endorsed by us to you on the 13th January last, at the exchange of 53d. per milrea, 458l. 6s. 8d. and requiring security from us for the amount; though such a proceeding is rather unusual, and we feel confident the draft will ultimately be duly discharged, yet we promptly comply with your request, and inclose an acceptance of Messrs. Morgan and Co., of this city, for 500l. (five hundred pounds), due the 1st November next, the receipt of which you will please to acknowledge; stating at the same time that it is for collateral security, and to be returned (or its value) in case the bill of exchange in question should be paid at maturity. We are, Sir, your obedient humble servant,

                                       Cumming & Co.

CCXX.

Messrs. Cumming & Co. *London.*   *London, 6th July, 18—.*

Gentlemen, — I beg to acknowledge the receipt of your draft, on Morgan and Co., of this city, for 500l. (five hundred pounds), due the 1st of November next, to be retained by me as collateral security for the payment of A. L. Pastor's draft, dated Lisbon, 22nd December last, on P. J. Fernandez, of Pernambuco, for 2,000 mil. 000 reis at 53d., equal to 458l. 6s. 8d. sterling, which now lies under protest for non-acceptance, in the hands of my friend Mr. A. P. De Carvalho; and I hereby engage to return the said draft, or its equivalent, in cash; on receiving advice that the above bill of exchange for 458l. 6s. 8d. has been duly paid; or, if not paid, such part of the said sum of 500l. as may exceed the amount of the said bill, with re-exchange and charges thereon. I remain, Gentlemen, your obedient humble servant,   Thomas Atkins.

CCXXI.

Messrs. Cumming and Co. *London.*   *London, 14th October, 18—.*

Gentlemen, Having this morning received advice that A. J. Pastor's bill on P. J. Fernandez, of Pernambuco, for 2,000 mil. 000 reis, referred to in my letter of 5th July last, was punctually paid when due, I beg to return you, inclosed, your draft on Morgan and Co., for 500l., held by me as collateral security for the payment thereof. Thanking you for the promptitude with which you furnished me with this security, and assuring you that I should not have required it, had the transaction been on my own account, I beg to subscribe myself, Gentlemen, your obliged and obedient humble servant,   Thomas Atkins.

CCXXII.

Thomas Atkins, Esq. *London.* *London, 14th October, 18—.*

Sir, — We are favored with your letter of this morning, returning our draft on Morgan and Co., for 500*l.*, held by you as collateral security for A. J. Pastor's bill of exchange on Pernambuco, for 2,000 mil. 000 reis, which latter, we are glad to learn, had, as we expected, been duly paid at maturity. We observe your reason for demanding security from us, and, under similar circumstances, perhaps we might have been induced to do the same. We are, Sir, your obedient humble servants,

CUMMING & Co.

Eighteenth Series.

CCXXIII.

Messrs. O, Clark, and Sons, *Huddersfield.* *Leipzig, 6th June, 18—.*

Gentlemen, — From the patterns sent us in your favor of the 20th. ult. we have made selections, and have the pleasure of handing you the following order, which we recommend to your immediate and best attention,

viz. 50 pieces of fancy valentias.
300 do. tartan plaids.
500 do. plain lustres.

In valentias, none but the patterns selected will suit us. In the tartan plaids, however, we can allow you some latitude, especially if there be any thing newer in this article than the patterns enclosed, which we forward rather to serve as your guide in selecting the style of the thing we wish, than for the purpose of restricting your choice too narrowly.

The lustres, on the other hand, we do not wish to have at all, unless you can procure them at 8 $^1/_2$d. per yard, and can execute the order in the exact colors prescribed.

You will oblige us by handing us in your next, a full report of the estate of your market, as we may, probably, have it in our power to give you orders for other descriptions of goods. We are, etc.

HOMEYER & SCHMIDT.

CCXXIV.

Huddersfield, 13th June, 18—.

Messrs. Homeyer and Schmidt, *Leipzig.*

Gentlemen, — We are in receipt of your favor of the 6th instant, with an order for valentias, lustres, and tartan plaids, which we have duly noted, and will endeavour to execute to your satisfaction.

Among all the lustres on hand, there were not twenty pieces in the colors which you require; we have consequently been obliged to bespeak the whole parcel, and have had great difficulty in getting it done at 8 $1/2$ d., particularly as the greater part consists of expensive colors; whereas we might have bought the goods on hand at 8d.

A few days since a parcel of 150 pieces of cassinets, of good quality and current colors, was offered to us at 8 $1/2$ d. per yard. Would not this price tempt you to take them?

Our market is now very brisk, and the prices of several articles are on the advance. Lastings are scarce; the last quotations were 50s. 6d. for No. 1; merinos, 14s. 3d.; bombazetts, A 1, 13s. 9d.; moreen, No. 2, 20s. 6d.; damask, of the quality of the enclosed sample, 48s. 9d.; three-fourths wide Thibets, No. 6, 32s.; six-fourths wide, 60s.

It is highly probable that prices may still rise, therefore we would advise you to give in your orders without delay. We are, etc.

O. CLARK & SONS.

CCXXV.

Frankfort on the Maine, 16th May, 18—.
Messrs. J. Parsons & Co. *Nottingham.*

Gentlemen, — When I had the pleasure of seeing your Mr. John Parsons, jun. here, in October last, I made him a promise that I would, in the spring, give your house an order for bobbin-net.

Accordingly, I will thank you to send me 5,000 pieces of various widths and qualities, as noted ad foot, and with all possible expedition. The invoice amount shall be duly remitted in good London bills.

If I find your goods not dearer than those of other Nottingham houses for similar qualities, and you evince a desire to oblige and accomodate, I will with pleasure give you the preference in future.
I am, etc. F. F. STEIBELT.

Nineteenth Series.

CCXXVI.

John Harris, Esq. *London.* *London, 1st. May, 18—.*

Sir, — Having been requested by Mrs. Charles Kempthorne to call on you for payment of her quarter's pension, due the 31st March last, amounting to 25l., I shall be obliged by your appointing a day and hour when I may send you a receipt for that sum. I am, etc.

T. OATES.

CCXXVII.

Timothy Oates, Esq. *London.* *London, 2nd May, 18—.*

Sir, — I shall be ready to pay Mrs. Charles Kempthorne's pension, on your furnishing me with your authority to receive it, accompanied by a certificate of her having been alive on the 31st March last, and your receipt for the amount, 25l. I am, Sir, your devoted humble servant, JOHN HARRIS.

CCXXVIII.

John Harris, Esq. *London.*   *London, 2nd May, 18—.*

Sir, — In reply to your letter of this morning, I beg to state, that I am not provided with any certificate of Mrs. Charles Kempthorne's having been alive on the 31st March last; but I have a letter in her own hand-writing, dated the 26th of last month, which I trust will be considered, in this instance at least, ample proof of her existence, as also a sufficient authority for my receiving her pension for the past quarter. Whatever regulations for the future you may be pleased to establish, shall be strictly conformed to. The bearer will produce the letter above alluded to for your inspection, and also a receipt, should you be disposed to comply with Mrs. Kempthorne's request. I know the cash would be very acceptable to her at the present moment; and I am sure she would be grateful for your kindness. Believe me, Sir, your obedient humble servant,

TIMOTHY OATES.

CCXXIX.

Timothy Oates, Esq. *London.*   *London, 2nd May, 18—.*

Sir, — I have acceded to your request in behalf of Mrs. Charles Kempthorne, in regard to her pension for the last quarter, but, in future, I must trouble you to produce a certificate of her actual existence from the mayor or clergyman of the town or parish in which she resides, and her power of attorney authorising you to receive her pension. I am, etc.   JOHN HARRIS.

Twentieth Series.

CCXXX.

R. H. Lynch and Co. *Havannah.*   *Hamburgh, 24th October, 18—.*

Gentlemen, — We have the pleasure to address you for the first time, under the auspices of your R. H. Lynch, Esq. who was lately in this city and with whom we had the gratification of becoming personally acquainted; and are induced, in consequence of an arrangement entered into with him, to give you an order for 400 boxes of sugar on joint and equal account.

Permit me to remind you of what will tend in a great degree to the fortunate issue of this our first undertaking: that is, the selecting sugars of good quality; we are well convinced that you will pay the most careful attention to this point.

The limits that we have resolved to fix, after mature deliberation, are 9*s.* (nine shillings) sterling per arrobe * net weight, for the whites,

---

* A Spanish weight equal to 28 lbs. English; 25 1/2 lbs. according to some authorities.

and 5s. 6d. (five shillings and six-pence) sterling per arrobe net, for the browns, first cost with you, and all charges of shipping, commission and freight included.

The assortment we leave entirely to you; but should the price of white sugars be a little higher than the limits given, and that of Muscovado proportionally lower, or *vice versá*, so that upon an average, the respective limit may not be exceeded, you will please to execute the order.

This shipment must be made in a strictly neutral vessel, giving the preference to the English flag.

The invoice and bills of lading of this sugar should be made out to our address, and forwarded to Joseph Vancouver, Esq. of London, who will, you may rest assured, on receipt thereof, honor your drafts for our moiety of the invoice amount. Be pleased to hand him by two or three opportunities, the requisite advice, to enable him to effect insurance in due time. We remain, with esteem, Gentlemen, your obedient humble servants, MÜLLER, Son & Co.

CCXXXI.

London, 9th November, 18—.

Messrs. R. H. Lynch and Co. *Havannah*.

Gentlemen, — Referring you to the inclosed letter from my friends, Messrs. Müller, Son and Co., of Hamburgh, I beg to assure you, that on your complying with their orders for the purchase of sugars as therein specified (forwarding me bills of lading and invoice of the same with advice in anticipation, for effecting insurance thereon), your drafts on me for the amount of their half share in 400 chests, or of any smaller number you may ship on joint account with them, shall meet due honor.

It is, I presume, almost unnecessary to add, that being merely an agent in this transaction, it will be requisite that you abide strictly and literally by Messrs. Müller, Son and Co.'s directions in the execution of their order, to authorise my acceptance of your drafts; for regularity's sake, however, I deem it best to put you on your guard, not doubting, at the same time, that you will fulfil their wishes in that and every other respect.

Should you desire to have your moiety insured by me also, you may rely on my paying every attention to your interest, and if you do favor me with the order, you had better, perhaps, desire our friends at Hamburgh to reimburse me, charging the cost of the insurance in the account-sales. Believe me, devoted to your service, Sir, your obedient humble servant, Jos. VANCOUVER.

Twenty-first Series.
CCXXXII.

Adolph Schmidt, Esq. *London.* *Charleston, S. C., 18th April, 18—.*

Dear Sir, — With inexpressible pleasure do I inform you, that I am at length liberated from the disagreeable situation in which I was placed by the customs here; they having given up the whole property on an appraisement. In this, the appraisers, one appointed by them, one by me, and one by the court, are now engaged to ascertain the duties, which latter, I now calculate, will average about 27 $1/2$ per cent. on the whole cargo. The expense and trouble attending this business seem to be interminable; and had I been aware how much anxiety and vexation it would cost me, the whole duties should not have led me into it; however, I am extremely fortunate in getting the property restored; and though I believe I shall not, in the end, be a gainer of one dollar, I am satisfied as things are. We commence selling by public auction on Monday next, and I shall use every endeavour to remit you amply. The commission agreed on sales was four per cent., but in consequence of this business I am obliged to pay seven per cent., i. e. three per cent. city-tax, and four per cent. auction-commission. You may reckon your property secure. Believe me, dear Schmidt, it is impossible for man to feel more than I have for these several weeks past, and do now, from knowing the agony of suspense you must endure until this relieves you. I have done no more than thousands before me, though many have been more fortunate. When I look back, it is dreadful to think what might have been my situation and what danger I have escaped. Pray make my kind respects to your family; assuring them that I shall ever be happy to hear of their welfare, independent of any commercial arrangements. Yours, very sincerely, W. LAURENT.

CCXXXIII.

Adolph Schmidt, Esq. *Philadelphia, 8th Aug. 18—.*

Dear Sir, — Your favor of the 31st May was duly received, and we immediately waited on Mr. Schröder, from whom we obtained the following goods, to be sold on your account, viz.: — 6 pieces pelisse cloths, No. 1; 23 pieces, No. 2; 25 pieces, No. 3; 34 pieces, tollenetts, N. 1; 1 dozen, No. 2; 4 dozen, N. 3; 4 $3/4$ dozen, No. 4; 3 $1/2$ dozen, N. 5; 2 dozen waistcoats; 168 dozen Madras handkerchiefs, which he had been trying to sell by auction; the remainder of your shipments to him, we presume, he has sold.

We are sorry to say that, from the prices Mr. S. handed to us, the goods are not likely to sell for their invoice value, as British manufactures are extremely low; however, you may rest assured that our best endeavours will be used to promote your interest.

Please to give our best respects to your family, and believe us, with great regard, your most obedient humble servants,

JOHN & EDWARD BLITHE.

CCXXXIV.

Adolph Schmidt, Esq. *London.*   *Philadelphia, 20th October, 18—.*

Sir, — On the 8th August, we informed you that we had received from Mr. Schröder a quantity of goods, as per list then inclosed, and that we intended to dispose of them as soon as an opportunity offered. Accordingly, when our fall trade* commenced, we put them up at auction, and we have now to inclose you the account-sales of the same. Although they nett considerably less than their cost, it is twenty per cent. more than the same goods would now sell for, as you will perceive by a few waistcoats, which were omitted in the first sale and sold yesterday. We are extremely sorry to have to render so unsatisfactory an account of sales. As soon as the proceeds are due, we will remit you for them, and hope that any further transactions you may intrust to our care, will prove more profitable.

Business is very bad here, — money extremely scarce, and above half of our dry-goods merchants have suspended payments. In fact, times were never so bad before; and it appears to be the same throughout the commercial world. By accounts from your side, we learn that prices are uncommonly low, which, no doubt, is the case; and if we have not too many goods sent out in the spring, our markets will probably improve, so as to encourage speculation. We shall always be glad to hear from you, and what is the state of your markets. With kind regards to all your family, we are, etc.

JOHN & EDWARD BLITHE.

CCXXXV.

Adolph Schmidt, Esq. *London.*   *Philadelphia, 16th Nov., 18—.*

Dear Sir, — Our last respects of the 20th ult., of which we hand you duplicate annexed, covered account-sales of the goods received from Mr. Schröder. Since that date Mr. W. Laurent has presented your order to us to pay over to him the nett proceeds, which order we accordingly complied with.

We are sorry to say business continues in the same dull state as when we last addressed you. Flour has advanced to 13 dollars per barrel in consequence of the failure of the crops (1) in England, and rather a deficiency here of most kinds of grain. This will, no doubt, have some effect on the exchange, as there are several shipments of

---

(1) Raccolti.
* The autumn is called in America the *fall.*

flour being made to Liverpool, so that the shippers of dry goods (1) may perhaps be a little benefited.
Please to give our best respects to your family, and believe us, etc.
JOHN & EDWARD BLITHE.

CCXXXVI.
Adolph Schmidt, Esq. *London.*   *Philadelphia, 30th Nov. 18—.*
Dear Sir, — Since we last wrote to you on the 16th inst. we have received your favor of the 1st October, covering a power of attorney for W. H. Levy, and our John Blithe. Mr. Levy not being here, and not knowing where he was to be found, we called on Mr. Schröder immediately, who informed us he had sent you the account-sales, and intended to interest you in a shipment of furs, which he had made on board the ship Electra, for your port, to the consignment of Burtwell Brothers. We saw the copy of his letter to you by that ship, but did not perceive how you were to know any thing about that interest. When we first applied to him respecting your affairs, he appeared to be very unconcerned, and observed he would not now give you any interest in the shipment of furs. At length, finding us determined not to be trifled with, he gave us the inclosed letter to Burtwell Brothers, containing an order for you to receive your proportion of the proceeds of the furs; and we trust it will enable you to get from those gentlemen the balance due to you from him. We should not have taken this, but he has no property here; so that it would be only throwing money away to pursue the thing farther: besides he is on the point of returning to England. From further inquiry, we find that he has made a shipment of furs to Messrs. Oppenheim, by the same ship, so that if Messrs. Burtwell Brothers do not pay you, you may perhaps recover from Messrs. Oppenheim. We regret that it is not in our power to hand you a bill for your claim, but trust that what we have done will be satisfactory.
With great respect, we remain, etc.   JOHN & EDWARD BLITHE.

CCXXXVII.
Adolph Schmidt, Esq. *London.*   *New York, 1st Nov., 18—.*
Dear Sir, — Pursuant to your instructions, I called on Mr. John Blithe, when at Philadelphia, from which place I am but just returned. He told me he had effected sales of all your property that he had received from Mr. Schröder, which sales he forwarded to you per Electra on the 21st ult. I shewed him your instructions, in compliance with which he paid me 1677 $^7/_{100}$ dollars, amount of sales, deducting interest on note till due, for which sums I gave him my account; the difference of exchange between this city and Philadel-

---

(1) Tessuti di cotone, lino, seta, ecc.

phia is 5 per cent., you therefore stand credited by me for $1595\ ^{21}/_{100}$ dollars: I shall appropriate this amount, in paying Mr. _____'s demand against the goods of yours yet in his possession. I mean to take them on Monday next, though I am sorry to say, I know not what to do with them. Had I not pledged myself to receive them, I would not do so; as it is, I will do the best I can for your interest. The hosiery, which is the heaviest, must lie over till the spring, they would not now realise within 50 per cent. of their sterling cost; the hard-ware (1) would not fetch the cost; the glass-ware considerably under. I have not yet made up my mind, but believe it will be most to your interest to take them on with me. The prints I shall sell on account of what I have to pay: If I can sell the remainder at Charleston at a small sacrifice, I will; if not, I shall sell sufficient to pay my demands: the balance I will leave with a safe house; and if I can procure an advance on them, I will forward it to you. I would not remove the goods, but for reasons already assigned; added to which, I know your demands are pressing, and here I cannot obtain any advance whatever: sales cannot be effected, unless a credit be allowed, on which no guarantee can be obtained; and without that I will not sell, as I will not take any responsibility on myself; at Charleston, I can procure a guarantee; and I think, on the whole, though a sacrifice must be made, it will by no means be so large there as here, and the proceeds certain. I shall write you from thence. I called on Mr. Schröder, who informed me that he had sold the property of yours in his hands, and transmitted account-sales to you, nor did he feel himself bound to give me any further information on the subject. I of course retired. I have no opinion of him whatever. I shall transmit any remittances I may make on your account, through the house of F. and J. Laurent. You may rely on my best endeavours being exerted for your interest, and should I not succeed to the extent of our wishes, you will accept the will for the deed. I remain, dear Sir, your obedient humble servant,

W. LAURENT.

Twenty-second Series.

CCXXXVIII.

Charles Simpson, Esq. *London.* *Surinam, 15th Jan., 18—.*

Sir, — We hope shortly to hear that the Columbia, Captain Jackson, has arrived safely at your port, and that the sugars shipped in her have met with a favorable market.

We have now the satisfaction of informing you, that we have sold one case of the cambrics C, and two ditto of the H and C at 37 $^1/_2$ stivers, 2 florins per ell; also one piece of the blue cloth at 10 florins per ell, and a few pieces of the coffee-bagging; but we have not been able, hitherto, to dispose of any of the pennistone.

---

(1) Chincaglieria.

With regard to remittances, we beg to state that we deem coffee at the present price of 12 stivers, preferable to sugars which are now at 7 1/2 stivers, and we request you to take notice that we shall ship, for your account, in the Elizabeth Sophia, sixty bags of coffee which we have purchased at the above price.

This vessel will sail at the beginning of next month, and you can effect insurance accordingly.

We hope soon to announce to you that we have closed the sales of the cambrics.

The Dutch being about to take possession of this colony, their troops having already arrived, we shall be glad to receive your instructions as to future remittances. We are, etc. HOOD & THOMPSON.

CCXXXIX.

Charles Simpson, Esq. *London.*   *Surinam, 16th April, 18—.*

Dear Sir, — I have to acknowledge receipt of your favor of 5th February last, in reference to yours of 8th August, 16—, the former covering a power of attorney to receive all the remaining stock of your goods in the hands of Mr. M. J. Hood, acting for the firm of Hood and Thompson, and to adjust and settle with him all balances due on your account. The packet arriving on the first day of the holidays, prevented me from doing any thing in the matter prior to its sailing again for Europe. I have seen Mr. M. J Hood, concerning your affairs with the above firm, and he has promised to deliver up to me without delay, whatever goods there may be on hand belonging to you, and to render to me a statement of your account with the said firm, which, when in my possession, shall be duly attended to, and I shall fully comply with your instructions in disposing of the articles that I may receive from Mr. Hood, *à tout prix*, either by private or public sale, as I may find to be more to your interest. The nett proceeds of such goods, and whatever balance I may receive on your account, shall be remitted by the first opportunity; and, as you direct, I shall, at all times, give the preference to good bills for remittances, if to be had. The account sales of each invoice shall be kept separate. As soon as the goods and accounts are in my possession, I will acquaint you with my proceedings in your behalf. In the mean time, I am, etc.   ISAAC ABENDANN.

    Sugars   7 dollars per cwt.
    Coffee   12   do.
    Cotton 30   do.
    Bills none to be had.

CCXL.

Charles Simpson, Esq. *London.*   *16th May, 18—.*

Sir, — Above, you have copy of my last respects, dated the 16th ult. I requested our common friend, Mr. S. J. Levy, to explain the cause of my not having addressed you per Queen Charlotte packet, and to give you notice of my having been furnished with a list of the articles unsold belonging to you, in the possession of Wood and Thompson.

I have since received the articles there enumerated, and likewise accounts of your concerns with said firm, correct copies of which you will receive herewith. The account-current shews a balance of 4,738 fls. 4 st. 12 pfening, in your favor.

I have disposed of the seventy pieces of cambrics and twenty-five pieces pennistone at auction, as per inclosed sales, nett proceeds, 3,087 fls. 3 st. — which amount, with the above balance, shall be remitted in good bills on London or Amsterdam, if such are to be had. Should I not succeed in procuring bills, I shall then remit produce to your per Martha, N. Humble, master, or Sarah Ann, J. Watson, for London.

The blue cloth is very coarse, and a quality which is not much used here. I shall dispose of it, as also of the billiard cloth, without delay, and add the nett proceeds to the other amount, in order to make one remittance of the whole. Is is much to be lamented, that at this moment no bills can be procured, as produce at the present prices cannot be so good a remittance as bills.

The cambrics that I sold at auction were of a very inferior quality.

Have the goodness to favor me with your opinion on the accounts inclosed, and say whether they meet your approbation or not, and whether I am to give a final acquittance to Mr. Good. Prices of produce remain the same as quoted in my last. I am, etc.

ISAAC ABENDANN.

Twenty-third Series.

CCXLI.

Gallatz,
Ibrail, } 1–13*th August,* 18—.

Messrs. Merivale and Bohte, *London.*

Gentlemen, — We are approaching the season in which the products of this country assume the most importance, and which is so much the greater this year, from the lamentable deficiency of our last crops being so abundantly compensated by the bounty of heaven on our present harvest.

Consequently, we deem it our duty to inform you of the state of our market, in order that you may take advantage of the low prices of all our export articles; not doubting that the considerable demand to be expected for our produce, will influence our import trade also, and impart to it more activity.

Our *agricultural products* form the principal branch of our commerce; and in a year of abundance, like the present, we can export to the extent of 1000 cargoes of moderate tonnage.

Although the *hard wheats* of Moldavia are equal, in several respects, to those of New Russia, and the soft descriptions, principally the growth of Wallachia, improve from year to year, still we cannot state them to be of prime qualities.

Wallachia alone is capable of exporting annually 500 cargoes, and even more, of this class of agricultural produce. Purchases have been made on delivery, which, on the quay of Ibrail, come to about 50 piastres of Bucharest per kilo of Ibrail, equal to about 400 occhs.

We have already some parcels of *barley* at market, the price of which on board, is estimated at 36 piastres of Bucharest per kilo above-mentioned.

Rye is to be had at about 10 to 12 piastres less than the soft wheat. Millet, and especially maize, promises a superabundant crop, and, consequently, low prices; but which, however, we cannot at present quote with any certainty. The same observations apply to beans and lentils. The culture of oats is totally neglected in this country.

Subjoined, we hand you details respecting the weights, measures, etc. of Gallatz, Ibrail, and Bucharest, and shall continue to quote our prices in the money of Bucharest, unless we especially name that of Gallatz. *

Linseed is exported in only small quantities, because the cultivation of the oily seeds has as yet made very little progress, having been but recently introduced by some of the farmers. The price varies from 60 to 80 piastres per 100 ocche.

Moldavia produces a good quality of ordinary *wool*, two thirds white, and one third black and grey, with a little Cigaja; in all about 500,000 to 600,000 ocche.

Wallachia produces but little, and that of ordinary quality, which is found mixed with the Cigaja wool, the aggregate of which is estimated at about five or six millions of ocche.

The price of *white wools*, of quite ordinary quality, has varied this year from 145 to 160 piastres per occa. Cigaja wool was bought at first at 3 piastres per occa, one moiety being paid in anticipation at the place of growth; subsequently the price went down to $2\,^1/_4$ piastres per occa, and again advanced to $2\,^3/_4$ per occa, deliverable at Ibrail. This wool is grown in the environs of Ibrail, where the quality is superior to that of the wool of the neighbouring provinces, and particularly to that of Wallachia Minor, which fetches only $1\,^1/_2$ to 2 piastres per occa. The wools are bought unwashed, and the purchaser has the washing

---

* See Appendix.

performed at his own expense. We refrain from entering more into detail on this article, the season for it having gone by.

Sheep skins.- It is the custom to kill, between Easter and Whitsuntide, those sheep the skins of which are intended for exportation; the major part of these skins are sent to Galicia and Germany.

Those most esteemed are the black, the very choice qualities of which fetched, this year, 375 to 400 piastres per 100 skins. The white 250 to 275 piastres per 100 skins.

Hare skins were formerly an article exported in considerable quantities for the Leipsic fair, and for France; but since the price has been so much depressed, the chase of the hare has been neglected, and there is not now one-third of the former quantity for sale. The winter is the season for purchasing this article.

Bullocks' hides. – These provinces are infinitely rich in cattle, which are either driven to the neighbouring countries, or are fattened and killed for the tallow and hides. The hides come to market principally salted, and are exported to Austria or Turkey. The cattle are killed in autumn; in the mean time the prices are not fixed, but that of 55 to 60 piastres is mentioned for a pair of bullocks' hides, or three calves' hides.

Tallow is prepared here of a quality called *Tscherwish*, which is in great request for Turkey, where it is used for culinary purposes in lieu of butter; about one-third is ordinary tallow; consequently it is not a perfect quality. It is usually sewn up in bulls' hides, and sold together with the head and horns. However, ordinary tallow can be bought on delivery, in the same hides of good quality; or it can be had in barrels at the price of two piastres per occa; two thirds of Tscherwisch and one-third of ordinary quality are worth 1 $^1/_4$ to 1 $^7/_8$ piastres per occa.

In Moldavia, this grease is subject to an export duty of half a piastre per occa. In Wallachia the exportation of tallow is permitted only where the farmer of the monopoly of candles is sufficiently supplied: which will, no doubt, be the case this year; when the export duty will not exceed 5 per cent.

Of *Wax* our home consumption is considerable, insomuch that last year we were under the necessity of importing this article.

This year, in consequence of the quantity promising to be very abundant, we expect tolerably low prices. Sales on delivery are effected at present at 10 $^1/_2$ to 10 $^3/_8$ piastres per occa. According to appearances we shall have plenty of honey this year, and at low prices.

The *Tobaccos* of these provinces are, with few exceptions, of very inferior quality, although the soil is favorable to their culture. We export only to Turkey, where they mix our tobacco with that of their own growth, and it is from that country that we receive in exchange the fine qualities. The crop bids fair to be excellent, but the prices are not yet fixed.

Cantharides are purchased in Moldavia up to 1 sequin per occa, and in Wallachia at 25 piastres per occa; but they are of rather inferior quality; from being generally salted.

Hogs' bristles are cropped in winter, and are principally exported to Germany. Parties have commenced some time ago to make purchases on delivery, with payment in advance, as is the custom with us, in the products of the country. The price is 17 to 18 piastres per occa, in their rough state unassorted.

Isinglass varies from 55 to 75 piastres per occa, according to quality. The quality is not superior.

We have some mines of *rock salt*, which are farmed out by our government every three years, without restrictions as to working them. The price is fixed at 9 $1/2$ florins fr. Auguste per 1000 ocche, duty free. The importation and transmit of this article are alike prohibited.

Barilla is an article of exportation to the Levant; the price is 25 to 30 piastres, per cantaro of 44 ocche.

The *cheese* called Cascavalho is exported chiefly to Turkey, and is worth about 90 piastres the cantaro; another quality called Pegorina, is used for home consumption.

Timber for building. - The situation of Gallatz, washed as it is by the Sereth, the Pruth, and the Danube, is extremely favorable to the timber trade, which has been carried on here since the peace, and becomes every year more extensive. In Wallachia this trade is yet in its infancy. When carriage is cheap, the timber is transported by land, and such is preferred to that which is floated down the rivers.

Pine trees are sold in bundles, called *plutts*, of 4 or 5 to 72 pieces each. The larger the trees, the fewer pieces there are in a plutt. The highest trees and the small ones vary in price, while the others are sold at about half the price of the largest, differing only in the number of pieces contained in a plutt. The relative prices are subjoined.

Timbers, deals, and deal ends of soft wood, are sold per plutt of 100 pieces, or by the piece, according to quality. Oak planks are sold by the thousand; however, as the dimensions are not always exact and uniform, it would be desirable to order them expressly.

Our *import trade*, already important, cannot fail to keep pace with the progress of agriculture and population. Moldavia possesses no other port than Gallatz; and all goods arriving from abroad, by sea, for Wallachia, have no alternative but to come to the port of Ibrail. In the month of May, and particularly in October, import articles find the readiest sale, from the afflux of numerous buyers, who assemble at these periods at our market, as at a fair, to supply themselves for the autumn and winter.

According to appearances, trade will be this autumn the more brisk, in consequence of our rich harvest, which will enable the people to satisfy all their wants, many of which they could not provide for last year, owing to the deficiency of the crops. The chief articles of home consumption are sugar, coffee, pepper, oil, lead, dried fruits, rum, plates of tin, etc.

At foot you will find a list of our prices; but we beg you to observe, that it is not at all desirable to send goods of prime quality to our market, as they would never fetch prices proportioned to their value. The middling and inferior qualities are more in request, being better suited to the wants and means of our consumers.

The export duty on wheat, both hard and soft, and on rye, is $3/_{10}$ piastres per kilo of Ibrail, and 4 piastres per kilo of Gallatz; on maize, 6 $3/_{8}$ piastres per kilo of Ibrail, and 4 piastres per kilo of Gallatz; and on barley, 4 piastres per kilo of Ibrail, and two piastres per kilo of Gallatz.

Tallow pays at Gallatz a half piastre per occa, while at Ibrail the duty is only 3 per cent.

All other articles of exportation, as well as those of importation, whether at Gallatz or Ibrail, pay indiscriminately a duty of three per cent., with the exception of *tobacco inwards*.

The brokerage on purchases and sales is . . . . . $1/_2$ p. cent.
Bank commission . . . . 1 p. cent.
Del credere for all sales on credit, and purchases by
    anticipation . . . . 2 p. cent.
Interest on our real disbursements, and anticipations
    in account current per annum . . . . 12 p. cent.
Warehouse rent and market dues according to their actual amount, with every possible attention to economy.
Commission on sales or purchases . . . . 3 p. cent.

You will not be surprised at our charging a commission somewhat higher than is usual at other commercial towns in Europe, if you consider the difficulties and hazard connected with our trade, which are greater, beyond all comparison, than those of any other. In the first place, we can never meet with entire parcels of goods; these, having, even prior to their maturity, passed through the hands of a number of petty dealers, who purchase them without fixing the price, by paying a small sum in advance, engaging to take the goods at the price which shall be determined on at the period of delivery. The majority of these dealers being persons without character or funds, those who treat with them are always exposed to imposition, and, in addition to the inconvenience of never obtaining from them any thing but very trivial parcels, we have no security for the anticipated payments, owing to their intrigues and bad faith.

Besides, these goods can never be purchased in one place, and it is necessary to go to a different quarter for almost every article.

The difficulty of transport, the number of coins current with us, and their different value in the neighbouring countries, as also the want of a well-organised post-office, are so many obstacles to our trade, which justify the charging a higher commission. It is the same with sales, which can only be effected in detail, or in small parcels on credit, to persons whose credit is very limited. However, we expect to procure for our friends a very considerable advantage in the exchange on our reimbursements, which will, in some degree, indemnity them for the high commission charged.

Measures. — A *Kilo of Ibrail* of about 400 ocche is equal to about —

    18   Kilos of Constantinople.
    9   Sacchi of Leghorn.
    7 $^9/_{10}$ Staro of Venice.
    5 $^1/_2$ - 5 $^3/_5$ Mines of Genoa, or 3 $^1/_2$ Cetvers of Russia.
    4   Charges of Marseilles.

The *Kilo of Gallatz* is only about $^9/_{10}$ of that of Ibrail, and the money differs from that of Bucharest, as is shown below.*

Weights. — 100 ocche of Gallatz and Ibrail are equal to 8 poods of Russia.

800 ocche of Gallatz and Ibrail are equal to 2 $^1/_2$ centners of Vienna.

Others reckon 44 ocche to 100 lb. of Vienna, which makes a difference of about two to three per cent.

Assurance. — Having the principal agency of the « Assicurazione Generale Austro-Italica, » of Trieste, reputed one of the most respectable, we are enabled to effect insurance for any voyage whatever, at the same premiums as those demanded by the first companies in the different maritime ports.

Freights depend on circumstances, so that we can only note the probable rates. At present they ask for —

Venice or Trieste, per staro of Venice $^2/_3$ to $^3/_4$ florins.
Genoa   per mine   4   • 5 livres.
Leghorn   per sacca   2 $^1/_2$ •
Marseilles   per charge   4 $^1/_2$ • 5 $^1/_2$ francs.

In conclusion, we refer to the specification of exchanges and prices at foot; and should any article interest you more particularly, we shall be most happy to procure it for you. In the mean time we are, etc.

BIENWERTH & Co.

CCXLII.

Messrs. Merivale and Bohte *London.*   *Hamburgh, 20th October, 18——.*

Gentlemen, — Having none of your valued communications to ac-

---

* See Appendix.

knowledge, we now beg to wait upon you with our price-current, and a few observations on the state of our markets.

Camphor is looking up. Of new Zante and Corinth *currants*, our stock on hand is considerable; the prices may be quoted a shade lower. *Coffee* very dull, and no business can be done except at reduced prices. The transactions of the last week amount to only 2000 bags of Brazil and Domingo; qualities, ordinary to fine ordinary. *Ginger* higher. *Pepper* and *Pimento* very firm. *Sweet Sicilian almonds* declining. *Olive-oil* is again on the advance. The stock is now very limited, and of some sorts we have none on hand. *Para cocoa* is held at 4 sh. *Cassia Lignea*, flat; middling 7 $1/4$; fine 7 $5/8$. *Cassia buds* 10 — 10 $1/4$. *Raisins*, none on hand.

Indigo, — prices firm, sales limited. *Cochineal*, — little doing.

Rice. In consequence of several large orders for good Carolina, the prices have again risen; and as we have only a moderate supply of 2,600 tons, of which 2,200 tons are in first hands, and not at market, a further advance may be anticipated. In Java there is more doing. From Maranham we have an importation of 500 bags of Brazil, which are to be had at 10 $1/2$; the quality is but middling.

Tobacco. The prices for Domingo are very firm, and those for Virginia and Kentucky cannot, at the present moment, be noted lower. The last accounts from the United States lead us to expect large shipments, so that a further improvement of the prices is improbable: 350 serons of Domingo were sold by auction. The imports of new Porto Rico continue, and our prices may be quoted rather lower.

Tea. 119 quarter chests gunpowder have been sold by the importers: in the other descriptions, nothing of any importance has been done.

Raw Sugars rather more in request, and the transactions at the former prices considerable. Fine whites have, indeed, been bought at an advance of $1/8$d. The sales consisted of 2,500 chests yellow Havannas, at 8 $1/8$ — 8 $5/8$; 1000 chests brown do. at 7 $1/2$ — 7 $3/4$ d. 350 chests of white Bahia at 9 $1/2$ — 10 d. 300 chests brown do. at 7 $1/8$ — 7 $3/8$ d. 100 chests white Rio, at 9 — 9 $1/2$ d. 150,000 of lumps at 9 $3/8$ — 9 $3/4$ d. In refined sugars, there was also some business done. Dutch and Belgian melis and lumps are in demand.

Corn. Wheat very steady. There is but little at market. Of *rye* we have had but small arrivals. In *barley* and *oats* nothing doing. *Pease* and *beans* flat. *Vetches* in request. *Rape-seed* has been bought at somewhat better prices. *Clover-seed:* from the probability that our supplies from the last crop will be very scanty, our prices are constantly looking up. For *red-seed* of last season 41 $1/4$ mks. have been paid for parcels on the spot, and 40 on delivery. For the finest, *white*, likewise, of last season, 50 mks. were paid.

In *Wools* there is much briskness, and prices remain very firm.

Good qualities, well washed, are in lively demand, at 27—29 sh. *
We remain, etc. HOMEYER & SCHMIDT.

Twenty-fourth Series.
CCXLIII.

T. Saunders, Esq. *London*.   *Halifax, 29th June, 18—.*

Sir, — We are, this morning, in possession of your letters of the 17th and 20th April, and are not much surprised at the contents, as you evidently write under an impression that we have neglected to acknowledge the receipt of some goods, which you had thought proper to consign to our address. Our communications, however, of the 9th April and 27th ult. will, we trust, remove the unfavorable opinion you appear to have formed of our mercantile correctness. It would have been, indeed, difficult to answer letters not delivered to us, or to acknowledge receipt of goods which never came into our possession.

Such as were handed over to us by Mr. Black we have disposed of, and we now remit the proceeds in the bills noted at foot. The deficiences in your invoice must, of course, be accounted for by that gentleman, who appears to have been authorised to hold the goods back on your behalf.

It has always been our desire, and, we may confidently say, our practice, to be regular in our correspondence and prompt in our remittances. We therefore feel your remarks the more keenly, as being what we are totally unaccustomed to; and we are extremely hurt that we should be subjected to them, through the mistake or negligence of another individual. At the same time, as the whole may prove to originate in some inadvertency or misunderstanding, we have only to assure you, that we shall always endeavor to render you, or your friends, our best services; conceiving, that by accuracy and attention we shall contribute most effectually to the advancement of our own interests, as well as those of our constituents. We are, etc.   ANDREWS & CORBYN.

P. S. Enclosed, you have account-sales of sundries, amounting to 233*l*. 10*s*. currency, equal to 210*l*. 3*s*. sterling, which we remit in Commissary Manby's draft on the Lords of the Treasury for 190*l*. 13*s*. 7*d*., being at 10 per cent. premium.

You will also please to observe, that we never received a bill of lading or invoice from you; and that if any of your letters to us contained such documents, they must, *in some way*, have miscarried.

---

* The quotations of prices in this letter are in marks, shillings, and pence, Hamburgh banco.

CCXLIV.
Thomas Saunders, Esq. *London.* *Halifax,* 8th *January,* 18—.

Sir, — We have to acknowledge receipt of your esteemed favor of the 12th October, and are much pleased to find that any unfavorable impression formerly entertained in regard to us is now totally removed. You may be assured, that it will always be our pleasure and pride to maintain our credit for mercantile regularity and exactness, and, more particularly, in cases where property is intrusted to our good faith and attention.

We sincerely hope that your friends, Messrs. M. and Co., being on the spot, will have no difficulty in arranging your business with Mr. Black, whom, it is but justice to say, we have always found to be very punctual and correct in his transactions with us.

We certainly felt extremely hurt at your shipments being withheld from us, as well as the letters, but Mr. B. accounted for it by stating that the arrangement was only conditional, and to be acted upon *in case of his non-arrival.* As this appears, by your own letter, to have been in some measure the fact, we have not made any comments upon the circumstances, but contented ourselves with handing him a copy of your letter.

We should be very happy to render Messrs. M. and Co. our best services; and we beg to assure you, that your recommendation will at all times, receive our most prompt attention. We are, etc.

ANDREWS & CORBYN.

P. S. We have only to repeat, that the seven packages to which you allude, were never handed to us, and that any accompanying letter must have been purposely withheld.

Twenty-fifth Series.
CCXLV.
James Turner, Esq. *Glastonbury.* *London,* 21st *Dec.,* 18—.

Sir, — I beg leave to trouble you with the enclosed draft for 35l., at thirty days' sight, on Mr. John Cummins of Axbridge, which I shall be obliged by your getting accepted, and retaining in your possession until due, at which time you can remit me the amount.

If acceptance be refused, please to have the bill protested. I am, etc.

EDWARD ROBSON.

CCXLVI.
Edward Robson, Esq. *London.* *Glastonbury,* 28th *December,* 18—.

Sir, — I despatched a messenger to Axbridge to present the draft of 35l. for acceptance, which, however, Mr. Cummins refuses, having no assets. We have no notary living nearer than Bristol, so that I could not employ one to protest personally, and shall, therefore, be glad of your instructions how to act. I can write on the bill • refuses to accept; • or I can keep it till due, which will be thirty days from the 24th inst., and then, if not paid, write • no effects. • I shall be happy to attend to your wishes. I am, etc. JAMES TURNER.

CCXLVII.

James Turner, Esq. *Glastonbury.*   *London, 29th December, 18—.*

Sir, — In consequence of Mr. Cummins' refusal to accept the draft of 35*l*., I must beg of you to have it duly protested by a notary from Bristol or elsewhere, as you may find most convenient, and return it to me without delay.

Regretting the trouble thus occasioned you, I am, etc.

EDWARD ROBSON.

Twenty-sixth Series.
CCXLVIII.

Abraham Meyer, Esq. *London.*   *Königsberg, 5th Jan., 18—.*

Sir, — We are very much indebted to our friend, Mr. P. Salomons, for recommending us to your worthy house, and, in reply to your favor of 1st ult., beg to say, that we have taken due notice of the shipment you have addressed to us for account of Mr. Behrends, as also of your directions concerning the delivery of the goods, as well as the credit we are to give that gentleman on account of them.

Thanking you for this kind proof of your confidence, we beg leave to assure you, that we shall act strictly according to your instructions; and we shall likewise use our best endeavours to promote the interest of Mr. Behrends, in any way that may be in our power.

We are already enabled to announce the safe arrival of our said friend with the goods in question. We have had the pleasure of seeing him, and have come to an understanding with him concerning your wishes and intentions.

We are not prepared at present to say more upon this subject, because the goods are not yet landed ; and Mr. Behrends having arrived only yesterday, has not had time to do any thing in the matter. In a few days you shall hear from us again, when we expect to give you more circumstantial advices. The insurance against fire shall be attended to, as soon as the goods are discharged from the ship.

We shall be extremely pleased, if this first transaction between us, the result of which will give you the best proof of our attention to our friends' interests, should lead to a permanent, and reciprocally useful and agreeable correspondence, to cultivate which, nothing shall be wanting on our parts.

Our trade is not very animated; there is but little demand for manufactured goods, or colonial produce. The prices of the former cannot be noted with any accuracy, since they depend so much upon the quality. Of the latter, we inclose a price-current, to which we refer, and are, with the greatest respect, Sir, your most obedient humble servants, TOUSSAINT & Co.

CCXLIX.

Abraham Meyer, Esq. *London.*   *Königsberg, 25th Aug., 18—.*

Dear Sir, — I am in possession of your kind letter of the 10th inst., handing me my account-current, shewing a balance, on the 1st of this month, of 1058*l.* 16*s.* 3*d.* in your favor. The account is quite correct, and I carry forward the balance in conformity. Against this balance you will, I trust, have received, ere this, a remittance of 332*l.* 11*s.* 6*d.*, through the medium of our friends, Messrs. Toussaint and Co.; and I have placed in their hands a further sum of 4,200 rix dollars, Prussian currency, to be remitted to you as soon as the exchange becomes a little more favorable.

By next post, Messrs. Toussaint and Co. will hand you a bill of lading of a small assortment of goose quills, which I have purchased, and instructed them to ship to your address for my account. At foot you have the invoice, wherein I have inserted the lowest prices at which I should wish them to be sold, and which I do not in the least doubt you will realise, these being summer goods, and very dry. Besides; the weight is Berlin, which you will please to note in effecting sales, as there is a difference of several pounds per cent. between it and the English weight in favor of the former; therefore I feel confident you will obtain, *at least,* the prices stipulated; and as soon as I find that this small parcel answers my expectations, I will make you consignments of some considerable quantity. Please to insure the quills for 130*l.*

With regard to the goods in the hands of Messrs. G. V. Branting and Son, at Gothenberg, I am much surprised at the negligence of that firm, in giving no reply to the letter which you wrote to them three months ago, when I was in London. I must request the favor of your writing to them once more, to desire them to use their best endeavours to dispose of the goods, if it be only at cost price, to put a stop to the expenses which are already so considerable on this unfortunate consignment. If they find it out of their power to sell, even on these terms, let them send the goods to the address of our friends, T. and Co., here, where I hope to be more successful, and may perhaps, realise a tolerable profit. It is truly vexatious, that so small a parcel of goods should remain on hand a whole twelvemonth.

I now beg to trouble you with a small order, as particularised at foot, and I shall esteem your kind and particular attention to its execution as a mark of personal regard. Believe me, always, dear Sir, yours very faithfully, W. BEHRENDS.

CCL.

Abraham Meyer, Esq. *London.*   *Königsberg, 8th September, 18—.*

Dear Sir, — Since I had last the pleasure of writing a few lines to you, on the 25th ult., I have been favored with your letter of the 16th of that month, the contents of which I duly note. Messrs. Toussaint and Co. will this day remit you 500*l.* on my account, for which you will please to credit me; another considerable remittance will follow in a few days.

I am anxious to know the result of the little speculation in quills, having lately been tempted to make further purchases on very favorable terms; but I deemed it better to lose the chance of this opportunity than to be working in the dark.

I am much gratified by your sentiments of friendship and esteem, and I trust that you will have no reason ever to think less favorably, than you now are kind enough to do, of my integrity and correctness in matters of business.

The small order contained in my last has, I have no doubt, received your immediate attention, and I may shortly expect the invoice and bill of lading.

Have the goodness to insure the amount of the former, with 10 per cent. imaginary profit.

At foot I mention a few articles, which I should be glad to have sent, in addition to those formerly ordered from Abrahams and Son, and which I imagine must be nearly ready by this time. Please to insure the whole of their invoice, with 10 per cent. added for profit.

I hope that you will not forget me, should it be in your power to procure any commissions for me from your friends; and you may rely on all occasions on my most strenuous efforts being used to do credit to your recommendation; a course, indeed, which is dictated by common prudence and the natural desire to extend one's connexions.

A cargo of coffee, sugar, and indigo, would, I think, answer very well, as our prices fos these articles, always rise very much in the winter. On this subject, however, I have written more at length to our common friend, Adolph Schmidt, from whom you may obtain further information, should you desire it. I am, etc.

W. Behrends.

Twenty-seventh Series.
CCLI.

Messrs. Harris, Curry & Co. *London.*   *London, 28th April, 18—.*

Gentlemen, — Inclosed I have the satisfaction to hand you an order from my friend, Mr. A. I. Martin, of Oporto, for your house at Riga, to ship 200 shippounds of outshot hemp to his address, furnlshing me with invoice and bills of lading, and also with timely advice for insurance, and valuing on me for the invoice amount.

As this quantity will not be sufficient to fill a vessel, and none may be on the berth at Riga for Oporto, to take it on freight; rather than my friend should be disappointed, I shall have no objection, if your house will charter a small vessel, to take an equal share with them in a further quantity of hemp, flax, or any other article suited to that market, provided my interest therein shall not exceed 500l.

Should they agree to this proposition, it is to be understood, that the goods and vessel shall go consigned to my above-named friend at Oporto. Your house will, of course, give me timely advice for insuring my moiety of the investment, together with invoice and duplicate bills of lading; when their drafts for my proportion shall be most punctually honored. Believe me, very truly, Gentlemen, your obedient humble servant,   WM. THOMAS.

CCLII.

Messrs. Harris, Curry and Co. *London.*   *London, 3rd May,* 18—.

Gentlemen, — By the mail, I have this morning received the enclosed letter from Mr. A. I. Martin, which you will be so good as to forward immediately to your house at Riga. The purport of it is, as I understand from Mr. M., to make an alteration in his order for hemp, reducing it from 200 to 100 shippouds, in consequence of advice received from Riga, stating that the quantity there was very limited, and the prices accordingly very high.

Under these circumstances, I think it would be advisable to countermand the order given your house on joint account; and as the packet may be detained at Harwich by contrary winds, a letter per post to-night may possibly be in time to go by the same conveyance as that of yesterday. Your house must embrace the first opportunity of shipping the 100 shipponds, without chartering a vessel on purpose, and filling her up on joint account, as I yesterday suggested; since I should by no means wish to enter into any speculation at a time when the price of an article is higher than usual; for, in my opinion, the chances in all such cases are, that one may sustain a heavy loss, while there is no probability of realising a handsome profit. I remain, very truly, Gentlemen, your obedient humble servant,   WM. THOMAS.

CCLIII.

William Thomas, Esq. *London.*   *London, 3rd May,* 18—.

Sir, — In compliance with your wishes, and the orders of Mr. A. I. Martin, of Oporto, we have written to our house at Riga this day, via Harvich, to countermand the order sent them yesterday for the purchase and shipment of hemp on joint account with you, for that port, and ordering only 100 shipponds of outshot hemp instead of 200, to be shipped for Mr. Martin's account, taking the chance of any vessel that might offer for that city.

According to recent advices from our friends at Riga, no alteration had taken place in the prices of hemp, though the quantity at market was certainly diminished. Whenever a favorable juncture occurs, we shall be ready to engage, on the part of our house there, to take a share with you in any shipment you may wish to make, either for Oporto or Lisbon. We are, etc.   HARRIS, CURRY & Co.

Twenty-eighth Series.
CCLIV.

Thos. Trelvar, Esq. *London*.   *Liverpool, 7th May,* 18—.

Sir, — Having recently received various orders from your agent at Cadiz, for the purchase and shipment of sundry articles of British manufacture, I should be glad to be informed what agreement exists between you and him as to commission; whether if, as I suppose you allow him a part of it, I am to credit him or you for such and what proportion; for, as it is understood between you and myself, that we reciprocally allow one half of the commission charged on invoices and account-sales, if I am to allow you a moiety of my charge on these purchases ordered by Mr. Robinson, it is clear I cannot make any division with that gentlemen without sacrificing my own interests. Pray explain how it is to be, for my government. And believe me, ever, Sir, your very devoted humble servant,

                                               JOHN ADAMS.

CCLV.

John Adams, Esq. *Liverpool*.   *London, 10th May,* 18—.

Sir, — Respecting the orders for goods which you have received from my agent at Cadiz, Mr. Robinson, permit me to state, that, when in Spain and Portugal, I desired all my correspondents to address any orders they might require to be executed at Liverpool direct to you, with a view to save time and postage; therefore you must consider those orders as coming from or through me, and, such being the case, I am entitled, by our agreement to half your commission. At the same time, it is understood between Mr. Robinson and myself, that he is to have a moiety of the commission on all goods bought and shipped by his orders. It certainly did not occur to me, at the time, to make any provision for cases like the present, where the order is executed by a third party; but I consider it as most reasonable and equitable, that the commission should be divided in thirds between all parties concerned, since it would doubtless be very unreasonable and unjust, that, after having undergone the fatigue, and incurred the expense of travelling to and from and through these countries, I should be deprived of all benefit from the emoluments accruing from my exertions.

I feel confident that Mr. Robinson will have no objection to this equitable adjustment, and, I have little doubt, that you will as readily agree to it; therefore, I conclude with assuring you of my earnest desire to make every thing agreeable and profitable to all parties interested. I remain, most truly, etc. THOMAS TRELVAR.

CCLVI.
John Adams, Esq. *Liverpool.* *London, 14th May, 18—.*

Sir, — Since I wrote to you on the 10th, I am without any of your esteemed favors, and therefore take your silence for consent to my proposition, respecting the division of your commission on goods ordered by Mr. Robinson of Cadiz. I have now, in reference to the same subject, to inform you that my friend, Mr. Ramos, of Rio de Janeiro, has shipped to your address some cotton on his own account, and some coffee on account of Mr. Dias Santos of Lisbon, as you will perceive by his letter of the 10th March, which is enclosed, having been left open for my perusal. You will please to note that I do not allow either of these gentlmen any share of my commission; consequently, when you furnish them sales, you will be so good as to credit me with a full moiety, since it is in consequence of my recommendation that they have made you these consignments, which will, most probably, be followed by others; a circumstance that will afford me great pleasure, as well on your account as my own. Believe me, etc. THOMAS TRELVAR.

Twenty ninth Series.
CCLVII.
Messrs. Crawford and Dunn, *Plymouth.* *London, 4th July, 18—.*

Gentlemen, — In reply to my letter, furnishing them with copies of my correspondence which you, relative to the order for wines with which you were so obliging as to favor me, my friends at Oporto inform me, that in order to open an account with your respectable house they will ship 10 pipes port, No. 1, at 164,000 reis; and 10 pipes, No. 3, at 136,000; the 10 first mentioned, and 5 of the latter, to be for your account, the other 5 on their account; it being at your option, however, to take the whole, should you approve of the qualities, conformably to your proposal of the 10th May last.

As soon as I am put in possession of any further particulars as to freight being engaged, etc., I shall not fail to give you the necessary information for your guidance in effecting insurance. I have no advice of any vessel loading there for your place; but, as the wines will be ready for shipment in the course of the present month, my friends will, in case no opportunity offers direct, ship 5 pipes,

No. 1, on board any vessel that may intend to touch at Falmouth, Darmouth, Exeter, Southampton, or Plymouth, as requested in your letter of the 15th May.

I have no doubt that my friends will pay such attention to the quality of these wines, as will insure them a continuance of your orders, which I shall be at all times happy to forward, and they to execute.

Should you wish me to effect the insurance, I will do it with much pleasure, and without charging commission. I think it might be effected at 12s. 8d. to 15s. 9d. per cent. Believe me, very truly, Gentlemen, your obedient humble servant, Wm. Thomas.

CCLVIII.

Messrs. Crawford and Dunn, *Plymouth*. *London, 5th August,* 18—.

Gentlemen, — My friends at Oporto inform me, under date of the 11th ult., that not wishing to send your wines too new, before they were perfectly bright, and in proper state for this market, they had not shipped them, in a vessel which had taken in some pipes for your port; but that they would avail themselves of the next opportunity that offered. In order to secure you the benefit of the summer premiums, I have opened a policy by ship or ships at 12s. 8d. per cent., which is the lowest rate at which similar risks have been done. Believe me, truly, Gentlemen, your obedient humble servant,

Wm. Thomas.

CCLIX.

Messrs. Crawford and Dunn, *Plymouth*. *London, 11th August,* 18—.

Gentlemen, — I am this morning favored with your much esteemed letter of the 9th instant, and am extremely sorry you should consider there has been any improper delay in shipping your wines; but I feel confident that my Oporto friends acted for the best. Shipping is very scarce there, and I am informed that freights had risen to 3 guineas per ton.

With respect to sending out the vessel you have at your port of about 350 tons: should you determine on so doing, and will consign her to my friends there, Messrs Dawson, Forbes and Co., I am certain they would do every thing in their power to serve you, not only by giving her a preference of what wines they might have to ship themselves, but by inducing their friends to do the same.

I would suggest that, as soon as you come to a determination on the subject, you should write to my friends not to engage freight for your wines in any other vessel, and the same to the company. It is possible they may have already succeeded in obtaining freight for them, for it being known that freights were high and vessels scarce, some may have been sent out from different ports. This is a

point for your consideration. Expecting your determination and orders for insurance, I remain, truly, Gentlemen, your obedient humble servant,
               W. THOMAS.

CCLX.

Messrs. Crawford & Dunn, *Plymouth*.   *London 16th August*, 18—.

Gentlemen, — Your esteemed favor of the 14th inst. is before me, and I note your determination to despatch the Snow, «Wellington,» for Oporto, addressed to my friends there. I feel much obliged for this preference, and am confident they will use their most strenuous endeavours to fulfil your wishes. Should no great number of vessels arrive out before the Wellington, the voyage will, no doubt, answer your expectation; and it is as well that you intend her to take wines for this port also, as she has too much tonnage for the western ports only.

Annexed, you will please receive copy of the policy, and an account of insurance, effected by your order on $^{14}/_{16}$ ths (fourteen sixteenths) of the above vessel, valued at 600*l*, amount to your debit 10*l*. 10*s*. Finding I could get it done at 30*s*. out and home, you will perceive I have embraced the opportunity, and hope you will consider the premium moderate. I deemed it more advisable to do so, than run the risk of an advance of premium on the homeward voyage, on account of the winter season, which is fast approaching.

I am thankful for your offer of Captain Tickle's taking any parcel out for my friends, but at present have no occasion to trouble him. I shall, however, be obliged, both to you and to him, if he will take charge of the two inclosed private letters, and deliver them personally. I remain, most respectfully, Gentlemen, your obedient humble servant,   W. THOMAS.

CCLXI.

Messrs. Crawford & Dunn, *Plymouth*.   *London, 17th August*. 18—.

Gentlemen, — I had this pleasure yesterday, and have now to inform you, that having made application on Change to the Oporto houses, I find there are some wines on order for your port, and I have secured a preference of them from Messrs. Hall and Co., and Mr. Dold; but I am told, that all wines arriving at your port are subject to 5*s*. per pipe, harbour or town dues, whether landed there or not. Please to inform me if that be the case; for if so, the Wellington had better come to this port first, and I can get the policy altered accordingly, to London and Plymouth, etc., instead of London, with liberty to unload at Plymouth, etc., and the policy for your wines also. I remain, Gentlemen, your obedient humble servant,
               WM. THOMAS.

CCLXII.

Messrs. Crawford & Dunn, *Plymouth.*   *London, 28th August, 18—.*

Gentlemen, — I duly received your letter of the 19th inst., and notice what you say relative to the 5s. per pipe exacted by your collector on all wines arriving at your port, an imposition which I hope, with you, will be done away with. However, as you have determined that this charge shall be paid by the ship-owners, and not by the consignees of the wines, the objection is removed, and several of my friends have, in consequence, ordered their wines to be shipped in the Wellington.

I have mentioned to my Oporto friends, your desire to substitute old wines for new, and have recommended their acquiescence in your wishes; and should you, at any time previous to the 31st December next, make up your order to 50 pipes, I shall with pleasure make you an allowance of 4,000 reis per pipe on the whole fifty.

By a letter of the 1st instant from Oporto, received this morning, I learn that my friend had not engaged freight for your wines, and that no vessel was offering direct for your port, few having arrived out; therefore feel assured the Wellington will be in good time. Freights were still 3 guineas per ton. Believe me, sincerely, Gentlemen, your obedient humble servant,   WM. THOMAS.

CCLXIII.

London, 13th September, 18—.

Messrs. Crawford & Dunn, *Plymouth.*

Gentlemen, — Inclosed, I beg to hand you a letter received this morning by the Dido, via Falmouth, from Oporto, and which will, no doubt, inform you of the arrival out of the Wellington on the 25th ult.; and that she was expected to be loaded in about three weeks from that time for your port and this. My friends advise me that they intended to ship your 15 pipes by her at 3 guineas per ton freight. I remain, Gentlemen, your obedient humble servant,

WM. THOMAS.

CCLXIV.

Messrs. Crawford and Dunn, *Plymouth.*   *London, 18th October, 18—.*

Gentlemen. — At foot I have the pleasure of waiting on you with an invoice of your 15 pipes port per « Wellington, » Captain Tickle, which vessel is, I hope, by this, arrived at Plymouth, having sailed on the 26th of last month; she was fortunate in obtaining 3 guineas per ton, which she would not have done, had not my friends exerted themselves powerfully. Another friend of mine, at my solicitation, shipped 80 pipes on board her to my consignment. The freight had fallen to 50s. per ton. On Captain Tickle's arrival here, I shall be most happy to render him every assistance in my power.

Inclosed, you will please receive bill of lading for these wines, and for the 5 pipes which it is at your option to take or not; likewise Messrs. Dawson, Forbes and Co's draft on you at 9 months' date, from the 26th ult., for the amount thereof, 2,320 mil. 000 reis, exchange as per Lloyd's list when due; as also for supplies to Capt. Tickle, 138*l*. 13*s*. 6*d*. at 50*d*. per milrea, at 90 days' date, both which drafts I will thank you to return me accepted at your convenience.

For your information, I beg to state that the exchange on Portugal has every appearance of rising, having been done yesterday at 49 $^1/_2$ on both Lisbon and Oporto. It comes from the former at 50 $^1/_2$ to $^3/_4$, and from the latter 51*d*. I call your attention to this circumstance, solely with a view to your interest, since it might suit you to pay the amount of the wines, under discount, at the present rate of exchange. It would make no difference whatever to my Oporto friends, who will receive the same amount in milreis, let the exchange be what it may. I confidently hope that the quality of the wines will be approved, and that the whole transaction will have been so ably managed as to merit a continuance of your favors. Should you resolve on sending the Wellington out again, my friends will be happy to see Captain Tickle once more.

I have valued your wines in the policy at 500*l*., which will fully cover the costs, after deducting charges, in case of loss, calculating the exchange at 50*d*. I hope this will meet your approbation, which I shall ever be anxious to secure, and I remain, Gentlemen, your obedient humble servant, WM. THOMAS.

CCLXV.

Messrs. Crawford & Dunn, *Plymouth.*   *London, 23rd October, 18—.*

Gentlemen, — I am duly favored with your letters of the 19th and 21st instant, to the former of which I should have replied in course, had I not been unavoidably prevented. These letters have put me in possession of two bills on this city, one for 235*l*., the other for 219*l*. 7*s*. 1*d*., together 454*l*. 7*s*. 1*d*, which sum, deducting interest at 5 per cent. per annum, as per statement at foot, and calculating the exchange at 49 $^1/_2$ per milrea, is equivalent to 2,286 mil. 408 reis: and consequently leaves a balance in my favor of 33 mil. 592 reis; or at exchange of 49*d*. is 6*l*. 17*s*. 2*d*., which small sum please to credit me in account.

The exchanges, as I predicted, are rising, having been to-day at 50*d*., and I doubt whether my Oporto friends will not be losers; but, of course, as I made the offer, and you accepted it, I must abide the consequence.

I am glad to find that you are pleased with the manner in which my friend attended to your wishes in procuring for your vessel so good a freight; and I perceive it is your intention to send the Wellington out again, provided I can get any outward-freight for her. This, I fear, will be impracticable, as the regular traders at all times command a preference. Besides, the time she would require to be on the berth, would absorb all the freight she could earn.

I shall dispose of the 'ork wood which may remain from the stowage, and account with you for the nett proceeds. Remaining, very truly, Gentlemen, your obedient humble servant, WM. THOMAS.

CCLXVI.

Messrs. Crawford & Dunn, *Plymouth.*   *London, 3rd November, 18—.*

Gentlemen, — I am in receipt of your much esteemed favor of the 31st ultimo, and have now the pleasure to advise you of the safe arrival of the « Wellington. » She is in the London Docks. Captain Tickle has made his entry, and will commence discharging his cargo to-morrow.

I shall endeavour, in conformity with your instructions, to procure a freight for the « Wellington; » but the navigation to the north being closed, and vessels more plentiful than cargoes, I am apprehensive there will be no alternative but to send her to Sunderland to load coals for your port, as pointed out by you as a « dernier ressort. » I remain, Gentlemen, your obedient humble servant,

WM. THOMAS.

CCLXVII.

Messrs. Crawford & Dunn *Plymouth.*   *London, 11th November, 18—.*

Gentlemen, — This morning's post has brought me your letter of the 8th instant, with an inclosure for Captain Tickle, which has been delivered to him, and you will hear from him in a day or two. The Wellington, I am sorry to say, has not yet discharged, owing to the number of vessels in the docks wihe-laden. I expect she will complete her discharge in two or three days, when, as there are no freights offering, she will proceed to Sunderland for coals.

In compliance with your instructions, I have endeavoured to effect insurance on her for 890l. to Sunderland, and back to your port; but I can get no one to look at it for 50s. per cent.; indeed, some have refused to underwrite her at 3 guineas. As your order is conditional, « if to be done at a moderate premium; » and as the vessel will not be ready for a few days, I shall await your further directions, which I hope to receive by return of post. If, in the interim, I can get the risk done at 50s., I shall do it provisionally, « subject to your approbation. » Believe me, truly, Gentlemen, your obedient humble servant,   WM. THOMAS.

CCLXVIII.

Messrs. Crawford & Dunn, *Plymouth.*   *London, 17th November, 18—.*

Gentlemen. — Referring you to my respects of the 11th instant, and not having since heard from you, I now beg to inform you that

I have effected the insurance for 800l. on the Wellington. Not having been able to induce any one of the underwriters at Lloyd's to take the risk at 3 guineas, much less at 50s. per cent., I was obliged to apply to the Royal Exchange Assurance Company, who agreed to do it at the 3 guineas, but without the clause « subject to your approbation. » Consequently, if you have done it at your port, one half of each policy must be cancelled. I am truly sorry that I could not do better for your interest, but it was impossible; and as the vessel is about to move into the river, I did not feel justified in delaying it. Cost to your debit per account. 17l. 4s. 11d.

The wines have all been landed, but are not yet gauged. The custom here is, to pay freights the Saturday week after the quantity is ascertained. I shall hand you the account of freight, and of Captain Tickle's disbursements, in my next.

I fear I shall not be able to obtain more than 21l. per ton. for the cork, which will scarce cover the cost: but Captain Tickle thinks I had better accept that price, than let him take it round first to Sunderland, and then to your port, at the risk of breakage, waste, etc. I shall, therefore, close with this offer in a few days, if I cannot get a better. I am, truly, your obedient humble servant, WM. THOMAS.

CCLXIX.

Messrs. Crawford & Dunn. *Plymouth*   London, 5*th December*, 18—.

Gentlemen, — I have to acknowledge receipt of your esteemed favor of the 19th instant, and am sorry it did not come to hand until after I had disposed of the cork, of which, inclosed, you will receive the account-sales, nett proceeds to your credit, 64l. 3s. 4d.

I am pleased to observe that you approve of the insurance per « Wellington », and now wait on you with an account of her freight, 198l. 18s. 4d. to your credit likewise.

On the other hand, I have debited you 214l. 12s. 10d. amount of my disbursements on account of the said vessel at this port.

You will observe the sum of 10 milrels deducted for plunderage of one pipe of wine, marked M, which the surveyors at the docks gave against the ship. There were other deficiencies, but which they gave against the shippers. I have the certificate, but do not transmit it on account of the postage; should you wish it to be forwarded to you, I will embrace the first opportunity by private hand.

The vintage in Portugal has proved very short of what it was last year, though the quality of the wines in general is expected to be superior, and nearly equal to that of the vintage of 1815. When you have formed an opinion of those per Wellington, I shall be glad to learn it; and at all times it will afford me much pleasure to execute your commands; being, most faithfully, Gentlemen, your obedient humble servant,   WM. THOMAS.

Anderson.

CCLXX.

Messrs. Crawford & Dunn, *Plymouth* London, 19th December, 18—.

Gentlemen, — I have received your favor of the 17th instant, inclosing a letter from Mr. R. L. Kingston, agent to Lloyd's at Dartmouth, communicating the unwelcome intelligence of the loss of the « Wellington »; which was, however, known here yesterday from the same quarter. I am much grieved at this misfortune, particularly as the cargo of coals is not covered. It now, however, proves fortunate that I sold the cork, or it would have increased your loss.

I have laid Mr. Kingston's letter and yours before the Royal Exchange Assurance Company, who approve of the steps taken, and expect to be furnished in due course with the captains's protest, and account-sales of what may be saved; when, if every thing is found correct, they will settle the loss on the policy without hesitation. Their payments are made within one week after the loss is adjusted. You will, therefore, do well to forward me the documents required, as soon as they can be procured. And the instant I have arranged with them, I will acquaint you with the amount which may be at your disposal.

Your draft, under date of the 7th instant, at 30 days' date to your own order shall be duly honored, although you do not state the amount; but I presume it will be in conformity with the account handed you. The primage and pierage on wines from Oporto are invariably 6 per cent. per pipe, and not 5 per cent.

The exchange on Oporto is on the decline, being to day at 48 $^1/_2$ per milrea. Should you be in want of wines, I shall be happy to forward your orders, and that you may secure the advantage to be derived from the present state of our exchange, I shall have no objection to accept the loss per Wellington in payment. Awaiting your determination, I remain, truly, Gentlemen, your obedient humble servant,   WM. THOMAS.

CCLXXI.

Messrs. Crawford & Dunn, *Plymouth.* London, 5th. January, 18—.

Gentlemen, — I received, in due course, Captain Tickle's protest, and Messrs. Kingston and son's account-sales of the stores saved from the « Wellington, » as also a note of your expenses attending the unfortunate loss of that vessel. I immediately submitted these papers to the Royal Exchange Assurance Company, and I have now the satisfaction to inform you, that they consent to settle the claim the ensuing week. They at first objected to the charge of 5l. for Captain Tickle's expenses and attendance; but on representing the exertions he had made, they withdrew their objection. The amount you will have to draw is 755l. 12s. 8d., as per statement at foot. Believe me, truly, Gentlemen, your most obedient humble servant,
                                            WM. THOMAS.

CCLXXII.
Messrs. Crawford & Dunn, *Plymouth.*   London, 15th January,—.

Gentlemen, — Your valued favor of the 13th instant has reached me; and having, since I wrote you on the 5th., inst., recovered the loss per « Wellington » from the Royal Exchange Assurance Company, your draft for the amount 755*l.* 12*s.* 8*d.* at 30 days' date, to the order of St. Aubyn and Co., your bankers, has [been duly accepted, and will be as punctually discharged at maturity; thus closing our accounts for the present; I trust, however, an opportunity will soon offer of opening a new one with your respectable firm. Requesting you, on all occasions, to command my services freely, I remain, most sincerely, Gentlemen, your most obedient humble servant,

WM. THOMAS.

Thirtieth Series.
CCLXXIII.
Messrs. Francis Lupton & Co. *London*   *Hamburgh* 12th. May, 18—.

Gentlemen, — By the Thought, Captain John Sinclair, we are shipping to your consignment fifty bags of Saxony wool, on our own account, on which we hereby request you will be so good as to effect a conditional [insurance to the amount of 2000*l.* On the shipment being completed, we will furnish you with bill of lading and invoice, and state the value of each bag, for endorsement on the policy.

We hope these wools will arrive at a good market, and encourage us to continue our speculations in this article, the present being our first essay therein.

You will please to observe, that this consignment will consist of an assortment of Electoral, Saxony, first and second qualities, and some locks. We will thank you, on receipt of this, to give us all the information in your power on the subject, and to furnish us with quotations of your present prices. We remain, very sincerely, Gentlemen, your obedient humble servants,   FELDHEIM & SONS.

CCLXXIV.
Messrs. Feldheim & Sons, *Hamburgh.*   London, 12th. May, 18—.

Gentlemen, — In reply to your esteemed favor of the 12th instant, we beg to thank you, in the first place, for your kind consideration in making us the consignment of the fifty bags of Saxony wool per Thought, Sinclair. Conformably to your directions, we have insured them provisionally in the sum of 2000*l.*, at 7 sh. per cent, and on receipt of invoice and bill of lading, shall be ready to accept your drafts for two-thirds the amount of the former, should you feel disposed to value on us at usance for the same.

Our market is not at present overstocked with Saxony wools, and sales are pretty brisk, at remunerating prices, say — Electoral, at 6s. 6d. to 8s. 6d; first Saxon, 5s. to 6s.; second ditto, 3s. 6d. to 4s. 9d.; locks, 2s. to 3s. 6d.; and in fleece, 4s. 3d. to 3s.; lamb's wool, 2s. to 5s. per lb. Nor do we anticipate any great deterioration or amelioration, so that, in your further speculations, we think you may safely calculate on the above quotations; but, of course, it will depend entirely on the quality, whether we shall be enabled to obtain the higher prices above given.

Repeating our thanks, we are, with great esteem, Gentlemen, your obedient humble servants,   FRANCIS LUPTON & Co.

CCLXXV.

Messrs. Thomas Goune & Co. *London.*   *Seville, 20th March, 18—.*

Gentlemen, — By this vessel, the Pendennis, Captain Rutter, we have shipped from Cadiz to your consignment, as per bill of lading and invoice enclosed, twenty-two bags of Spanish wool, of excellent quality, and which we have no doubt you will be able to dispose of per samples, which go under the care of Captain Rutter, in a parcel addressed to your firm. These twenty-two form part of the 100 bags, on which we requested you, in our letter via France, of the 30th ultimo (and of which you have a copy annexed), to effect insurance, per ship or ships; the remainder we shall ship as occasion offers. Being confident that you will find the 100 bags as nearly as possible of the same quality, we expect the price you obtain for these twenty-two, will regulate that of the whole; we must, therefore, strongly urge you to use your utmost endeavours to fix the best possible price for this first parcel.

We trust you will be able to find a purchaser at 3s. per lb.; but we do not limit you, relying confidently on your accustomed zeal in promoting your correspondents' interests. The amount of invoice, you will perceive, is 2,666 dollars, 4 reals; 17 maravedis, which is the actual cost, for your government in effecting sales. We remain, Gentlemen, your obedient servants. RICHARD THOMAS & Co.

CCLXXVI.

Messrs. Richard Thomas & Co. *Seville.*   *London, 14th April, 18—.*

Gentlemen, — We have the pleasure of acknowledging the receipt of your highly valued letters of the 30th Feb. and 20th ult. The provisional insurance ordered in the first mentioned has been effected, in 2000l. on 100 bags Spanish wool from Cadiz to this port, on ship or ships, at 15s. 9d. per cent.; the cost we shall charge on the respective account-sales.

The twenty-two bags, of which your second letter furnished us an invoice and bill of lading, have arrived safe, but have not been landed, the Pendennis having only taken her berth in the dock yes-

ACCOUNT-SALES OF WOOL.

terday. Captain Rutter has, however, delivered us the parcel containing the samples, which are certainly of a very good quality; and although we despair of obtaining the price you mention, 3s. per lb.; yet we hope to sell them at one that will give you entire satisfaction leaving you a handsome profit. We shall certainly attend to your recommendation, and use our best endeavours to fix a price for the whole lot.

Our market is amply supplied at the present moment, and we would recommend your not shipping more than twenty to thirty bags at a time. Expecting, in our next, to be enabled to furnish you with the account-sales, and in the mean time to be instructed how to dispose of the nett proceeds, we remain, very truly, Gentlemen, your obedient humble servants, THOMAS GOUNE & Co.

CCLXXVII.

Messrs. William Roberts and. Co. *Bilboa*   *London* 10th *April*, 18—.

Gentlemen, — Inclosed, we beg leave to wait on you with the account-sales of your fifty bags of Spanish wool, received by the Gratitude, Captain T. Rowe, nett proceeds of 1238*l*. 11s. 6d. to your credit, in account current. You will perceive that, for the thirty-four bags, first quality, we were so fortunate as to obtain 3s. 6d. per lb.; for the eleven ditto, second quality, 2s. 3d.; and for the remaining five, of the third quality, 2s., which we consider very excellent prices, and, we assure you, it was not without considerable difficulty and much negotiation, that we obtained them.

We have no doubt you will approve of these sales; indeed, so well pleased are we with the result, and the probability of having it in our power to place a similar assortment at the same prices, that, should no rise have taken place with you, we will gladly join you in the purchase of 100 bags, to be shipped in moieties by two different vessels, to sail about a month apart.

The usual credit on wool is eight months, with a month for delivery; 5 per cent. discount for cash; 2 1/2 per cent. at four months. We have charged the usual *del credere* of 2 per cent. If you wish us to allow the discount, as above stated, please to inform us per return of mail. We are, etc.   THOMAS GOUNE & Co.

Miscellaneous Letters.

CCLXXVIII.

St. John's, Newfoundland, 30th *June,* 18 —.

To the Directors of the Phœnix Assurance Company, *London*.

Gentlemen, — At the instance of several persons of consideration and influence in this quarter, who are anxious for the more general adoption of the admirable system of Fire Assurance, I am induced to make application for an agency of your company.

Should I have the honor to be appointed agent to the association, I shall be prepared to give satisfactory security, either in this province or in England, for the faithful discharge of my duties.

Being attached to the profession of the law, and enjoying the office of notary public, I am let to believe that my interest might be exerted to the advantage of the institution, as well as of this community and of myself.

For any information that you may desire, regarding my character and fitness for the office I solicit, I beg to refer you to Messrs. Burton and Smith of your city; and requesting the favor of your reply at an early date, I am, etc.   JAMES FORMES.

CCLXXIX.

To the Secretary of the Royal Exchange   *Dantzic, 14th August, 18—.*
Assurance Company, *London*.

Sir, — Conversing with our highly respected friends, Messrs. Hellman and Co., on the subject of the insurance business of this port, which is of great magnitude, and might acquire much more importance if the number of respectable underwriters were increased, our friends suggested to us the propriety of applying to your company for their agency.

It being our candid opinion, that the agency in question, if well conducted, may be productive of considerable profit to the company, we avail ourservels of this encouragement; and under the auspices of the above-mentioned firm, and other influential houses here, beg leave to make you a tender of our services at this place.

Should you deem this proposal worthy of consideration, we shall be happy to afford you every information in our power; requesting, in return, to be made acquainted with your terms and regulations, and the wording of your policy.

We subjoin, for your guidance, a list of our premiums, and remain, etc.   KLEIN & SCHILLER..

CCLXXX.

Liverpool, 8th May, 18—.
To the Secretary of the London Assurance Company. *London*.

- Sir, — A highly respectable and influential house at the Mauritius, with whom we are connected, lately intimated to us their wish to obtain the agency of a London Assurance Office. We should feel obliged, therefore, by your acquainting us, as early as may be convenient, whether your company either have, or are desirous of having, an agent in the Isle of France; as, in the latter case, we shall be happy to explain to you the grounds on which we hazard the opinion, that a connection between your company and our correspondents would prove mutually andvantageous. Soliciting the favor of an answer, we are, etc. HEMMING & RAY.

CCLXXXI.
Hamburgh, 10th August, 18—.

Messrs. Andrew Hilson & Co. London.

Gentlemen, — We have just heard that several drafts, of considerable amount, on Messrs. ——, of this city, have been protested for non-payment.

The manner in which these gentlemen have been carrying on their business for some months past, sacrificing their consignments, and jobbing in bills to a ruinous extent, must, we doubt not, have brought them to the alternative of an accommodation or a failure.

We deem it, therefore, our duty, to apprise you of this state of things by express, in the hope that it may still be in your power to save some of your property. In the mean time we have taken measures to stop any consignments of yours, that may be on the way hither to their address, although to render these steps effectual, we shall require your power of attorney, which, if you have any goods so circumstanced, please to transmit forthwith. In haste we are, etc. GUMPELL & BECKER.

CCLXXXII.
Messrs. Andrew Hilson and Co. London. Stettin, 18th October, 18—.

Gentlemen, — At the instance of our common friends, Messrs. Possart and Co., of Berlin, and, in conformity with arrangements made with your traveller. M. Curtis, I use the freedom of requesting you to send me, by the first vessel for this port, about fifty puncheons of molasses, and 180 to 200 cwt. of fine-ordinary Surinam coffee; *provided* the former can be purchased at 35s., and the latter at 85s. No other than such as is of merchantable quality will suit me. The molasses must be thick; the coffee small-berried, even, of a bright color, and thoroughly clean.

For the amount of your invoice you will be so good as to draw on Messrs. Gumpell and Becker, of Hamburgh, at three months' date, and forward them a bill of lading, requesting them to effect insurance.

I should be happy if you would keep me advised, from time to time, of the fluctuations of your markets; and with a tender of my best services here, whether in commission business or other matters, I am, etc. GUSTAF GUMPELL.

CCLXXXIII.
Madeira, 17th January, 18—.

Messrs. Edward Wallis & Co. London.

Gentlemen, — We take the liberty of annexing our shipping-prices of wines for the current year, and solicit the favor of your patronage.

Since the return of our senior to this island, he has devoted himself to the selection of a stock of wines, that will, we venture to hope, merit the approbation of all who may honor us with their commands. Our constant study is to purchase fine, flavory, ripe, full-bodied wines; and to reject all such as are thin, or have the least tendency to acid. Our last vintage has proved exceedingly good, and we live in hopes that REAL Madeira will yet obtain the estimation and preference it deserves amongst white wines. If this island produced an inferior wine to the Cape of Good Hope, Teneriffe, Fayal Sicily, etc., its name would not be borrowed as it is, and applied to much of the poor made-up stuff that is sold in England.

We think our standing and experience justify the assertion, that no house in the island can execute your orders more to your satisfaction than ourselves; and we assure you that the utmost attention shall be paid to any with which you may oblige us. We are, etc.

Ross & Turner.

CCLXXXIV.

Adolph Schmidt, Esq.   *Gibraltar, 1st June, 18—.*

Dear Sir, — Your valued favors of the 19th and 20th ult. came safely to hand. The Hope has not yet arrived. Part of your goods, per Harriet and John, are landed, and we have this day disposed of five dozen chairs, Nos. 71 to 73, and 39 & 42, for five hundred hard dollars; and one secretary, No. 31, for sixty. The chairs not being delivered, I cannot have the pleasure of handing you the proceeds by this conveyance.

There is some mistake respecting the package No. 30, which is in your invoice, but not in the bill of lading, therefore I cannot demand it of the Captain.

As you have seen Mr. Barnard in England, I have no doubt he has given you every information regarding the trade of this place, so as to render it unnecessary to enter into details on that subject by this opportunity.

The plague is reported to have broken out in Malta; and there have been long quarantines appointed for all vessels coming from the East, which will be a great impediment to our commerce. I am, etc.   I. C. Martin.

CCLXXXV.

Messrs. John Backhouse & Co. *Liverpool.*   *London, 10th June, 18—.*

Gentlemen, — I had last the pleasure of addressing you under date of the 29th ult., and have since been favored with your esteemed letters of the 3d, 7th, and 8th inst.

Your acceptance for 209*l.*, Castendyk and Co., to the order of Ide, Beugh, and Co., due 26th August next, payable with me, will be duly honored, and your account debited with it when paid.

I have filled up the exchange at 54d. per milrea, on your draft for 130*l.* on C. I. de Almeide, of Oporto, and forwarded it per mail to your friends there, Messrs. Adams and Co.; and that on G. I. Perreira, of Lisbon, for 31*l.* 2*s.* 8*d.* I have endorsed at 50 $^1/_4$ *d.* being the current course on that city (as 51 is in Oporto). This bill I have enclosed to Mr. George, agreeably to your orders.

You observe that the rates of exchange endorsed by me, on some occasions, do not correspond with those contained in Lloyd's list. The reason is this: the brokers are furnished with printed lists, in which, at the commencement of 'Change-time, they insert such courses on different places as they consider fair between the drawers and the takers, according to the quantity of money and bills offering; and in Lloyd's list, these imaginary prices are always inserted; whereas, when business commences, they are seldom or ever abided by, but every holder and every taker makes the best bargain be can. Of course, it depends on the proponderance of money or paper, whether the actual course of exchange be above or below the nominal or printed price.

The two bills sent me for acceptances in yours of the 7th instant, for 410*l.* 17*s.* 2*d.* and 286*l.* 1*s.* 3*d.* (not 285*l.* 1*s.* 3*d.* as stated by you) are duly accepted; and I have also in my possession the first for 119*l.* 7*s.* 9*d.* which I procured with the second contained in your last letter, likewise duly honored; all of which I shall retain until an opportunity offers of returning them free of expence.

Your remittance of 170*l.* on Thompson and Co., and 200*l.* on W. Bonar, both due to-morrow, will duly appear at your credit. I am, etc.   JAMES ROLFE.

CCLXXXVI.

Peter Barnshaw, Esq. *London.*   *London, 1st June,* 18—.

Sir, — I am in possession of your letter of yesterday; and in answer to your proposal on the subject of taking orders for wines in Ireland for my friends at Lisbon and Oporto, I beg to state that I am ready, and hereby engage to allow you one guinea per pipe on all wines, the orders for which may be forwarded to me by you, or through your influence, accompanied by reference to parties in this city; when, if satisfactory answers are given to the inquiries which I may deem it proper to make, the shipment shall be immediately ordered.

And I further agree to allow you commission, at the same rate, on all the wines that any of the parties so introduced by you may be pleased to order direct from my friends, at either of the places already named. With respect to the settlement of such commission, I shall be ready to pay to you, or to your order, the amount due on the respective parcels, when in cash for the wines; it being always understood that no commission is recoverable on wines wich are not paid for in full. I am, Sir, your obedient humble servant,

THOMAS JONES.

CCLXXXVII.

H. I. Dos Santos, Esq. *Rio de Janeiro.* *London,* 10th *October,* 18—.

Sir, — Above is a copy of the few lines which I addressed to you on the 5th instant. Since that date, I have received your much esteemed favor of the 28th of July last, inclosing bill of lading and invoice of forty-six chests of sugar, which, for my account, and by your order, Mr. A. F. Cunha, of Bahia had shipped in the Prussian ship, Freundschaft, Captain Becher, for Hamburgh. For the amount of this shipment, I have credited you in my account 2,473 mil. 553 reis. The manner in which these gentlemen have executed your orders, leave me nothing to desire, and not doubting but the quality will turn out good, I expect to have every reason to be perfectly satisfied. The ship is already arrived at the Texel, as I learn, but, I regret to say, with some damage.

I take due note of what you write, relative to my guaranteeing the underwriters, in future, on all risks insured for your account, which I shall attend to; although I assure you, that I am very cautious in the selection of underwriters on my policies, whether I stand guarantee or not. I remain, etc. THOMAS JONES.

CCLXXXVIII.

London, 10th *October,* 18—.

Messrs. Graves, Dobson, & Co. *Lisbon.*

Gentlemen, — Since I last had this pleasure on the 30th August, I have been without any of your valued favors; the present is, therefore, merely to enclose you a copy of an account furnished me by Messrs. R. Saunders and Co., of short gauge and deficiency on their 10 hhds. wine per Fortune, amounting to 5*l.* 9*s.* 11*d,* which I have allowed them, and debited you with. Inclosed, you will find particulars of the gauges and a certificate from the Dock Company. Believe me, truly, etc. ROBT. MYLES.

CCLXXXIX.

Mr. F. P. Dos Santos, *Lisbon.* *London,* 20th *March,* 18—.

Sir, — Inclosed, you have copies of my respects under date of the 14th and 17th instant, Nos. 59 & 60, which I beg leave to confirm, and proceed to answer more fully that part of your favor of the 26th ult. No. 7, to which I only partially replied in my last.

As the vessels by which I have effected an assurance for account of Mr. I. P. Da Costa sailed with convoy, he will be entitled to a return of premium, by virtue of the clause inserted to that effect, *provided they arrive at their ports of destination,* and of which I must be furnished with an authentic certificate in due time, that I may claim the return from the underwriters. He may rest satisfied on this head.

The necessary declaration has been made in the policy per Flor do Mar, respecting the alteration in the numbers of the bales of hare-skins.

You must endeavour to procure orders for hemp, flax, tallow, and cordage, from St. Petersburgh; then I will see what can be done in regard to obtaining orders for a cargo of fruit from your port, and I will, in due time, let you know what share I may be disposed to take in such an adventure.

You will have seen, by my last communication, that your orders for vitriol and turpentine could not be executed, not only on account of the price being above your limits, but the freight also. Should you be disposed to extend your limits, let me know, and your wishes shall have immediate attention.

I take due note of the progress you have made in the sale of the hare-skins, and hope you will very shortly be able to close that transaction.

I am much pleased with the promptitude of your remittance of the Spanish dollars, and for the amount of invoice of 550, per Duke of Kent, have credited you in my account 525 mill. 795 reis, having found the same correct.

I must strongly recommend you to close the sales of the cotton and silk stockings per Matilda and Gleaner, as the manufacturer who made you the consignment at my solicitation, is very anxious to have the transaction wound up, even at some sacrifice, perceiving, from the glutted state of your market and consequent low prices, that it will not answer to ship any more.

The warehouseman of whom I purchased the cloths for Mr. B. I. Perreira, wishes to know if Mr. P. was satisfied with them, and will be glad to execute any further orders, when he will exert himself to the utmost to give entire satisfaction.

Mr. I. G. Marqueza has written to me under date of the 26th ult. and appears very well pleased with the manner in which his orders for insurance were executed. I inclose my answer to him, left open for your perusal. Please to seal it and deliver it to him personally, and see if you cannot prevail on him to give you some further commissions. He is a valuable correspondent; and although he has other friends of long standing in this city, yet I think we may come in for a share of his business, if he is well looked after.

The arrangement you have made with Mr. F. A. Ponte is very satisfactory to me, and no more than in honor we (both you and I) were bound to do.

In my letter, No. 44, I informed you that there was no discount on the buckles, as you will more fully perceive from the copy of the manufacturer's letter from Scheffield, which I inclose.

I refer you to No. 54, as to the sugars, and hope you will be able to execute the order at the extended prices given hi No. 60. I say nothing as to quality, confident that you will not neglect a point of such vital importance. Believe me, most truly, Sir, your obedient humble servant, WM. JAMES.

CCXC.

London, 21st November, 18—.

Messrs. S. F. Bragança & Jones, *Oporto.*

Gentlemen, — Having none of your favors to reply to, I now write to inform you that I have received a dividend of 8s. in the pound from the estate of J. Morreira, on the sum of 216l., amount of your debt proved, being 86l. 8s. to your credit. For this sum, less commission and charges, say 84l. 10s. 6d, I now enclose you a draft on Bowden and Co. of your city, at 60 days' date, which, when discharged, will close this transaction. It is quite uncertain when another dividend may be paid, but you may rely on my attending to your interest, and remitting you, in due time, any further sum that may be recovered.

The assignees did not oppose my proving the protested bill for the above amount, on my exhibiting your power of attorney; but they objected to the 6l. 7s. re-exchange thereon, and the commissioners of bankrupts refused to allow this latter sum to be proved. I am, etc. RICHARD MATTHEWS.

CCXCI.

Edward Brown, Esq. *Lisbon.* London, 21st November, 18—.

Sir, — Confirming the above copy of my last respects, I have, on the present occasion, merely to wait on you with account-sales of the nine elephants' teeth, received per Reynolds, nett proceeds 55l. 18s. 4d. of which I have placed $^1/_3$ to your credit, say 18l. 12s. 11d. and the like sum to the credit of Mr. Bosson for his third share. Both of these accounts I shall remit you separately, *per appoint,* on the 19th of next month, that being the first post-day after the amount falls due.

I am truly sorry this small trial should have turned out so disadvantageously. It is owing, in the first place, to the teeth not being of primo quality; and, in the second, to the sale of a large parcel at the same time, by the East India Company. Some of ours were broken and split, as you will perceive by the broker's report and observations inclosed, and to which I refer for your future government in effecting purchases.

The Orchilla weed per Matilda will, I trust, turn to better account; it is landed and will be sampled to day. It is rather of a pale colour, I am told; but the broker thinks he will obtain 140*l.* per ton for it, in bond, that is, without the duty, which the purchaser pays. At this price it will answer well, and compensate us for the loss in the teeth. For good, dark-colored weed, 160*l.* per ton is the nominal price, duty paid. The duty is 16*s.* 8*d.* per hundred weight. In due course I shall hand you account-sales; meanwhile, believe me, truly, Sir, your obedient humble servant,   JOHN JENKINS.

CCXCII.

John Britton, Esq. *Lloyd's.*   *Old Broad Street, 16th February, 18—.*

Sir, — I beg leave to acquaint you, that I have authorised Mr. Richard Collins to underwrite policies of insurance in my name; and I hereby hold myself responsible for all claims on account of losses or averages that may occur upon any policies so underwritten by him, for me and on my behalf.

Allow me to solicit the favor of a share to your Insurances; being, Sir, your very obedient servant,   WM. CAREW.

CCXCIII.

Adolph Schmidt, Esq. *London.*   *Malta, 14th January, 18—.*

Sir, — On the 25th of December, we had the pleasure of writing to you by the Saragossa, William Grice, and informed you that the Augustus Caesar had arrived. Since this date, your two bales of furnitures have been delivered to us, and we have discovered No. 1 to be damaged. We have got it condemned, agreeably to the enclosed certificate, and shall sell it on the 16th inst. for the underwriter's account. There will be a general average to pay. It is a pity that both bales are not damaged, for we cannot obtain any thing near their worth for them sound, as they are much too expensive for this market. ⁹/₈ handsome patterns used to sell very well, but at present they are not in request. Your buttons hang heavily on hand; and there is very little probability of our finding a purchaser for them, owing entirely to the balls being hollow instead of solid.

By our next, we shall hand you account of sales by auction; In the interim, we remain, etc.   RANDAL & CO.

CCXCIV.

Jacques de Ville, Esq. *Bourdeaux.*   *London, 6th March, 18—.*

Sir, — I have before me your esteemed letter of the 17th ult. containing various documents and vouchers relative to the ship Etoile, detained on suspicion of being a slaver. I am endeavouring to establish the claim for indemnity for that vessel, and will acquaint you with the result in due time.

Our common friend, Mr. Bourdon, has transmitted to me the legal instrument by which you have transferred to him your claim of 1,440*l*. by that vessel, on account of Mr. I. M. Da Cunha, and of course I shall act upon it; but it would have been better had you sent all the documents connected with this particular transaction.

I am extremely sorry that you should have found yourself under the necessity of suffering my draft on you to be dishonored. Perhaps you are not aware of the discredit attached to such an occurrence in this country, or of the expense incurred by it for re-exchange and charges. And I the more regret it, as the drafts in question were totally distinct from your account with me.

Mr. Peters has refused acceptance to the bill of exchange you remitted me for 200*l*. for reasons, he says, with which he will acquaint you by this mail. I have not had a protest drawn out, as you requested me not to do so; but I have had the bill noted and shall keep it till due; when, if not instructed to the contrary, I shall have it presented for payment. I know nothing of the origin of this transaction, but suppose you were authorised to value on the party for the amount of this bill; if not, you did wrong, for such irregularities as these will soon destroy the credit of any house. I am, etc.

GEORGE DOUBT.

CCXCV.

London, 12th January, 18——.

Messrs. Samuel Symonds & Co. *Exeter.*

Gentlemen, — I beg to hand you, inclosed, your account current to the 31st ult., shewing a balance in my favor of 466*l*. 56., of which the sum of 283*l*. 4*s*. is due in cash that day, and the premiums of insurance on the 31st of March next, agreeably to the established practice of my house. If found correct, you will please to transfer the above balance in conformity.

Some time ago I recommended Mr. Long, of the house of Long, Lynch, and Co. of St. Michael's, to make you a consignment of fruit. I now learn, with much satisfaction, that they have complied with my solicitation, and have shipped to your address a cargo of Oranges by, I believe, the Pallas. As this consignment is in consequence of my introduction, I presume you will have no objection to divide the commission with me, agreeably to the understanding between us.

Messrs. Long have an establishment in this city under the firm of Michael, Lynch and Co., and should you be obliged to give them a share of your commission, of course, I cannot, in that case, expect any participation therein. I remain, with esteem, Gentlemen, your obedient humble servant, JACOB MORRIS.

CCXCVI.

Messrs. Sealy & Walton, *Southampton.*   *London, 14th May, 18—.*

Gentlemen, — In consequence of my conversation with your Mr. Walton yesterday, I have desired my friends at Oporto, Messrs. Richards and Whistler, to select, and put by twenty pipes of very good wine of the last vintage, for your account, and to await your orders for the shipment of them. As soon as the purchase is made, and the price ascertained, I will inform you at what they will be invoiced. My friends will value on you, as usual, at 9 months' date, from the 1st May next, for the amount of invoice; and, when the wines are shipped, at 60 days' sight for the warehouse rent and expences of filling up. I am confident that my friends will select such wines as will give you satisfaction; and I remain, very respectfully, Gentlemen, your obliged humble servant, THOMAS ROGERS.

CCXCVII.

Messrs. Paul, Berthon & Co. *Cork.*   *London, 11th June, 18—.*

Gentlemen, — Mr. Thomas Andrews, of your city, having informed me and Messrs. March and Co. of Liverpool, that he had written to you respecting the Latona, Captain Griffiths, which vessel had put into your port on her voyage from Liverpool to Villa de Conde, and was detained in consequence of the captain's not having been furnished with a letter of credit, I beg, in addition to what our common friends at Liverpool may have written to you on the subject, to request that you will use your best endeavours to prevail on Captain Griffiths to raise money on bottomry; but, should he not succeed in obtaining it, rather than the property on board should be detained or deteriorated, I have no objection to your advancing him a small sum on my account, to enable him to proceed on his voyage, provided the shippers of the rest of the cargo will do the same, in proportion to the amount of their respective freights.

The goods shipped by my orders are twelve crates of earthenware, marked IM, 800 bundles of rod, and 731 bars flat iron, the freight of which amounted to 3*l*. 3*s*. 5*d*., of which 120*l*. has already been paid Captain Griffiths, leaving 22*l*. 3*s*. 5*d*. to be paid at Villa de Conde, on delivery of the cargo.

Should you be under the necessity of making any advances to Captain Griffiths, you will please to advise the consignee of the above goods, Mr. Jose Azevedo, at Villa do Conde, by packet, what proportion he will have to deduct from the freight on the vessel's arrival out, and your draft on me for such proportion shall meet due honor. Tendering you my best services in this city, without interference with your old connections, I remain, Gentlemen, your very obedient humble servant, ROBERT NEWMAN.

CCXCVIII.
Messrs. Paul, Berthon & Co. *Cork.*   *London. 28th June, 18—.*

Gentlemen, — I am in receipt of your esteemed letter of the 19th instant, and feel much obliged by the manner in which you anticipated my wishes relative to advancing Captain Griffiths, of the Latona, a small sum to enable him to prosecute his voyage to Villa do Conde: I am happy to find that vessel has sailed with a fair wind. It is satisfactory that you advised Mr. Azevedo of the amount advanced to Captain Griffiths, 5l. 4s. 6d. sterling, for his government, which amount I have paid to your friends here, Messrs. Berthon Brothers, agreeably to your request. And with many thanks, I remain, Gentlemen, your obedient humble servant,   ROBERT NEWMAN.

CCXCIX.
London, 19th September, 18—.
Messrs. Daniel Brothers & Co. *Lisbon.*

Gentlemen, — I annex a copy of my last respects, which I now confirm; and being without any communication from you since, I have, on the present occasion, merely to hand you an account-sales of the 5 bags of dollars received by the Lady Arabella packet, on joint account, one half of the nett proceeds, 522l. 2s. 8d., with interest thereon 1l. 7s. 2d., say 523l. 9s. 8d. is passed to your credit: which, if found correct, please to enter accordingly. Believe me, truly, Gentlemen, your obedient humble servant,   WM. WILLIAM.

CCC.
Messrs. Sillem & Co. *Hamburgh.*   *London, 26th January, 18—.*

Gentlemen, — I am in receipt of your valued favor of the 23rd instant, accompanied by my account current and interest account to the 31st ult., which having been found correct, the balance in your favor of 10,525 marks banco, has been passed to a new account in conformity.

Inclosed, you will find your account current, with interest account to the same period, balance in my favor 1,605l. 7s. 4d, which you will please to examine; and, if found in order, pass to my credit under date the 1st instant. I am, respectfully, Gentlemen, your obedient humble servant,   JAMES ROBINSON,

CCCI.
London, 26th September, 18—.
To the Honorable the Commissioners of Her Majesty's Customs,
  Custom-House, *London.*

Honorable Sirs, — Being informed that your honors' land-surveyor at the London Docks, has detained 6 pipes of wine marked A. B., imported by the Diana, Captain James Collins, from Oporto, and now lying on the quay in the said Docks, because the marks thereon do not correspond with the manifest, which states the mark to be B. A., we beg leave to enclose for your honors' Inspection, the bill of lading for the same, in which your honors will perceive that the mark agrees with our entry, and that actually on the casks. And as there are no wines on board the said vessel, or imported by her, of the mark B. A., it is evident that there must have been some mistake in making out or copying the manifest, at the consul's office at Oporto.

We therefore entreat that your honorable board will be pleased to take the case into your honors' immediate consideration, and allow the said wines to be bonded and warehoused as really marked: giving the necessary directions to your honors' land surveyor, to liberate the said wines without remuneration.

We have the honor to remain,
Honorable Sirs,
Your Honors' most obedient humble servants,
JOHNSON & JACKSON.

CCCII.

To the Right Honorable the Lords Commissioners of Her Majesty's Treasury.

The Memorial of James Nixon of the City of London, in the County of Middlesex, Merchant,

Humbly Sheweth,

That the Portuguese ship Flor do Mar, Captain H. G. da Costa, bound from Oporto in Portugal, to Rio de Janeiro in the Brazils, was captured on or about the 26th of March, 18—, by a pirate, and carried into Nassau, New Providence, where a part of the cargo was taken possession of by the Vice Admiralty Court, and sold under the directions of the same.

That by a decree of the said court, bearing date the 17th May, 18—, a part of the proceeds of the goods sold was ordered to be paid to the agent of the underwriters at Nassau, and the remainder to be remitted to Her Majesty's Exchequer, to be paid over to the rightful owners, agreeably to the provisions of the act, 12th of Queen Anne, chapter 17th.

That your memorialist is fully authorised by the legal owners of the above-mentioned goods, to receive the proceeds thereof, for their use and benefit.

Your memorialist therefore humbly prays, that if the proceeds of the said goods have been remitted into His Majesty's Exchequer, in pursuance of the decree of the Vice Admiralty Court at Nassau, your lordships will be pleased to order the same to be paid over to your memorialist for the use and benefit of the said legal owners thereof.

And your memorialist, as in duty bound, will ever pray, etc., etc.

JAMES NIXON.

London, 10th January, 18—.

CCCIII.

George Hanmer. Esq. *Treasury Chambers*. London, 20th June, 18—.

Sir, — I was duly favored with your letter of the 20th January last, informing me, that until the proceeds of the Portuguese ship Flor de Mar and her cargo, should be remitted from the Admiralty Court at Nassau, New Providence, to Her Majesty's Exchequer, my petition of the 10th of that month, relating thereto, could not be taken into consideration by the Lords Commissioners of Her Majesty's Treasury.

Several months having since elapsed, and learning by advices from Nassau, bearing date November, 18—, that the proceeds were expected to be remitted from thence in a few weeks, I shall be very much obliged by your informing me, at your earliest convenience, whether the registrar at Nassau has, or has not, made the promised remittance to Her Majesty's Exchequer.

I trust that you will excuse the liberty I thus take, the parties concerned being very desirous of bringing this unfortunate transaction to a close.

I have the honor to be, with great consideration, Sir, your obedient humble servant,

JAMES NIXON.

CCCIV.

Messrs. Field and Blake, *Falmouth*, London, 26th May, 18—.

Gentlemen, — By the Marlborough Packet, from Lisbon, daily expected at your port, I am informed Mr. C. D. De Moraes will come passenger, and will be the bearer of a letter of introduction to you from my friends, Messrs. O. Bertrand and Co. of that city.

Permit me to solicit your kind and particular attention to the recommendation of the above highly respectable house; and further, to request that you vill be so obliging as to advance any cash that Mr. De Moraes may require during his stay with you. The sum so advanced shall be immediately paid into your London bankers, on your furnishing me with his receipt.

I need not say, that should Mr. De Moraes have arrived and taken up cash prior to the receipt of this letter, I shall have equal pleasure in reimbursing you, and shall be equally obliged for your attentions to him.

On any similar occasion, I hope you will make no scruple of availing yourselves of my services here, and I remain, etc.

RALPH RIDPATH.

CCCV.
(Per Dryade.)

Messrs. W. Simpson & Co. London, 20th April, 18—.

Dear Sirs, — Since the date of the annexed duplicate of my last respects, I have not had the pleasure to receive any of your esteemed favors.

The wools, received from you, per Auriga, were disposed of at public sale, on the 14th inst., and realised the following prices, viz. —

				s.	d.
Lot 102	W. S. 31, 32, 33, 34,	4 bales.	. . .	1	9 ¹/₂
103	— 29, 30,	2 —	. . . .	1	9 ¹/₂
104	— 18, 26, 27, 28, 4	. .	. . . .	1	10 ¹/₂
105	— 23, 24, 25,	3 —	. . . .	2	0 ¹/₂
106	— 19, 20, 21, 22, 4	—	. . . .	2	0
107	— 5, 16, 17,	3 —	. . . .	1	9
108	— 13, 14, 15,	3 —	. . . .	1	8 ¹/₂
109	— 10, 11, 12,	3 —	. . . .	1	11
110	— 7, 8, 9,	3 —	. . . .	2	0
111	— 2, 3, 4,	3 —	. . . .	1	10
112	— 1, 6,	2 —	. . . .	1	6
113	D. B. 22,	1 —	. . . .	2	1 ¹/₂
114	— 19, 20, 21,	3 —	. . . .	2	2 ¹/₂

Account-sales shall be handed you as soon as possible. It is considered that the market prices have been fully maintained; there was a large attendance of buyers, and the sales went off with much spirit. Fine wools were not in such demand, nor did they sell so well as the middling qualities.

Enclosed you have duplicate invoices and bill of lading for sundries shipped per Kinnear, Captain Millar, which vessel sailed from the Downs on the 13th inst.; also invoice and bill of lading for sundries shipped on your account per Dryade, Captain Beard, amounting to 2,897l. 11s. 6d. at your debit. This small shipment I hope will arrive at a favorable market. The Auriga, Captain Chalmers, will sail in about a fortnight. I have given an order on you, favor Mr. Walter Biggar, for 200l., which you will oblige me by protecting. The Mansfield has not yet arrived, but I look for her daily. The John sailed yesterday from the Downs; by her you have consignments from Messrs. Curtis & Tudor, etc. The Brothers, Captain Towns, leaves to-morrow. With best wishes, I remain, etc. GEORGE KIRKPATRICK.

CCCVI.
(Per Royal Sovereign.)

Messrs. William Simpson & Co. Sydney. London, 39th May, 18—.

Dear Sirs, — The above and enclosed are the duplicates of my last two letters, since the date of which I have had the pleasure to receive your esteemed favors of 27th December, 12th and 15th January; that of the 12th January handing me E. Wilson's draft on John Lechmere for 155*l*., which I regret to have to return you enclosed, with protests for non-acceptance and non-payment. I have to acknowledge receipt of bill of lading for 120 bales of wool to my consignment, per Henry. I am glad to see the progress you are making with this vessel, and I hope you will be able to get her away at the time you anticipate. I notice you intend also shipping to my consignment, by her, about 55 tons sperm oil. Conceiving it an omission on your part, that you have not ordered insurance, I have deemed it advisable to effect it; say, on 55 tons sperm oil, as interest may appear, at 45*s*. per cent., valuing the oil at 60*l*. per ton, or per invoice valuation, if any.

	L.	*s.*
Your drafts, favor Captain Williams	159	10
Roebuck and Co.	1000	0
Hart and Co.	1210	0

have been duly protected and passed to the debit of your drawing account.

Enclosed you have duplicate invoices for sundry orders received from you, and shipped per Kinnear, Captain Millar. The order for W. W. is not quite completed. I could not meet with any colored lastings to my satisfaction; I shall, however, endeavor to procure and forward them by an early opportunity. The small shipment I made to your firm, at Hobart Town, per Kinnear, I hope will arrive at a favorable market. I have made you a small shipment per Dryade, Captain Head, which vessel sailed from Gravesend yesterday.

Herewith I have the pleasure to hand you account-sales of 68 bales wool received per William Metcalfe, Captain Phillips, the nett proceeds of which, 1306*l*. 7*s*. 10*d*., are passed to the credit of your account. I have not yet received the sales of the wools sold by Messrs. Edwards and Co., the Prompt being not yet up.

The wool and oil markets continue to look well, and prices remain firm. I am, dear Sirs, your obedient servant, GEORGE KIRKPATRICK.

CCCVII.
(Per Derwent.)

London, 14*th* June, 18—.

Edward Ball, Esq. *Clarendon, New South Wales.*

Dear Sir, — Since I last wrote to you, I have had the pleasure of receiving your letter of 26th January last.

I now beg to inform you of the result of the last series of sales, from the 9th to the 17th ult., numbering above 7,000 bales of wool from your colony. The prices obtained at these sales are allowed to be very fair, but not equal to the preceding one of 1500 bales; perhaps, had not the sale been so large, and the German and Spanish Wools begun to arrive, the prices might have averaged a little higher; it is, however, proper to state that so large a sale has its advantages as well as disadvantages, by bringing up a numerous assemblage of buyers from the country, as was observable in these sales, they were literally crammed with purchasers from all parts of the country, much more so than has been witnessed hitherto. Upon a comparison of the prices of various marks at these sales, with the prices of the corresponding marks at the sales of the two preceding years, you will not fail to observe that the better wools have not fetched their relative value; it is not that the inferior wools have advanced, but the superior fleeces have declined; the causes assigned for this, are, that superior wools are not now so much sought after, as they have lately discovered a mode of spinning the medium qualities so as to answer nearly all the purposes of the fine; besides which, very fine goods made from your wools are not now so much in vogue. For these reasons it is strongly recommended, that wool to bring about 1s. 10d. to 2s. 8d. should be cultivated, as being more likely to be advantageous to the cultivator. As the trade of this country this season has been remarkably good, it is not expected it will undergo any augmentation the next; therefore a further advance must not be very confidently looked for, unless a failure in the supplies should take place. On the other hand, I have no reason to think there will be any decline, even should the trade of this country not be so brisk. Many of these wools were purchased for export to the continent, not only by the French but by the Germans; a further proof of their increasing reputation. The late wool sales being large, it is not considered advisable that another should follow for the next six weeks, when I shall again have the pleasure of writing. Enclosed are my broker's remarks and some catalogue for your inspection. I remain, dear Sir, etc. GEORGE KIRKPATRICK.

CCCVIII.

(Per Spartan, viâ Liverpool.)

Melbourne Warehouse, Sydney, New South Wales, 25th March, 18—.
Messrs. Robert Jamieson & Co. *London.*

Gentlemen, — We are now enabled to announce to you the conclusion of our sales of your consignments per ships « Rubicon » and « Sir Joseph Banks, » and to transmit to you herewith the account sales thereof, nett proceeds altogether amounting to 917l. 18s. 2d. from which the remittances already made to you being deducted, the balance still remaining in your favour amounts to 361l. 18s. 2d. as shewn by the accompanying accounts current. For this sum we have obtained the two enclosed drafts:

	L.	s.	d.
One for	201	11	8
the other for	162	2	9
together L.	363	14	5
Exchange at $1/_2$ % deduct	1	16	3
L.	361	18	2

nett cost of our remittance, which finally closes your account with our firm. We are, Gentlemen, your obedient humble servants,

JOHN WILSON & Co.

CCCIX.

Messrs. Robinson and Co. *Trinidad.*   *London, 28th July,* 18—.

Gentlemen, — With this I have the pleasure to hand you invoice and bill of lading for sundries shipped per Royalist, Arthur, master, to your address, amounting to 392l. 17s. 8d. at your debit.

This shipment comprises all your late orders (with one or two, exceptions which I shall notice hereafter), and which I hope will please. The Galloons are sent as near to former prices as possible. I have very great difficulty in procuring Blue-Black Silk Handkerchiefs; those now sent are the nearest I can get to the color, — here they will not sell at all, and consequently none are made. I could not get Silk Lace Gloves at 4s. 3d., those now sent at 6s. 4d. are much under the price. The De Laines are an extremely cheap lot, and very varied in their patterns; they are all sent at a sacrifice on their original cost. The Cloths have been purchased as near your figure as possible. I cannot procure the Ribbons to your colors — matching Ribbons is at all times very difficult. I regret I cannot send the Glass Squares this opportunity, as one of them was broken in stoppering it, they will be forwarded by first opportunity. I shall have this pleasure again per packet. Meanwhile I remain, Gentlemen, your obedient servant,   GEORGE HORNEMAN.

APPENDIX

Mercantile Technicalities.

Abandonment. — In marine insurance, under certain circumstances, the assured may abandon his property to the underwriter, and claim indemnity as for a total loss. In this case, the underwriter becomes the legal owner; and if the produce of the salvage be greater than the sum insured, he is entitled to the profit.

Acceptance. — The act by which the drawee of a bill of exchange binds himself to pay the same when due.

Accommodation-paper. — Bills of exchange or notes given without value for the accommodation of some person, which, being based upon no real transaction, and representing no real funds, are termed *fictitious capital*. This is one of the most common modes of raising money, and the incautious act *of lending an acceptance* has led many an individual to ruin.

Account Current. — A running debtor and creditor account, bearing interest, and balanced generally once, if not twice, in the year. Sometimes, however, is it kept open for a much longer period, as will be seen by the second of the following specimens.

There are two modes of stating the interest principally in use wich are likewise here shewn. Some mercantile houses keep an interest account apart from the account current, and bring forward the balance merely on closing the latter; but this seems quite useless, since they are obliged to furnish a copy of both to their correspondents.

Dr.   Henry Harvey, Esq. of St. Vincent, in Account

		Days.	Inter. 5 p.ct.	L.	s.	d.
18—.						
June 30	To Balance of last account. . . .	184	1,142	620	13	4
July 10	His draft, order of H. Martin, due Nov. 6............	55	137	250	0	0
»	Ditto P. Brand & Co. due Nov. 11.	50	83	160	16	0
Aug. 14	Invoice of stores, per Atala, Roberts, due Oct 4...........	78	375	482	6	7
» 24	Ditto of a horse and 10 asses, per Hope, Wilson, due Oct. 8	84	141	168	0	0
Sept. 1	Cash paid Mrs. Hepburne for board and tuition of Miss Annette Harvey to Midsummer	121	82	67	10	0
Oct. 5	Ditto Morris and Smith, Tailors .	87	47	54	12	6
Nov. 6	Ditto Wiltshire and Co. Bootmakers.	55	19	36	0	0
Dec. 31	Bank Commission on payments 568l. 18s. at 1/2 per cent.			2	16	10
»	Ditto on receipts 837l. at ditto . .			4	3	8
»	Postage and petty expenses			1	12	7
»	Balance of Interest			1	13	2
»	Balance to his credit in new account			92	8	4
		2026	l..1942	12	11	

Errors Excepted—London, 31st Dec. 18—
HOLDSWORTH & SONS.

Most English counting-houses are provided with interest-tables, which nearly supersede calculation in all these operations, and where these are used, the account may, perhaps, be as quickly made up in the common way, as in that shown in this first formula. But, in the absence of these tables, this mode is preferable, as saving time and trouble. It is managed thus: the sum is multiplied by the number of days, and the product (*after cutting*

Current with Holdsworth and Sons, London. Cr.

18—.		Days.	Inter. 5 p.cl.	L. s. d.
July 4	By proceeds of 18 hogsheads of sugar, ex Emily, Smith. due Aug. 4 . . .	149	352	249 12 6
„ 5	Ditto of 10 hogsheads of ditto, ex Favorite, Ray, due Aug. 18 . . .	135	203	150 14 0
„	Cash received of Forbes and Turner on his account	179	767	429 0 0
Aug.10	His remittance on Harper and Ramsden, due Oct. 1	91	409	450 0 0
„	Proceeds of 20 puncheons of rum, ex Emily, due Oct. 18	74	407	550 7 8
Oct.26	Proceeds of 15 puncheons of rum, ex Aladdin, due Dec. 25	6	6	112 18 9
Dec.31	Balance of interest		121	
			2026	L.1942 12 11

18—.
Dec. 31 To Balance of last account, due this day . . . . L. 91 16 7

off the two right-hand figures) entered in the interest column. Both sides are of course treated alike, and the balance is divided by 73 which gives the sum to be carried to account at 5 per cent. If the rate of interest be 4 per cent., deduct one-fifth; if 3 per cent., two-fifths; and so on. In computing interest, all fractions of a pound under 10s. are reckoned as nothing; and all above, as 1l.

Dr.   *James Ferguson, Esq. London, in Account*

		yr. days	L. s. d.	L. s. d.
18—. Jan. 11	To bill due ..... 13 Jan	1 186	13 7 9	221 11 0
»	» ...... 24 »	1 175	2 2 7	36 11 0
»	» ...... 27 »	1 172	16 19 10	288 13 3
» 15	Amount received of			
	Mr. Henry Sharp. 13 »	1 186	7 1 5	117 3 0
» 23	Bill due...... 18 Feb.	1 150	7 0 3	132 6 7
Feb. 10	» ...... 16 »	1 152	16 19 11	300 0 0
May 4	Two .... 26 June	1 22	12 5 10	289 16 0
Sept. 4	Balance of drawing acct. due			
	2 Sept.	319	1 0 3	29 7 2
18—.				
July 18	Balance of interest up to this			
	day...........			37 18 5
			L.76 17 10	L.1452 15 5

18—.
July 18   To balance from above, due this day ...... L. 737 16 4
        Errors Excepted — Liverpool, 21st. September, 18—.

Drs.   *Messrs. Simmons and Co., of Amsterdam.*

		L. s. d.	Days	L. s. d.
18—. Jan. 1	To Balance due .... Jan. 1	65 10 0	365	3 5 6
Feb. 26	Invoice of 6 chests of Indigo due			
	26 Feb.	340 10 0	308	14 7 0
May 26	Their draft, order of Lass and Co.			
	1 Aug.	1500 0 0	152	31 4 6
July 30	Their drafts, order of sundries			
	20 Oct.	2100 0 0	72	20 14 2
Nov. 7	Invoice of 200 boxes of sugar			
	7 Nov.	825 10 0	54	6 2 0
Dec. 31	Bank commission on 2790 l. at 1/2			
	per cent. .... 31 Dec.	13 19 0		
	Bill-brokerage and stamps ..	1 19 0		
	Postages............	2 5 6		
	Balance of interest.......	19 17 1		19 17 1
	Balance...........	231 4 5		
		L.5100 15 0		L. 95 10 3

     London, 31st December, 18—.   J. P. DRAYTON and Co.

MERCANTILE TECHNICALITIES.

with R. & F. *Marchmont, of Liverpool.*   Cr.

		gr. days	L. s. d.	L. s. d.
18—. Jan. 7	By acceptance due this day	1 192	2 17 4	47 0 0
» 18	Remittance on Portugal, due 19 Jan.	1 180	21 3 11	354 19 0
Feb. 10	Our acceptance 13 Feb.	1 155	8 10 11	150 0 0
» 29	Our acceptance 10 June	1 38	4 6 9	96 5 0
Dec. 17	Transfer balance owing by our Lisbon firm, due 2 Sept.		319	2 0 6	58 1 2
»	Commission on receiving 1116*l*. 5*s*. 4*d*. at ¹/₂ per cent.				5 11 8
»	Brokerage on 746*l*. 7*s*. 4*d*.				14 11
»	Postage				7 4
	Balance of interest			37 18 5	
18—. July 18	By balance to debit, due this day				737 16 4
			L.76 17 10	L.1452 15 5

R. & F. MARCHMONT.

In Account with J. P. Drayton and Co.   Crs.

		L. s. d.	Days.	L. s. d.
18—. Feb. 10	By their remittance on Smith & Co. due 13 March	400 0 0	203	16 1 1
Apr. 10	Do. on Baring Bro. & Co. 31 May	1100 0 0	214	32 4 6
May 3	Nett proceeds of wheat, ex James due 3 July	960 5 0	181	23 16 0
July 5	Remittance on Hammersleys and Co . . . . 8 Oct.	300 0 0	84	3 9 0
» 30	Our drafts on Paris, 10,000 fr. 3 Aug.	390 10 0	150	8 0 2
» »	Remittance on Curtis and Co. 3 Nov.	1000 0 0	58	7 18 10
Nov. 1	» J. Martin 30 »	950 0 0	31	4 0 8
		L.5100 15 0		L.95 10 3

18—.
Jan. 1 By balance . . . . . 1 Jan. . . . . L. 231 4 5

Messrs. Robert Jamieson and Co. in Account with John Wilson and Co.

Drs.   Crs.

18—.		*L. s. d.*	18—.		*L. s. d.*
June 30	To Bill on H. M Treasury and premium...	101 10 0	March 15	By nett proceeds of Sales per Rubicon N. 1 ..	483 9 0
Nov. 22	Ditto on ditto & ditto.....	304 10 0		By ditto ditto of ditto, Coffin Furniture per ditto, No. 2	266 19 10
18—. May 3	Ditto on H. M. Treasury ..	150 0 0		By ditto ditto, 168 Casks Bottled Beer, per Sir Jos. Banks ..	167 9 4
	Balance carried down....	361 18 2			
		L.917 18 2			L.917 18 2

By Balance brought down L. 361 18 2

Errors Excepted.
    Sydney, 18th March, 18—.

        JOHN WILSON & Co.

Account Sales. — It is the practice of merchants to render a separate account-sales for every parcel of goods received, and not to include several consignments in one, although they happen to be sold at the same time and to the same parties. The forms here given are to be considered merely *as forms*, and not as guides in regard to the rate of commission, etc., because this varies according to circumstances, the old-established houses continuing to charge 2 or 2 $^1/_2$, and, in some trades, 3 per cent. commission on sales, while the younger houses do business on much lower terms.

MERCANTILE TECHNICALITIES.

I.

Account Sales of Sundries received per Ship Rubicon, Daniels, Master, from London, and sold by order and for account and risk of Messrs. Robert Jamieson and Co. of that place, viz: —

					L. s. d.	*L. s. d.*
Out of J. & Co. 32	Case, 8 ends Silk Waistcoating, as per Invoice........ Advance 23 per cent... Add for Package....				25 7 2 6 6 10 0 6 6	32 0 6
	15 Hogsheads Hollands ... 5 Puncheons Brandy	Impl. Gls. 785 531 ½	*s.* at 4 » »		....	157 0 0 106 6 8
	6 Cases, 100 Muskets with Bayonets	14 12 72 2 100	*s.* at 14 » 13 » 12 » 9	9 16 0 7 16 0 43 4 0 0 18 0		61 14 0
R. J. 1 to 168	168 Casks Bottled Ale and Porter: —	Casks 16 » 11 » 44 » 8 » 50 » 39	48 dozen 33 » 132 » 24 » 150 » 117 »	*s.* at 11 » 10 » » » » » 5 » »	26 8 0 16 10 0 66 0 0 12 0 0 37 10 0 29 5 0	187 13 0
		» 168	500 dozen			544 14 2

CHARGES.

To Cash paid Wharfage................ 5 5 9
Auction Duty on 66*l*. 15*s*. at 1 ½ per cent. 20*s*. and expenses 10*s*................... 1 10 0
Commission and Guarantee at 10 per cent....... 54 9 5

                                                                                           61 5 2

Nett proceeds . . L. 483 9 0

Errors Excepted.
    Sydney, 15th March, 18—.
           JOHN WILSON & Co.

APPENDIX.

II.

Account Sales of Sundries received per Ship Rubicon, Daniels, Master, from London, and sold by order and for account and risk of Messrs. Robert Jemieson and Co. of that place, viz: —

J. & Co.		No.	Price.		L. s. d.	L. s. d.
			s.	d.		
1 case	40 Sets White Coffin Furniture	18	7	3	14 10 0	
	40 Ditto » » »	19	8	4 1/2	16 15 0	
	20 Ditto » » »	25	11	3	11 2 6	
	Case				0 10 0	
						42 17 6
2 ditto	40 Sets White Coffin Furniture, gilt	18	10	1 1/2	20 5 0	
	40 Ditto » » »	19	12	0	24 0 0	
	40 Ditto » » » »	25	14	4 1/2	14 7 6	
	Case				0 10 0	
						59 2 6
3 ditto	100 Sets. Same as No. 2				58 12 6	
	Case				0 11 6	
						59 4 0
4 ditto	10 Sets White Coffin Furniture	9	3	5	1 14 2	
	10 Ditto » » »	10	3	4	1 13 4	
	40 Ditto » » »	11	3	6	1 15 0	
	10 Ditto » » »	27	4	11	2 9 2	
	10 Ditto » » »	29	5	0	2 10 0	
	10 Ditto » » » oil					
	40 Single Black Plates, each {	18	0 10 1/2		3 18 4	
		19	1 1			
	20 Ditto » »	25	1	1 1/2	1 5 10	
	Case				0 7 0	
						15 12 10
32 ditto	49 Pieces 6d. Love Ribbon		6	0	14 14 0	
	6 Dozen Men's White Silk Gloves	1	20	0	6 0 0	
	9 Ditto » » »	2	21	0	9 9 0	
	2 Ditto » Black » »	3	20	0	2 0 0	
	22 Ditto » » » »	4	21	0	23 2 0	
	10 Ditto » » » »	5	21	6	10 15 0	
	50 Yrds. 4 inch Black Bullion Fringe		0	8	1 13 4	
	30 Black Worsted Pall Tassels		1	2	1 15 0	
	12 Black Silk » » »		3	0	1 16 0	
	1 Dozen Frame Saws				1 4 0	
	Part Tin and Wood Case				1 0 0	
						73 8 4
33 ditto	10 Packets 16 in. sup, Black Crape		90	0	45 0 0	
	Tin and Wood, Case				1 13 0	
						46 13 0
						296 18 2
	CHARGES.					
	To Cash paid Wharfage, 6 Cases				0 4 6	
	Commission and Guarantee, at 10 per cent.				29 13 10	
						29 18 4

Nett Proceeds . . . . L. 266 19 10

Errors Excepted,
    Sydney, 15th March, 18—.
        JOHN WILSON & Co.

III.

Account Sales of 17 bales of Wool received by the Swift, John Perkins, Master, from Hamburgh, for account of Ludwig Kann, Esq. of Vienna.

17 Bales Wool. $\begin{matrix} O \\ LK \\ O \end{matrix}$ 1 to 17

	L.	d.	s.
City dues and entry	1	2	1
Freight on 49 cwt. 2 qr.			
1 lb. at 2s.	4	19	0
Primage, 10 per cent.	0	10	0
Duty on 5230 lb. at 1d.	21	15	10
Entry	0	6	0
Warehousing	0	8	6
Cartage and Watching	0	18	6
Weighing inwards	0	8	6
Mending cases	0	15	4
Dock charges	1	11	2
Mending and making merchantable	1	2	9
Sampling	0	7	6
Opening and examining	0	6	4
Weighing on delivery	0	8	6
Warehouse rent	0	8	6
Taring and sewing up	0	7	0
Interest on advances six months	3	12	6
Stamps and petty expences	0	11	6
Fire Insurance	1	12	6
Brokerage, 1 per cent.	12	9	3
Discount 2 1/2 ditto	31	3	0
Del credere, 2 ditto	24	18	5
Commission, 2 ditto	24	18	5
	135	1	3
Nett proceeds	848	19	0
	L. 984	0	3

No.	ct.	qr.	lb.
1.	2	2	27
2.	2	3	10
3.	3	0	8
4.	2	3	13
5.	2	3	9
6.	2	3	17
7.	3	1	25

20 2 25=2321 lb.

Tare & Draft 70

Nett 2251 lb.

at 4s. 9d. L.534 12 3

8.	2	2	12
9.	2	3	26
10.	2	0	8
11.	2	2	25
12.	2	3	13
13.	2	3	27
14.	2	2	10
15.	2	3	26
16.	2	3	25
17.	2	3	12

27 2 16=3096 lb.

Tare & Draft 100

Nett 2996 lb.

at 3s. . . . 449 8 0

L. 984 0 3

E. E. — London, 17th December, 18—.   FLETCHER & BRINK.

IV.

Account Sales of 168 Casks Bottled Beer, received per Ship Sir Joseph Banks, Edward Smith, Master, from London, and sold by order and for account and risk of Messrs. Robert Jamieson and Co. there, viz: —

GL 1 to 168	168 Casks Bottled Ale and Porter viz.: —							
			s.	d.	L.	s.	d.	L. s. d.
48 Casks	144 doz.	at	10	0	72	0	0	
5 "	15 "		7	4	5	10	0	
82 "	246 "		7	0	86	2	0	
20 "	60 "		6	8	20	2	0	
5 "	15 "		5	4	4	0	0	
8 "	24 "		5	0	6	0	0	
								193 12 0
168 Cask	504 doz.							

CHARGES.

	L. s. d.	
To Cash paid Wharfage (168 barrels, at 6d.)	4 4 0	
Auction Duty on 121l. 12s. at 1 ¹/₂ per cent., 36s. 4d., and expenses 15s.	2 11 4	
Commission and Guarantee, at 10 per cent.	19 7 4	
		26 2 8
Nett Proceeds		L. 167 9 4

Errors Excepted.

Sdyney, 15th March, 18—.

JOHN WILSON & CO.

V.

Account Sales of 17 pipes of Linseed Oil, received per Philadelphia, Morgan, and sold for account of George Hayter & Co. of London.

| G. H.
C.
17 to 34 | Sold at 6 months. Dollars Cts.
17 pipes, or 2140 gall, at
100 cts. . . . .
Charges.
Freigh., 12*l.* 17*s.* 7*d.* at 4*s.*
6*d.* . . . .
Duty on 2120
gall. at 25 cts. 530
deduct 10 per
cent. . . . 53
———477
ad 2 per cent. 9 54
———— 486 54
Bond, Permit, etc. . . . 5 50
Cartage, labor 17 50
Gauging 4 25
Cooperage, hoops, etc. . . 8 50
Rent . . . . 12 —
Fire Insurance, ¹/₈ per cent. 2 75
Interest on freight and duty 9 10
Brokerage, 50 c. per pipe . 8 50
Commission and guarantee,
5 per cent. . . . . . 107 —
———
Nett proceeds, due 1 Dec. . Dollars | Dollars Cts.
2140

718 88
1421 12 |

New-York, 3 *June* 18—.   John Rider.

Anderson.

VI.

Account Sales of 1000 bags of Manilla Sugar, received by the Sylla, Jones, from Manilla, and sold for account of Messrs. Versluys and Co. of Antwerp.

Oct. A.	Sold at Public Sale, 1 April. Lot.		L. s. d.
	1 to 8 — 328 bags, gr. 230 2 1		
	Tare 2 } Draft 1 } 8 2 6		
	Nett 221 3 21 at 26s.		284 10 4
	9 to 15 — 280 bgs, gr. 199 0 18		
	Tare 2 } Draft 1 } 7 2 0		
	Nett 191 2 18 at 25s.		239 11 6
	16 to 25 — 400 bags, gr. 291 1 20		
	Tare 2 } Draft 1 } 10 2 24		
	Nett 280 2 21 at 2's.6d.		343 17 6
	Charges.		
	Freight on 721 cwt. 11 lbs. at 5s. per cwt. . L. 180 5 6		
	Pierage, 3 1/2 d. per ton. 10 6		
	180 16 0		
	4 months' Interest, at 4 per ct. 2 8 3		
	Dock rates, 721 cwt. 11 lbs. at 5d. 15 0 5		
	3 months' Interest 0 3 0		
	carried over . . L. 198 7 8		71 19 4

		L. s. d.
Brought forward . . L. 198 7 8		871 19 4
Sorting and lotting 4 7 2		
Fire insurance 1 2 6		
Brokerage, 1 per cent. . . . 8 14 5		
Commission and guarantee, 2 ½		
per cent. 21 16 0		
		234 7 9
Nett proceeds, due 1 April . .		L. 637 11 7

London, 17th January, 18—.

JAS. JOHNSON & Co.

VII.

Account Sales of 76 bales of Madder Root, received per James, Hill, and sold for account of Messrs. Julilan and Co. of Trieste.

| A.
1 to
76 | Prompt 3 months and 1 month.
75 bales, gross . . 269 0 27
draft, 4 lb. per bale . 2 2 24
―――――
266 2 3
tare, 10 lb. per bale 6 3 4
―――――
at 54s
Nett 259 2 27 per cwt.

Charges.
Insurance, 800*l* at 40s. L. 16
Stamp. 2
――――― 18 0 0

Carried over . L. 18 0 0 | L. s. d.

701 6 0

701 6 0 |

APPENDIX.

	L. s. d.	L. s. d.
Brought forward . L. 18 0 0		701 6 0
Entry, bond, dock and town dues	2 0 4	
cwt. qrs. lbs.		
Duty on 261 3 3 at 6d. per cwt.	6 10 10	
Freight on 269 0 27 at 63s. per ton. L. 42 8 1		
Primage 10 per cent. . 4 4 8		
	44 12 9	
Cartage and porterage on landing	2 17 0	
Warehouse rent, 10 weeks, at 1d.	3 3 4	
Porterage delivering, mending, canvas, ecc.	1 2 6	
Fire Insurance, L. 800 at 7s. 6d. per cent.	3 0 0	
Interest on charges 76l. 8s. 11d. 164 days	1 14 2	
Postages and petty charges . .	0 18 2	
Brokerage, ¹/₂ per cent. . . .	3 10 0	
Commission and guarantee, 4 per cent. 28 1 0		117 10 1
Nett proceeds, per 4 Jan. 18—. . .		L. 583 15 11

Liverpool, 7th September, 18—.

GRIFFIN & Co.

Pro forma* Account Sales of 10 bags of Orchilla Weed.

10 bags of Orchilla Weed, duty paid.		*L. s. d.*	
Weighing gross . . . cwt. qrs. lbs. 21 3 17 draft, 1 lb. per bag . . 10			
Tare, 6 per cent. 21 3 7 . 1 0 19			
{ at L.250 { per ton. 20 2 16 Discount, 2 1/2 per cent.		258 0 9 6 9 0	
Charges. Housing, landing, and wharfage, at 9d. per bag. . . . . 7 6 Weighing, 3d. per bag . . . . 2 6 Freight, per ton . . . . Primage, per cent. . .		251 11 9	
Duty, 16s. 8d. per cwt. . . . . 17 4 0 Warehouse rent, 1d. per bag per week. . Brokerage 1 per cent. if sold by auction; 1/2 per cent. if by private contract. . Postages 17s. 6d. and petty charges 10s. . 1 7 6 Brokerage on remittance, at 2s. per cent. Premium of insurance from 15s. 9d. to 25s. per cent. according to the season of the year, ship, etc. . . . . Policy stamp, if premium under 20l. 2s. 6d. per cent. above, 5s. per cent. . . . . . Commission on amount insured 1/2 per ct. Del credere (if required) 1/2 per cent. . . . Commission on 251l. 11s. 9d. at 2 1/2 per cent. . . . . 6 5 9 Del credere, when not sold for cash. 2 per cent.			
Nett proceeds			

Errors Excepted. — *London,*

* See the term « pro forma. »

APPENDIX.

Act of Honor. See *Bills,* page 202.

Ad valorem duty. — One levied on the value of the article, not by weight, numbers, or package.

Administrator. — A person empowered by the Ecclesiastical Court to manage the estate of an individual deceased, when the latter has died intestate, or the executor appointed by him declines to act.

Advances — are made by merchants on account of goods consigned to them, either by the remittance of bills, or the acceptance of the shipper's drafts.

Adventure. — A commercial operation, or speculation, entered into by a merchant for his own account, or on joint account with another, consisting usually, of the import or export of goods.

Advice. — Notice of a bill drawn.

Advices. — Reports of the state of trade, the course of exchange, and general commercial intelligence communicated by letter.

Agio. — The difference between *Banco,* or bank money, in which accounts are kept, and the current money of a country.

Appoint. — *Per appoint.* See note, page 46.

Arbitration. — An amicable adjustment of a dispute by the decision of one or more private individuals, nominated by authority, or by the parties concerned. — Their judgment is termed an *award.*

Arbitration of Exchanges. — A comparison made between the exchanges of different places, with the view of buying or selling bills to advantage. When three places only are concerned, it is termed *simple arbitration:* when more, *compound.*

Assets. — Cash or property of a bankrupt, an insolvent, or deceased person. Means to pay the debts of an estate or commercial house.

Assignee. — One to whom the management of an insolvent's affairs is confided. If appointed by the insolvent Court, he is called an *official assignee.*

Assurance. — See *Insurance.*

Assured. — The party who holds a policy of any kind is thus designated.

Attorney. — A person legally substituted to sign and act for another.

Attorney, Letter of, Power of. — The legal instrument conveying such authority.

Averages — In marine Insurance, are of two kinds; particular and general.

A *particular average* is a contribution *pro rata* by the underwriters, to make good damage done to the property insured by what are termed *accidents of the seas*, as when a vessel loses an anchor or part of her rigging, or goods are washed overboard, or injured by the salt-water.

A *general average* is a contribution by all the parties concerned — that is, the owners of the ship, freight, and cargo — to make good any loss incurred for the preservation of the whole, as when a mast or an anchor is cut away, or a part of the cargo thrown overboard. The under-writers are liable to pay this contribution, or a part of it, *pro rata*, when the property is only partially assured. The act of cutting away the rigging or cable, or throwing goods overboard, is called a *jettison*, which see.

Average, free of. — From the difficulty of ascertaining the causes of such trifling damages and deteriorations as most frequently occur to the ship and cargo, it has been found necessary to stipulate on behalf of the underwriters, that they shall not be liable to pay any particular average at all on certain articles; nor any, on certain others, that shall not amount to so much per cent. This exception is specified in what is termed the memorandum of the policy (See *Policy*). When goods so excepted, as corn, flour, fruit, fish, etc. are damaged, the loss falls upon the owner, not upon the underwriter, which will explain the allusion, in one of the foregoing letters, to the average consuming the profit.

Award. — The decision of arbitrators.

Balance of Trade. — When one country exports to another more goods than it imports from thence, the difference must be paid to it in cash; this difference is called the balance of trade between the two countries, and is chiefly instrumental in fixing the rate of exchange.

Banco. — Bank money. See *Agio*.

Banker. — A person who trades in money; who acts as an agent for the receipt and payment of money; who receives sums of money at interest or for safe custody.

Bankrupt. — An insolvent merchant or tradesman, who, by a legal process, is made amenable to the Bankrupt laws. None but persons in trade can become bankrupts.

Bankrupt's Certificate. — A document signed by the creditors, which releases him from all further claims for liabilities then subsisting. When this certificate is refused, the party is termed an *uncertificated bankrupt*.

Bank * *Banking-house.* — Establishments wherein the various ope-

---

* « The term *bank* is derived from *banco*, the Italian word for bench, as the Lombard Jews in Italy kept *benches* in the market-place where they exchanged money and bills. When a banker failed, his bench was broken

rations of banking are carried on. The former term is more properly applied to such as belong to Joint Stock Companies trading under an assumed title, whose capital is subscribed by a numerous body of shareholders, and whose affairs are managed by a committee, or board of direction; the latter to such as belong to a few individuals in copartnership, trading on their own capital, and in their own names. Some writers designate the first *public*, the second *private* banks.

Some banks issue their own notes, payable on demand; others do not. In London, and for a distance of sixty-five miles around, the Bank of England enjoys the exclusive privilege of issuing its own notes.

The system of banking affords many advantages and facilities for business, the principal of which are the following. It provides places of safety for the custody of money. It obviates the inconvenience of carrying cash from place to place at the risk of loss or robbery. It effects a great saving of time, and consequently of expense, to merchants and tradesmen, who would otherwise have to count out every sum of money they had to pay, and to send their own clerks to all parts of the town to demand payment of their bills of exchange. It affords a most efficient safe-guard against peculation on the part of clerks, shopmen, and servants. It presents the means of making payments in distant parts without the transmission of money. In country places it supplies a want very commonly felt, that of an appropriate circulating medium.

On opening an account with a banker, every person is required to write his name in a book, in order that his signature may be known, and always referred to when necessary. He is then supplied with a cash-book and printed checks. In the former, all the sums received and paid on his account are entered to his debit and credit, as frequently as he chooses to leave the book for that purpose.

When he has occasion to pay an account, or to draw cash for his own use, he has only to fill up and sign a check, and his banker immediately pays it. In like manner he transfers to his banker the trouble of paying all his acceptances, by writing on the bills, « *Payable at Messrs.* —— ».

On the other hand, he sends to his banker all checks paid to him, and all bills of exchange, payable in London, that may come into his possession.

He is thus relieved from the trouble of presenting them himself; and if any neglect or mistake occur in regard to a bill thus transferred, the banker is responsible for the consequences.

---

by the populace; and from this circumstance we have the term *bankrupt*. »
— See A *Practical Treatise on Banking*, by James William Gilbart, 3d edition, London, 1834. — See also M*^c Culloch's Commercial Dictionary*.

Another very important advantage to a person in business is this. He can both refer to his banker for testimony of his own respectability, and obtain, trough him, information as to the credit and stability of other parties.

Bankers will take charge of boxes of deeds, chests of plate, jewels, or other valuables, for their customers, and place them in their strong room, which is generally fireproof and well secured with iron doors, etc.

Through the medium of the country bankers, who all have correspondents in London, and many of them direct communication with each other, a person residing at one end of the kingdom may pay a sum of money to a correspondent at the other, and avoid all risk of loss or robbery, at the expense of a small commission, charged by the banker in whose hands he places it.

There are two modes in which bankers are remunerated for their trouble and responsibility. The first, which was, until recently, the universal custom of the banking-houses, is, to charge no commission, but to require a certain balance to be left in their hands by each customer; that balance being proportioned to the extent of his banking transactions throughout the year.

The interest of the cash so deposited, constitutes to profit of the banker.

The second mode is, to require no floating balance (or to allow interest if there be one), and to charge a stipulated sum annually for agency, or a commission on all the transactions, of an eighth or a quarter per cent.

Upon this principle, all the country bankers and two London establishments * now do business.

Merchants act as bankers to their foreign correspondents, receiving their bill, paying their acceptances, and interfering, when requisite, for their honor. † In these cases the merchant is remunerated like the country banker, by a commission of an eighth, three-eighths, or a quarter per cent. (according to agreement) charging interest on payments and allowing it on sums received. See *Check* and *Clearing*.

Barratry — signifies any illegal act on the part of the master or crew of a ship, whereby the owners may be injured or defrauded; as smuggling, which renders the vessel liable to seizure; running away with the ship; cruizing in quest of prizes without consent of the owners, and thus exposing the ship to injury or capture; engaging without a licence in any exclusive trade, as the East India, before the restrictions were removed, etc. **

---

* The London and Westminster Bank, and Messrs. Lawson, Newham and Co. † See « Bills, » page 202 ** No act in which the owner participates can be an act of barratry, since a man cannot commit a fraud against himself.

APPENDIX.

Bears and Bulls. — Terms used on the Stock Exchange. A *bear* is one who has agreed to sell more stock than he possesses, and is consequently obliged to buy in at a loss to settle his account. A *bull* is one who agrees to purchase more than he can pay for, and so is obliged to sell again before the time of payment (called *settling day*) arrives.

Bill of Exchange. — An order to pay a certain sum of money at a time specified. When the party, to whom such order is addressed, has signified his intended compliance with it, by accepting the bill, it becomes an *engagement* to pay, which is as binding as any obligation in law.

The principal use of bills, and that, no doubt, for which they were invented, is to effect the settlement of accounts, or payment of debts, between parties residing at a distance from each other, without the transmission of money or bullion.

When a commercial intercourse is carried on between two cities, as, for instance, Amsterdam and London, it must always happen that there are parties in each city who are indebted to persons in the other. Thus, A, at Amsterdam, has to pay Y, of London, 300*l*.; and Z, of London, has to pay B, of Amsterdam 200*l*.; and C, of the same place, 100*l*. Now, if A buys of B an order on Z for the payment of 200*l*., and of C an order on Z for the payment of 100*l*., and remits these two orders to Y, of London, the latter receives of Z, the 300*l*. due to him, and all the claims are adjusted in a simple, safe, and expeditious manner.

Bills, however, are now employed for many other purposes; they form a principal feature in the modern system of credit, and are given by buyers of goods to the sellers; by debtors to their creditors; and under many other circumstances, both as security for money due, and a means of obtaining the immediate use of cash not payable till a given time.

Bills of Exchange are principally of two kinds, inland and foreign. The following is the form of

An Inland, or Domestic Bill.

L. 280 14*s*. 6d.   London, 20th November, 18—.

Two months after date, pay to me or my order, two hundred and eighty pounds, fourteen shillings, and sixpence, for value received.   EDWARD HART.

Messrs. Kittson & Co. Bristol.

A Promissory Note.

L. 200 0 0.   London, 28th November, 18—.

Three months after date, I promise to pay to Mr. John Millhouse, or his order, two hundred pounds, for value received.

         CHARLES RUSSELL.
         141, Oxford-street.

A bill requires the acceptance of the person on whom it is drawn (legally termed drawee) to render it valid. A promissory note is valid the moment it is signed and delivered, its form precluding acceptance. In all other respects these documents are precisely similar. They must both be drawn « to order » to make them negotiable, and in both, the words « *for value received*, » are indispensable.

The acceptance of a bill is usually written across it in the centre. Some merchants write « accepted » for so much, payable at such a banker's; but many use only the word « accepted, » which is all that the law requires in addition to the signature. Indeed, it has been decided, that if the latter be omitted, the acceptance is not the less binding in law. Domestic bills are either endorsed *in blank*, by writing the name only on the back, which is the usual way; or *specially*, for a particular purpose; as thus — « pay to the order of A. Newman, for value received. »

The law requires that a bill should be left for a day at the office, or house of the drawee, for acceptance, and if he refuses to accept, it must be immediately placed in the hands of a notary, to be noted for non-acceptance. The notary presents the bill again, and notes the answer of the drawee upon a small slip of paper which he affixes to the bill; and upon the same slip he marks his charge for noting, which charge is added to the amount of the bill, and recovered from the person who ultimately pays the latter. When the bill becomes due, it is presented for payment by the holder; if payment be refused, recourse is again had to the notary, who, having presented it himself as before[*], draws up a legal document called a protest, armed with which the holder can commence proceedings against the drawer, and all or any of the previous endorsers. When a bill is dishonored, merchants usually send a notice to the parties of whom they received it, a specimen of which is given at page 124.

If a bill be not presented for payment on the day on which it falls due, the drawer and all the endorsers are exonerated by law, and the holder has no claim but on the acceptor, if the bill be accepted; or, in the case of a promissory note, the party by whom the note was issued.

Bills falling due on a Sunday, or Good Friday, or Christmas-day, are payable the day before.

A Foreign Bill.

London, 30th November, 18—. Marks Bco. 5000.

Three months after date, pay this our first of exchange (second

---

[*] The law does not require that the notary should see the drawee personally; it is sufficient if he present the bill at the place indicated therein.

and third not paid) to the order of Messrs. Hellman and Son, five thousand marks banco* for value received, as advised by

Messrs. P. H. Fürst & Son.   Edw. Collins & Co.
Hamburgh.

The chief difference between inland and foreign bills consists in the latter being usually drawn in sets of two or there, all exactly alike, excepting the words «first,» «second,» and «third,» by which they are distinguished from each other.

As merchants, in writing to distant parts, generally send duplicates of their letters lest the original should miscarry, so, in remitting a bill, they guard against loss by transmitting a second, and sometimes a third, by different opportunities, or at different times.

The first that comes to hand is presented for acceptance, all being equally valid.

Foreign bills should always be endorsed at length, thus: —

London, 28th November, 18—,

Pay to Messrs. C. U. and Co., or order, for value received. N. N.

Firsts for Acceptance.

When a merchant purchases a foreign bill (for the first, second, and third constitute but one bill), he transmits the first immediately to a correspondent in or near the town on which it is drawn, to procure acceptance to it. By this means he secures the responsability of the drawee, without delay, and without incurring any risk whatever, since the first not being endorsed is not negotiable; and in the mean time he can dispose of the second, writing upon it at foot, «First, with Messrs. ———.» The second, travelling, as it must ultimately do, to the place on which it is drawn, is presented to the house indicated in the above notice; and the first is immediately given up, being, in the language of merchants, *held at the disposal of the second.*

Case of Need, or Acceptance and Payment for Honor.

Every individual, whose name is found upon a bill, whether as drawer, drawee, or endorser, is alike responsible to the last holder for its payment when due; and, as the return of a bill is not only prejudicial to the credit of a merchant, but is also attended with considerable expense, a plan has been devised for guarding against this unpleasant occurrence.

This plan consists in adding what is called « *A case of Need,* » or reference to a correspondent in the same place, who is thus called upon « *to interfere for honor* » of the merchant by whom the bill is referred to him. This reference is made by writing at

---

*Or it is drawn in pounds sterling, and the course of exchange stated at which the bill has been negotiated and at which it is to be paid abroad.

the bottom on the bill, thus: — « In case of need, with Messrs. ———» When the acceptance or payment is refused by the drawee, the holder applies to the house thus indicated, who accept or pay as the case may be, *under protest and act of honor*; such being the name given to the notarial instrument drawn up to enable their correspondent, for whose account they interfere, to recover from the drawers of the bill.

Bill of Lading. — A receipt on a stamped and printed form, given by the master of a vessel for the goods shipped on board her. This document is considered sufficient evidence of their being so shipped, in case of loss, and insurance being effected thereon.

Bills of lading are transferable like bills of exchange, either by blank or special endorsement, and the holder can claim the goods of the captain under any circumstances, when the bill is endorsed by the consignee, and he can prove that he has given a fair consideration for it.

A Bill of Lading.

B 1 to 12

Shipped in good order and well conditioned by *John Brooks*, in and upon the good ship called the *Lady Pellew*, whereof is master for this present voyage, *Captain Charles Cobbin*, and now riding at anchor in the *London Docks*, and bound for *St. Petersburgh*, *five cases printed cottons, and seven bales woollen cloths*, being marked and numbered as in the margin, and are to be delivered in the like good order, and well conditioned at the aforesaid port of *St. Petersburgh* (the act of God, the king's enemies, fire, and all and every other dangers and accidents of the seas, rivers, and navigation, of whatever nature or kind soever excepted), unto *Messrs. John Barton and Co.*, or to *their* assigns, *on paying* freight for the said goods, *three pounds eighteen shillings, and five per cent.*, primage and average accustomed. In witness whereof, the master or purser of the said ship hath affirmed to *four* bills of lading, all of this tenor and date: the one of which *four* bills being accomplished, the other *three*, to stand void.

Dated *in London*, 11*th Sept.* 18—.
Weight and contents unknown.   CHARLES COBBIN.

APPENDIX.

Bill of Parcels. — A bill of goods sold. See note, page 46.

Blank Credit. — Permission to draw on a house to a certain amount, without restriction as to time, and without making remittances against the drafts.

Bonded Goods, Goods in Bond. — Such as are permitted to be warehoused in certain *Bonded Stores*, without payment of the duty, on the owner giving bond for the payment of such duty and other charges, on their removal for home consumption, or re-shipment to some other country.

Bottomry Bond. — A bond given by the captain for money advanced on the keel or bottom of his ship.

Bottomry Loan. — The money so advanced. The condition of a loan on bottomry or respondentia, is, that if the ship be lost, the lender shall lose the entire sum lent; if she arrive safe, he shall recover his money with the interest agreed upon. The law, in consideration of the great risk incurred by lending cash on such precarious security as the hull or cargo of a ship, permits an interest to be charged in this case, which in every other, would be illegal, and sometimes as much as 25 or 30 per cent. is paid for the accommodation.

It sometimes happens that a master of a ship is obliged to borrow money twice or thrice on bottomry, being under the necessity to repair again, after he has left the port where he first took up money on bottomry, etc.: in that case, the sum advanced last must be paid out of the value of the ship's cargo before the preceding loan is, because, without the last loan being furnished, the ship could not have proceeded to her destination.

The sum lent may be insured; but the lender cannot insure more than the difference between the amount of the loan and the value of the Ship or goods. See *Respondentia*.

Bounty. — A premium paid by government for the exportation of certain articles of British growth or manufactures, or for the importation of foreign corn, etc. Also for the imployment of ships in the herring and whale fisheries.

Brokers. — Persons licensed to act as intermediate parties between one merchant and another in the purchase of goods, bills of exchange, etc. their office being very similar to that of a notary public. They are restricted from trading themselves, and are witnesses to the transactions in which they are employed.

Brokerage. — The charge made by the broker for his trouble.

Broker's Note. — A voucher signed by the broker, and given in every case in which he is called upon to act. It states, briefly, the names of the buyers and sellers, the description and quality of the goods sold, and the prices and terms of sale.

Bullion. — Uncoined gold or silver.
Case of Need. — See *Bill of Exchange,* page 204.
Charter Party. — A contract entered into by the owner or master of a vessel who *lets,* and the merchant who *hires* the ship, either wholly or in part, for a specified time, or a stated voyage. A perusal of the following specimen will clearly explain the nature of this engagement.

CHARTER PARTY.

London, 20th May, 18—.

It is this day mutually agreed between *Edward Griffiths, master* of the good ship or vessel called the *Freedom,* of the measurement of *one hundred and forty* tons or thereabouts, now lying *in the River Thames,* and *Messrs. Curtis, Ross and Co.,* of *London,* merchants.

That the said ship being tight, staunch, and strong, and every way fitted for the voyage, shall *in due time proceed to Cadiz (with liberty to take a cargo to any port on her way out)* or so near thereunto as she may safely get, *and there load a full and complete cargo of wool or other lawful merchandise, but not exceeding six hundred whole bags, or what may be equal thereto,* and not exceeding what she can reasonably stow and carry, over and above her tackle, apparel, provisions, and furniture; and being so loaded, shall forthwith proceed to *London to discharge at such place as the charterers may appoint,* or so near thereunto as she may safely get, and deliver the same on being paid freight, *at and after the rate of fourteen shillings per bag of wool, of two hundred and twenty four pounds nett weight at the Queen's beam, and so in proportion for other lawful merchandise, with* 10s. per cent. on *the whole* (the act of God, the king's enemies, fire, and all and every other dangers and accidents of the seas, rivers, and navigation, of whatever nature and kind soever during the said voyage, always mutually excepted).

The freight to be paid on unloading, and right delivery of the cargo, *one half in cash, and the other half by an approved bill at three months' date from the said delivery.*

Forty working days are to be allowed to the said merchant (if the ship be not sooner despatched) for loading the ship at *Cadiz* and discharging at *London, to commence when she shall have arrived out, shall have received pratique, and shall be in every respect ready to load,* and *ten* days on demurrage, over and above the said laying days at *three* pounds *three* shillings per day. Penalty for non-performance of this agreement *three hundred pounds.*

And the said master engages that the said vessel shall be ballasted with iron, stone, or shingle, and not with sand or mud, or anything prejudicial to a cargo of wool; likewise, that she shall be stowed in the usual and customary manner. And the said merchants engage to

advance the said master as much money as he may require at Cadiz for ship's use, but not exceeding one hundred pounds; the said master reimbursing them by his draft on his brokers, Messrs. Rothwell and Smith, of London. In testimony of this our mutual agreement and undertaking, we hereunto affix our hands and seals.
Witness.

Check, or *Cheque*, sometimes called a draft. An order addressed to a a banker, or other person, for the payment of money to the individual named, or bearer, on demand. Checks are negotiable like bills, but require no endorsement, and are payable instantly on presentation. All checks should be presented for payment with as little delay as possible; for, if retained beyond the day of their dates, and the bankers on whom they are drawn should fail, the holder cannot recover from the drawer.

Clearing. — The name given to a daily exchange of bills and checks, which takes place between most of the bankers resident in the city of London, at the clearing house in Lombard-street. The banking houses who « clear, » are, as appears by Mr. Gilbart's « Treatise on Banking, » thirty in number, and a clerk from each attends first at twelve and then at three o'clock, with all the bills and drafts on the others that have been paid in up to those hours. There is a drawer appropriated to each house, and in these all the drafts and bills are distributed by the respective clerks. Each being provided with a printed list of the clearing bankers, called a balance sheet, he enters to the debit side all the sums the other houses owe him, and on the credit all that he owes them. If he has money to receive, he takes it from any body who has money to pay; for it is obvious that the amount to be paid, must be equal to the amount to be received; and the only point to be attended to is, that each shall obtain the balance due to him on the clearing.

Checks *crossed*, i.e. having the name of a banker written across them, are payable to that banker only, and are therefore useless if stolen or lost, since no other person can receive the money.

Composition. — An agreement between an insolvent and his creditors, by which the latter accept of a portion, in lieu of the whole of their respective demands. The per centage so paid is also thus called, as « a composition of 10s. in the pound. » etc.

Compromise. — To adjust a difference by mutual concession.

Consignee. — A merchant to whom goods are sent to be sold on commission.

Consignment. — The goods so sent.

Consols (for Consolidated Funds). — Certain public stocks formed by the consolidation of different annuities.

Consul. — An accredited agent of government at a foreign port, appointed to protect the maritime interest of the country more especially. Documents of any kind attested by the consul, under his hand and seal of office, are admitted as evidence in courts of justice.

Contingent. — The share of any one concerned with others in an adventure.

Convoy. — One or more ships of war appointed to protect a fleet of merchantmen.

Coupons. — Small slips, cut from a foreign bond, bearing date, amount, signature, etc., and forming so many orders (or *dividend warrants*) for payment of the dividend or interest.

Customs. — Duties levied on goods imported or exported.

Debenture. — A custom's certificate to enable a shipper to receive the bounty, or drawback, on goods exported.

Debts, active and *passive.* — The former are such as are owing to us; the latter such as we owe to others.

Decrease. — An allowance made by the Customs, to importers of liquors, for the quantity *decreased* during the time they remain *in bond.*

Del credere. — See note, page 51.

Demurrage. — In maritime affairs, an allowance of so much per day made to the owners of a vessel for her detention in port beyond the time agreed upon. See *Charter Party.*

Despatch. — A despatch in insurances, is the statement made out in case of a general average, in form of a certificate, setting forth, 1st, the value of the ship, freight and cargo, which together have to contribute to a loss or an expense incurred for the general benefit or safety; 2nd, the amount of this expense; 3rd, the extent to which a party is interested in the goods; and 4th, the per centage he has to contribute towards the whole expense.

Deviation. — In marine assurances, a wilful departure from the regular course of voyage, by which the policy is vitiated.

Discount. — A deduction of so much per cent. for present payment. Discounting a bill, is giving the money for it at once, charging interest for the time it has to run. See *Interest.*

To *Dishonour.* — To refuse acceptance or payment of a bill of exchange.

Dividend. — A share of anything divided. The *dividends* on stock, are simply the interest due thereon to the holders.

Domiciliated — made payable; applied to bills of exchange that are either drawn on one town, with the condition that they shall be paid in another, or are made so payable by the acceptor for his own convenience, or to facilitate the negotiation of his acceptances.

Draft. — A bill of exchange drawn by A upon B, is called in commercial language, A's draft on B. A check is also sometimes called a draft. See *Check.*

Draught. — An allowance on goods sold by weight.

Drawback. — A return of duties allowed on the re-exportation of certain foreign goods, or on the exportation of certain British goods that are subject to an excise duty when consumed at home.

Drawee. — The person on whom a bill is drawn.

Drawer. — The person who draws a bill.

Dunnage. — Loose wood, faggots, mats, etc., used in stowing a cargo.

Embargo. — An arrest on ships or goods by public authority.

Entrepôt. — This word signifies, 1st, Bonded Warehouses; 2nd, Private Warehouses, for the reception of merchandise *in transitu,* or on transit.

Exchange. — See *Bill of Exchange.*

Exchequer Bills. — Notes issued by Goverment bearing interest.

Excise. — An inland tax on goods manufactured or consumed in the country.

Execution. — The process of seizing a person's goods by a sheriff's officer.

Firm. — A house of trade, as the firm or house of Bradford and Co.

Free Port. — One where goods may be warehoused and exported free of duty.

Freight. — The cargo of a vessel; the sum paid for the hire of it; the rate paid per ton, per last, etc.

Funds. — See *Stocks.*

Gallats. — Table of monies and exchanges referred to at page 146.

		Money of Buckarest.	Of Galats.
1	Florin ct. d'Auguste of Vienna	8 $^3/_4$ piastres —	8 $^5/_8$ piastres.
1	Silver rouble	10 $^1/_2$ » —	13 $^1/_2$ »
1	Zechin (full weight) . .	31 $^1/_2$ » —	39 $^1/_2$ »
1	Ditto, called rather light	30 $^1/_2$	39 »
1	Austrian lire of 20 kreutzers	2 $^1/_2$ » —	2 $^3/_4$ to 2 $^{24}/_{40}$
1	Yermeliky	14 $^{14}/_{40}$ » —	18 $^1/_4$ » 18 $^{12}/_{40}$
100	Piastres of Costantinople	67 »	— 86 $^{28}/_{32}$
115 to 116	ditto, ditto . .	77 $^1/_{80}$ »	— 100.

In addition to the money of Vienna and Constantinople, it has been attempted to introduce that of Marseilles and Genoa, and it may be estimated that 100 piastres of Bucharest are equal to about 38 $1/2$ franks.

Garble. — The dust, dross, and refuse of spices and drugs.

Garbling. — The picking out the worst of any commodity.

Grace, Days of. — Those days which are allowed by law or custom for the payment of a bill of exchange, beyond the day on which it strictly falls due. In some countries, no days of grace are allowed; in others, they vary in number from three to thirty. In Great Britain and Ireland, the days of grace are three; so that a bill at two months from the 1st of June is not payable until the 4th of August, and the date is generally thus marked by merchants, viz. « due 1st — 4th of August. » Bills drawn « at sight » are an exception, being payable on presentation.

Groundage. — A small duty levied, in some ports, on ships coming to an anchor.

Husbandage. — An allowance made to the husband or managing-owner of a ship.

Jettison. — The act of throwing overboard any part of the cargo or of cutting away masts, anchors, sails, rigging, boats, etc. This act is justified by stress of weather; by being chased by an enemy; or by running aground. The owner of property so sacrificed for the preservation of the whole, has a claim upon the owners of the property preserved, who are bound to share his loss with him *pro rata.*

Indorsee. — The person to whom a bill is indorsed.

Indorsement. — The act of writing the name of the holder of a bill on the back of the same, for the purpose of transferring it to another person. See *Bill of Exchange.*

Indorser. — The person who writes his name on the back of a bill.

Insolvent. — One who is unable to pay his debts.

Insurance. — A contract by which the one party undertakes, for a consideration called a premium, to indemnity the other against certain losses, or to guarantee the payment of a stipulated sum.

Insurances are of three kinds, namely: —

1st. On ships and their cargoes, and on their freight: whereby the owners are secured against the perils of the sea, capture, barratry, etc.

2nd. On houses and moveable property of all descriptions, farming-stock, crops, growing timber, etc. against the risk of fire and lightning.

3rd. On lives; the operations of which are complicated, and the advantages numerous and diversified.

All insurances are founded upon these principles; first, the distribution of the hazard to be incurred among many, so that each individual, instead of bearing his own risk, wholly and exclusively, shall bear but a small portion of his own, and the same of every other person's risk; secondly, the sacrifice of a small portion of his property to secure the rest; thirdly, the condition that the sacrifice so made by each individual, shall be commensurate with the nature and degree of his particular hazard *.

Goods to a large amount are frequently bought for shipping on credit, which could not be done to that extent if the sellers were not aware that their creditors could secure their property by a policy of insurance.

Insurances, Fire — are effected in England with incorporated bodies (of which there are a great number), and are subject to a duty of 3*s.* per cent. In some countries, were the necessities of government do not compel them to tax institutions of so beneficent a character, there exists a system of mutual insurance under the sanction of the legislature; and in others, an office under its immediate control, in which all the proprietors of houses and other buildings are required to assure them for a value fixed by the official surveyor.

The risks of fire insurance are usually divided into four classes, termed, Common, Hazardous, Doubly Hazardous, and Special.

The first of these is chargeable with a premium of 1*s.* 6*d.* per cent; the second 2*s.* 6*d.*; the third 4*s.* 6*d.*

For the last, which comprises all risks of extraordinary hazard, no premiums are fixed, because they vary according to the peculiar circumstances of each case.

Full particulars of the rates of premium, and conditions of the policy, may be obtained on application at any of the insurance offices.

Merchants usually keep open a floating assurance on « *goods their own in trust, or on consignment,* » by which means all the merchandise in their hands, wherever it may be deposited (within the limits of the town or district to which the insurance is made to extend), is covered either wholly or in part, according as the value of such merchandise, in the aggregate, shall happen to be under or above the sum insured. See *Floating Policy*.

---

* Policies of insurance were first used in Florence about the middle of the 16th century, although some conjecture that the system of insuring ships and merchandise was invented by the Romans. Be this as it may, it is only within the last 70 or 80 years, that the practice of insurance has become at all general, or properly understood, even in this commercial country.

Life Insurance — is better known and appreciated in Great Britain than any other part of the world; but still, the system is very far from being generally understood, or commonly resorted to, in the numerous exigencies in which it alone can afford relief.

We have many companies that undertake this species of contract, and which may be divided into three classes.

The first is founded on the mutual system, that is, a number of persons agree to assure each other; to divide among themselves all the profit (or surplus of their annual payment above the sums paid on policies and for the expenses of management); and to make good all deficiencies. Under this system every policy-holder is a proprietor to the extent of his insurance. The second class consists of Joint Stock Companies (i. e. companies formed by a number of individuals who subscribe a capital to be embarked in the business), who assure lives at fixed premiums; and bind themselves to the payment of the sums insured, whether there be a profit or a loss on their transactions. The third class consists also of joint stock companies, but which are formed on principles that unite, in some degree, the two systems above mentioned. They likewise bind themselves to the payment of fixed sums, and exempt the assured from loss under any circumstances; while, at the same time, they admit them to a participation in the profits of their business. The last are called, by modern writers, *mixed companies*, and are by many considered to rest on the safest and most satisfactory basis.

The system of life insurance is founded upon actual experience of the duration of human life, and the *expectation of life* (or chance of living a certain number of years) at a given age.

The tables which are framed on these data are calculated for healthy lives only; i. e. for such person as are supposed to have the ordinary chances of attaining an advanced age. When, therefore, a person afflicted with any serious malady, which may shorten the term of his existence, is desirous of insuring his life, he is required to pay an extra premium commensurate with the increase of risk which will fall upon the company in consequence. This regulation is far more humane, than one which would exclude such individuals altogether from the advantages of a system to which the very circumstance of their ill health would induce them to have recourse.

The modes in which life insurances may be effected are too numerous, and the objects to be attained by them too diversified, to be more than cursorily noticed in this place.

First, as regards the duration of the contract. It may be made for any specific number of months or years; or during a stated voyage; or for the whole term of life.

Secondly, as regards the payment of the premium. It may be done by one payment; by annual and equal payments during the whole of life; by equal payments, annually, during a certain number of years; by payments increasing annually; by payments decreasing annually.

Thirdly, as regards the nature of the guarantee itself.

A man may assure a sum on his own life, payable at his death: or for a given number of years, to be paid to himself, if living at the expiration of the term. He may assure the life of a debtor, for an amount equivalent to his claim upon him. A person who is entitled to a sum of money, or on estate, on the death of another individual, provided he survive that individual, may assure his own life against the life of the latter, and thus secure his inheritance. The holder of a valuable lease, who has to pay a fine on the death of a certain person, may assure the life of that person, and thus obtain the means of paying the fine.

In short, any party having a pecuniary interest in the life of another, may legally insure such interest by any mode that best suits his purpose.

Life policies acquire, after a number of years, a value, proportioned to the age of the assured and the amount of annual premiums to be paid upon them; and may, of course, be sold like any other property. Thus, a person of advanced age, having nobody to provide for at his decease, may convert his policy into cash or an annuity, and augment his means of comfort in the decline of life.

All life policies are subject to a stamp-duty, which before the recent alteration, fell very heavily on the assurers of small sums. The following is the present scale:

All sums not exceeding 50*l*. . . . . 2*s*. 6*d*.
Exceeding 50*l*. and not exceeding 1000*l*. . . . . 5*s*.
Exceeding L. 100 and under 500 . . . . *L*. 1.
    500 » » 1000 . . . . . . 2.
    1000 » » 3000 . . . . . . 3.
    3000 » » 5000 . . . . . . 4.
    5000 and upwards . . . . 5.

Insurances, Marine, — are effected either with the chartered companies, or individual underwriters. The latter are accustomed to congregate in London at LLOYD'S subscription-rooms in the Royal Exchange; an establishment that stands unrivalled in the whole commercial world, for the admirable management of its affairs, and the amazing mass of information which is collected daily from all quarters, through the medium of its numerous agents.

There his scarcely a sea-port of any importance throughout the globe, in which the COMMITTEE OF LLOYD'S have not an agent, whose duty is to give intelligence from time to time of all departures and arrivals of vessels; ships spoken with at sea, or passing the port; wrecks, accidents, the state of the weather, prevailing winds, etc. etc.; likewise to survey all ships launched; and, in case of damage to goods insured, to examine them as soon as discharged, and make affidavit as to their condition, the extent of damage, etc., and generally to watch over the interests of the underwriters.

From sources such as these, the subscribers to Lloyd's are supplied with every information that it concerns them to possess; and there is scarcely a trading vessel afloat which is not registered in their books, with every minute particular of her name, captain's name, build, port of building, tonnage, age, character, etc., so that they have no more hesitation in accepting insurance on a foreign vessel than one of British build, having the same means of ascertaining her character.

It is a maxim in all insurance business, that the more the risks are distributed, the better it is for the assurers; and hence few underwriters at Lloyd's will hazard more than 500l. or 600l. on a single ship.

The average of the subscriptions, indeed, may be reckoned nearer to 250l. or 300l.; and yet assurances to an almost unlimited extent may, in some cases, be effected at Lloyd's, for it has been stated in evidence before a committee of the House of Commons, that one firm alone got 63l, 100l. subscribed on the Diana Frigate.

The business at Lloyd's is usually done through the medium of brokers. When a broker receives an order to effect an insurance, he notes the particulars on a slip of paper, and applies to such of the underwriters as form his more immediate connexion, to know if they will subscribe the risk, at what premium and to what amount. Upon this slip he then writes the names of those who agree to take the risk, and the sum that each is willing to undertake upon it; and having completed his order, or finding that he cannot complete it, draws up a policy upon the proper stamp, and procures the signatures of the parties with whom he has concluded the bargain, as soon as possible. Supposing his amount incomplete, he then continues his exertions to procure further subscriptions, if necessary, even at a higher premium.

In effecting an insurance with one of the chartered companies, there is less trouble and delay; for the particulars of the risk being given in on a slip of paper, it is accepted or rejected at once.

The insurance of human life during a voyage, belongs to the province of life insurance.

Animals may be insured with the stipulation that they shall be delivered alive at the place of destination, or paid for as a loss.

APPENDIX.

The present duties on marine insurance are as follows: — *s. d.*
For every 100*l.* insured on a voyage in the coasting trade of the kingdom, where the premium does not exceed 20*s.* per cent. 1 6
For ditto, the premium exceeding 20*s.* per cent. . . . 2 6
For every 100*l.* insured on a voyage to a foreign or colonial port, where the premium does not exceed 15*s.* per cent. 1 3
Ditto, where the premium exceeds 15*s.*, and does not exceed 30*s.* per cent. 2 6
Ditto, where the premium exceeds 30*s.* per cent. . . . 5 0
For every 100*l.* insured for a period not exceeding three months 2 6
Ditto, exceeding three months. 5 0
** No ship can be assured for a longer period than 12 months by one policy.

Interest. — In marine assurances, the property insured or intended to be insured. In life assurance, where one individual assures the life of another, it signifies the debt due to him, or the amount of the contingency against which the insurance is to be effected.

———— Money *paid* for the use of money *lent*, calculated at a certain rate per cent, per annum. If this rate exceeded 5 per cent., except for a short period, it formerly became usury, which see.

Interest. — Protecting the interest of a commercial house, is doing all that may be practicable, under certain circumstances, to save them from loss by frauds, the failure of houses, etc.

————, *Short.* — In marine insurance, signifies the amount over-insured; *i. e.* the difference between the sum assured, and the value of the goods shipped, when the former exceeds the latter.

Invoice. — An account of goods purchased and shipped. See note, page 46, and the following specimens.

Invoices.

I. London, 20th July, 18—.

Messrs. Robinson and Co., per Royalist, Arthur,
London and St. Vincent.   To Smith & Co.

R.	1-100	100 Casks, each 3 dozen, Porter, 300 dozen, at 6*s.* 6*d.*	*L. s. d.*	*L. s. d.* 97 10 0
301-303		3 Cases, 60 packets Windsor soap, 1cwt. 2qr. 18lb., at 63*s.* . . . . . Cases, etc.	5 4 8 18 6	
				6 3 2
304		36 Gents. Black Beaver Hats, at 5*s.* . . Case	9 0 0 0 12 0	
				9 12 0
305-307		3 Cases as above		28 16 0
308	1	5 gross, Black galloons, at 4*s.* 6*d.* . . Carried forward	1 2 6	142 1 2

MERCANTILE TECHNICALITIES. 217

					L. s. d.	*L. s. d.*
			Brought forward	. . . .		142 1 2
2	10 ditto,	ditto,	» 4s. 10d.	. . 2 8 4		
3	10 ditto,	ditto,	» 5s. 6d.	. . 2 15 0		
4	20 ditto,	ditto,	» 5s. 10d.	. 5 16 8		
5	20 ditto,	ditto,	» 6s. 0d.	. 6 0 0		
6	6 ditto, 4 doubles,		» 7s. 0d.	. . . 2 2 0		
7	6 ditto,	ditto,	» 7s. 5d.	. . . 2 4 6		
8	6 ditto,	ditto,	» 8s. 10d.	. . 2 13 0		
9	10 ditto, 6 doubles,		» 9s. 10d.	. . . 4 18 4		
10	10 ditto,	ditto,	» 10s. 2 1/2d.	5 2 1		
11	20 ditto,	ditto,	» 10s. 10 1/2d.	10 17 6		
	3 dozen 34 inch Blank Bandanas (handkerchiefs), at 26s.			. . . . 3 18 0		
			Tin and wood case	. . . 0 6 6		
					50 4 5	

309

	3 dozen Chall handkerchiefs, (job) at 50s.	7 10 0	192 5 7
1	6 dozen Habits, Black Nett Mitts, at 25s.	7 10 0	
2	6 ditto, ditto, at 30s. . . .	9 0 0	
	20 yards, Black Satin, at 2s. 6d.	2 10 0	
	12 ditto, ditto, » 2s. 8d.	1 12 0	
	30 ditto, White, » 3s. 0d.	4 10 0	
	12 ditto Sky, » 2s. 10d.	1 14 0	
	6 dozen Curling Fluid	6 6 0	
	Case, etc.	0 6 0	
			40 18 0

310

20 pieces, Black and lavender De Laines, 30 yards each, at 10d.	25 0 0	
10 ditto, colored, ditto, at 0s. 6d.	7 10 0	
24 De Laine dresses, » 5s. 6d.	6 12 0	
6 ditto » 6s. 0d.	1 16 0	
10 colored, ditto, » 8s. 0d.	4 0 0	
6 ditto, ditto, » 9s. 6d.	2 17 0	
10 ditto, (job) » 10s. 6d.	5 5 0	
Case	0 9 0	
		53 9 0

311

20 dozen, Japan Blacking, at 4s. . .	4 0 0	
Cask	0 1 6	
		4 1 6

312

10	15 dozen, Habits, Black Silk Gloves, at 12s.	9 0 0	
11	10 ditto, Elastic Tops, at 14s. 0d.	7 0 0	
12	10 ditto, Cordanet Lace, » 6s. 4d.	3 3 4	
13	10 ditto, Black Satin Stocks, at 21s. 6d.	10 15 0	
	2 End Black Cloth, 60 yds, at 6s. 2d.	18 10 0	
	1 ditto 25 1/2 yds. » 7s. 2d.	9 2 9	
	1 ditto, Drab, 26 yds. » 6s. 5d.	8 6 10	
	1 ditto, bottle green 25 yds. » 7s. 11d.	9 17 11	
	Case	0 9 6	
			76 5 4

Carried forward 366 19 5

APPENDIX.

	L. s. d.	L. s. d.
Brought forward		366 19 5
Charges.		
To Entry and Duty, 40s., Dock charges, etc., 45s.	4 5 0	
To Freight, Primage, and Bills of Lading	17 4 3	
		21 9 3
		388 8 8
Insurance on L. 395, at 20s. per cent.	3 19 0	
Policy	0 10 0	
		4 9 0
	L.	392 17 8

E. E. — London, 28th July, 18—.

SMITH & Co.

II.

Invoice of 16 chests of East India Indigo, bought by order and for account of Messrs. Schuback and Co. of Hamburgh, and shipped to their address by the John Bull, Corbyn.

S. & C.	16 Chests of Indigo.		
No. 1 to 16	No.	Gross	Tare.
	1	334 lb.	55 lb.
	2	333	56
	3	336	56
	4	338	57
	5	340	56
	6	337	55
	7	332	56
	8	339	57
	9	335	60
	10	336	56
	11	336	56
	12	328	53
	13	330	58
	14	342	55
	15	342	57
	16	341	58
		5,360	897
		929 { 32 draft	

Net lb. 4,431 at 6s. per lb.   L. 1,329 6 0

MERCANTILE TECHNICALITIES.

Brought forward	L. 1,329	6 0
Charges.		
Entry, bond, fees, etc. . L. 1 10 0		
Packing, 5s. each ... 4 0 0		
Lighterage, shipping, etc. . 4 2 0		
Brokerage ½ per cent. .. 6 13 0		
L. 16 5 0		
Insurance 1,600l. at		
10s. ... L. 8 0 0		
Stamp 1 0 0		
9 0 0		
	25 5 0	
	L.1,354 11 0	
Commission 2 per cent.	27 1 10	
	L.1,381 12 10	

E. E. — *London, 14th August, 18—.* J. SMITH.

III.

Invoice of 200 bales of Cotton, shipped on board the Julia, Black, for Leghorn, by order and for account of Messrs. Girolamo and Co. of Leghorn.

G. & Co.	200 Bales of Cotton,	
1 to 200	Weighing gr. 560 cwt.	
	Draft 2. lb. 3 2 8	
	356 1 20	
	Ropes 2 0 0	
	354 1 15	
	Tare 19 3 4	
	Nett 334 2 10	
	or 37,474 lb. at 8d. per lb.	L. 1,249 2 8
	Carried forward . .	L. 1,249 2 8

Brought forward. . .	L. 1,249 2 8
Charges.	
Bond, dock, and town dues and entry. . . . . L. 4 1 0	
Cartage and Porterage . . 5 0 0	
Bills of lading and petty charges 0 10 6	
Brokerage $1/_2$ per cent. . . 6 5 0	
	15 16 6
	L. 1,264 19 2
Commission 2 per cent.	25 6 0
	L. 1,290 5 2

E. E. — *Liverpool, 5th November, 18—.*   RAINES & Co.

IV.

Invoice of 500 bales of Cotton, shipped by A. Johnson and Co. on board the South America, Captain Gray, for account of Messrs. John Gray and Co. of Liverpool.

J. G. 1 to 500	500 Bales of Cotton. bales weighing	Dollars
	260 93,600 lb. at . . . *15 cts.	14,040
	240 86,400 » . . . 14 cts.	12,096
	500 180,000	26,136
	Charges.	
	Brokerage at 12 $1/_2$ cts. per bale. 62 50	
	Cartage at 8 cts. . . . . . 40 —	
	Petty expences. 3 50	
		106
	Carried forward. . . .	26,242

---

* 100 cents. are one dollar.

	Dollars. Cts.
Brought forward . . .	26,242
Commission for purchase and drafts, 4 per cent.	1,049 68
	27,291 68

E. E. — *New York, 31st October, 18—.*   A. JOHSON & Co.

V.

Invoice of 1000 boxes of Sugar, shipped by James Jones and Co. of Havana, to Hamburgh, by the Mary, Smith, Master by order and for account of Messrs. P. Smith and Co. of Hamburgh.

C. W. 1 to 1000	1000 boxes of yellow sugar, weighing, as per specification annexed,			Dollars. Cts.
	Nett 424,000 lbs. at 8 rls. per aroba of 25 lb*		16,960	
	Boxes 26 r. each.		3,250	
				20,210
	Charges.			
	To export duty, 4 r. per box.	500		
	Weighing, cartage, etc. . .	312		
	Brokerage 1/2 per cent. . .	101		
				913
				21,123
	Commission for purchase 2 1/2 per ct.			528 4
				21,651 4
	Commission on drafts 2 1/2 per ct. .			555 4
		Dollars		22,206 · 2

E. E. — *Havana, 3rd August. 18—.*   JAMES JONES & Co.

---

* One aroba is equal to 25 lb.; rls. stands for reals *de plata*, of which eight are one Spanish dollar.

VI.

Invoice of 103 casks of Crushed Sugar, bought by order and for account of Messrs. E Müller and Co. of Trieste, and shipped to their address by the Metternich Meyer.

E. M. 1 to 103	103 casks of crushed sugar, (specification of weights annexed.)		
	cwt. qr. lbs. cwt. qr. lbs.		
	Gr. 1416 2 Tare 125 3 4		
	126 0 23 dft. 1 0 19		
	Nett 1289 2 5		
	———— at 40s. on board	L. 2,579	1 9
	Charges.		
	Brokerage 1/2 per ct. . L. 12 13 0		
	Bills of lading, etc. . . , 9 6		
		13	7 6
	Insurance 2700l. at 25s. L. 33 15 0		
	Stamp. . . 3 7 6		
		37	2 6
		L. 2,629	11 9
	Commission 2 per ct. , .	52	11 10
		L. 2,682	3 7

E. E. — *London, 1st November, 18—.*

JOHN CRAVEN.

Lame Duck, — in the language of the Stock Exchange, is a person who his unable to fulfil his engagements, and is consequently expelled.

Letter of License. — A permission granted by the creditors of an embarrassed trader to conduct his own affairs, for a certain time without molestation.

Letters of Marque — are issued by a government, in time of war, to private individuals, to authorize the capture of the enemy's ships.

Lighterage. — The hire of a lighter or barge.

Liquidation. — The settlement or winding up of the concerns of a house of trade, by the recovery of claims, payment of debts, etc.

Lloyd's Register. — (See the remarks under the head of « Marine Insurances. ») A book in which the name, build, tonnage and character of every vessel afloat is registered for the use of the underwriters.

Manifest. — One of the ship's papers. It is a list of goods on board of a ship, a copy of which the captain is obliged to hand over to the custom-house on his arrival at the port of destination.

Mulcts. — Fines levied on ships or their cargoes, for the maintenance of consuls, garrisons, etc.

Navy Bills. — Notes issued by the Navy Board, bearing interest like Exchequer bills.

Notary. — A person duly appointed to attest deeds and writings; also, to note and protest bills of exchange and promissory notes. Documents and copies, or translations of documents, attested by a notary, under his official seal, are usually admitted as evidence in the courts of law, especially when countersigned by a consul or envoy.

Par of Exchange. — The intrinsic value of the money of one country in that of another, comparing gold with gold and silver with silver.

Parcel, — among merchants, signifies a lot of good purchased at one time and one price.

Permit. — A license from the Excise for the removal of goods on which the duty has been paid.

Pierage. — A duty levied for the support of a pier.

Policies. — Stamped forms on which contracts of insurance are written.
——————— *valued,* in marine assurance, are those in which the value of the goods is specified.

A Marine Policy.

In the Name of God. Amen. *John Bell, Agent*, as well in *his* own name, as for and in the name and names of all and every other person or persons to whom the same doth, may, or shall appertain, in part or in all, doth make Assurance and cause *himself* and them and every of them to be insured, lost or not lost, at and from

Liverpool to Montreal,

including the risk of craft and lighters from shore to shore. Upon any kind of goods and merchandises, and also upon the body,

tackle, apparel, ordnance, munition, artillery, boat, and other furniture, of and in the good ship or vessel, called the ARETHUSA, whereof is master, under God, for this present voyage, *John Price*, or whosoever else shall go for master in the said ship, or by whatsoever other name or names the same ship, or the master thereof, is or shall be named or called; beginning the adventure upon the said goods and merchandises, from the loading thereof aboard the said ship at *Liverpool*,
upon the said ship, etc.

and so shall continue and endure, during her abode there, upon the said ship, etc. and further, until the said ship, whith all her ordnance, tackle, apparel, etc. and goods and merchandises whatsoever shall be arrived at *Montreal* upon the said ship, etc. until she hath moored at anchor twenty-four hours in good safety; and upon the goods and merchandises, until the same be there discharged and safely landed. And it shall be lawful for the said ship, etc. in this voyage to proceed and sail to, and touch and stay at any ports or places whatsoever, *and wheresoever, and to land, exchange, and take on board goods or passengers at any place or places she may touch at without being deemed a deviation*, and without prejudice to this insurance. The said ship, etc. goods and merchandises, etc. for so much as concerns the assured, by agreement between the assured and assurers in this policy, are and shall be valued at . . . .
. . . . Touching the adveutures and perils which we the assurers are contented to bear, and do take upon us in this voyage; they are of the seas, men of war, fire, enemies, pirates, rovers, thieves, jettisons, letters of mart and countermart, surprisals, takings at sea, arrests, restraints, and detainments of all kings, princes, and people of what nation, condition, or quality soever: barratry of the master and mariners, and of all other perils, losses, and misfortunes, that have, or shall come to the hurt, detriment, or damage of the said goods and merchandises, and ship, etc. or any part thereof. And in case of any loss or misfortune, it shall be lawful to the assured, their factors, servants, and assigns, to sue, labour, and travel for, in and about the defence, safeguard, and recovery of the said goods and merchandises, and ship, etc. or any part thereof, without prejudice to this assurance; to the charges whereof we the assurers will contribute each one according to the rate and quantity of his sum herein assured. And it is agreed by us the insurers, that this writing or policy of assurance shall be of as much force and effect as the surest writing or policy of assurance heretofore made in Lombard Street, or in the Royal Exchange, or elsewhere in London. And so we the assurers are contented, and do hereby promise and bind ourselves, each one

for his own part, our heirs, executors, and goods, to the assured, their executors, administrators, and assigns, for the true performance of the premises, confessing ourselves paid the consideration due unto us for this assurance by the assured. — At and after the rate of

Forty Shillings per Cent.

In Witness *whereof, we the assurers have subscribed our names and sums assured in* London.

N. B. Corn, fish, salt, fruit, flour, and seed are warranted free from average, unless general, or the ship be stranded. — Sugar, tobacco, hemp, flax, hides, and skins are warranted free from average under five pounds per cent., and all other goods, also the ship and freight are warranted free of average under three pounds per cent. unless general, or the ship be stranded.

On 9 *Bales Woollen Goods, marked* XL. *No. 33 to 41, valued at Six Hundred and Fourteen Pounds. To pay average separately on each bale.*

No. 33 ... valued at ...... L. 64 3 2
    34 ..... do. 69 8 4
    35 ..... do. 65 15 3
    36 ..... do. 68 2 6
    37 ..... do. 66 3 9
    38 ..... do. 66 7 0
    39 ..... do. 66 15 9
    40 ..... do. 69 16 3
    41 ..... do. 77 9 0

L. 214 G. *Robson per* W. *Travers, Two Hundred and Fourteen Pounds, premium received* 17 *June,* 1819.

L. 200 J. *Rabson per* W. *Travers, Two Hundred Pounds, premium received* 17 *June,* 1819.

L. 200 W. *Pritchard* ————— *Two Hundred Pounds, premium received* 17 *June,* 1819.

Policies, open, those which do not express the value of the goods insured.

————— *floating,* in fire assurance, are such as extend to goods deposited in various buildings not designated, or to two or more buildings which are designated, but without limitation as to the amount to be covered on each. A loss under a floating policy is settled on the average principle. Thus, if a merchant had effected an insurance of 50,000*l.* without specification, and a loss of 9,000*l.* occurred, he would be called upon to show the total value of the property covered by his policy. Suppose it proved to be 150,000*l.* exactly thrice the amount insured, then he would be entitled only to recover 3,000*l*. since he must bear his own risk on the 100,000*l*. uninsured.

Premium. — See *Insurance*, p. 211.

——— *of Exchange.* — The per centage paid in British North America, the United States, etc. for the purchase of a bill on England. The mode of calculating this is shown at page 232.

——— *on Shares.* — The amount paid on a share being 50*l*. for instance, and the market price 53*l*., it is said to be « at a premium of 6 per cent. » If the same share would fetch but 48*l*. it would then be « at a discount of 4 per cent »

Primage. — An allowance made by the shipper or consignee to the captain, for loading the goods. It is usually a per centage on the freight; but sometimes it is reckoned at so much per package.

Prisage. — The king's share of such merchandise as is captured at sea by way of lawful prize.

Procuration. — The power given to an agent or clerk to sign and act for a commercial house.

Pro forma. — Imaginary, fictitious. The utility of a *pro forma* account is this: — A Hamburg merchant is desirous of shipping a parcel of wools to London on speculation and in order to ascertain whether he can realise a profit by such a consignment, applies to his correspondent for a *pro forma* account-sales of wool. The London merchant, in this case, either transmits him a copy of a real account, suppressing names, marks, etc. or makes up one altogether fictitious, but which suffices to show the duties, charges, commission, and expenses of all kinds on wools in the port of London.

Promissory Note. — See *Bills of Exchange*, under which head a formula is given at page 202.

Prompt. — The credit or time allowed for the payment of a parcel of goods.

Protest, Captain's. — The solemn declaration, or report of the captain and crew of a vessel, detailing the circumstances of any misfortune, stress of weather, or accident, that has occasioned injury to the ship or cargo. An important document in the settlement of a loss on a sea policy.

——— *Notarial.* — The evidence required by law of the due presentation of a bill for acceptance or payment. See *Bills of Exchange*.

Quarantine. — The time that a ship suspected of having the plague or other malignant disease among her crew, must ride at a certain place, called the *quarantine ground*, before she can be *admitted* to *pratique*, or allowed to have intercourse with the shore.

MERCANTILE TECHNICALITIES.   227

Quotations. — The prices of goods, course of exchange, rates of freight, etc. as advised by one merchant to another, or published by brokers in a price-current.

Quoted on board — free on board. — It is common in quoting the price of an article, to state what it will cost including all charges incurred in shipping it; this is the price *free on board;* it is *quoted on board.*

Register. — A ships's document, attesting the place where the ship is built, its tonnage, etc.

Respondentia. — A loan *in respondentia* is money lent on the security of a cargo. See *Bottomry.*

Returns. — The value in goods or money returned by the consignee to the consignor. A remittance in return for one received. The amount of a trader's sales in a given time.

Reversion, reversionary interest. — A right to the possession of property after a certain number of years, at the death of some person, or after the expiration of a lease.

Salvage. — The property saved from a wreck or a fire. In maritime affairs, it signifies also the expenses attending the recovery of the ship or cargo, when captured, wrecked, or abandoned by the crew for their own preservation. A salvage loss is a total loss, with the deduction of the property saved.

Seaworthy. — A term implying that a ship is tight and staunch, and stored, manned, and in every way fitted for her intended voyage.

Sleeping Partner. — One who has money embarked in a trading copartnery, but has no concern with the management of its affairs.

Solvent. — Able to pay one's debts.

Specie. — Coin as distinguished from paper money.

Stocks, or *Public Funds.* — The debts of government, for which interest is paid from revenues set apart for the purpose. These, with the unfunded debt mentioned below, constitute the National Debt, amounting to above 840 millions, and the annual interest and expenses of managing which are about twenty-nine or thirty millions. The public creditor or stock-holder cannot claim repayment of the capital, but he may sell his stock and thus transfer his claim to any other person, from whom he recovers his money more or less, according to the price of stock, which fluctuates from various causes. The stocks are denominated *Three per Cents., Four per Cents., Three and a half per Cent. reduced, etc.* The notes issued by the Exchequer, Navy, Victualling, and Ordnance departments, form the *unfunded debt;* for paying the interest of this debt no specific provision is made by the appropriation of taxes.

Stock — is a term applied also to the capitals of the Bank of England, the East India, and South Sea Companies, which are transferrable like government funds.

Stock-broker. — One who makes transfers of stocks.

Stock Exchange. — The building where the business of the stocks is transacted.

Stock-Jobber. — One who speculates in the public stocks for his own account.

Super-cargo. — A person employed to go a voyage, to superintend the sale of the cargo, to freight the vessel for her return, etc.

Time-bargain. — An agreement to purchase and sell goods or stock at a certain time and fixed price. A species of gambling which is declared illegal by act of parliament.

Tonnage. — The number of tons burden that a ship will carry.

Transfer Days. — Certain days appointed for the transfer of stock from the name of the seller to that of the buyer.

Transit. — A custom-house warrant or pass.

Trinity House. — An ancient corporation (the members of which are styled Brethren) for the promotion of commerce and navigation, whose province it is to erect lighthouses and land marks, appoint pilots, settle the rates of pilotage, etc. They issue Trinity Bonds bearing interest.

Underwriters. — Insurers — undertakers of the risk. This name, derived from the fact of their subscribing or underwriting the policies, is limited chiefly to private individuals, and to marine assurance; although incorporated insurance companies, whether for marine, fire, or life risks, are equally underwriters in the full acceptation of the term.

Usance. — There is, in every commercial city, an established custom, in regard to the number of days or months at which foreign bills of exchange are drawn; this is termed the usance of that place. Usances vary from fourteen days after date to six months after sight.

Usury — signifies the taking illegal interest for money. The legal interest in England is 5 per cent., but an exception was made in 1838, in favor of bills of exchange, on which any rate of discount may be charged, provided they do not exceed twelve months' date.

Voucher. — A document or paper proving that some payment has been made, or other transaction effected.

MERCANTILE TECHNICALITIES.

Example referred to at page 185.

249l. 12s. 6d. for 149 days at 5 per cent. (the first item on the credit side of the account current, in pp. 184 and 185).

   149 days
   250 pounds (12s. 6d. reckoned as 1l.)
   ―――
   7450
   298
   ―――

Sum to be 372 (50 cut off.
 entered
 The balance of 164 reduced into money, viz.
   73) 164 (2l. 4s. 11d.
   146
   ―――
    18
    20
   ―――
   73) 360 (4s.
    292
   ―――
    68
    12
   ―――
   73) 816 (11d.
    803
   ―――
    13

The real divisor is 7300, the number of days in 20 years; but by striking out the cyphers of the divisor and two figures of the dividend, the same result is obtained within a fraction.

THE GERMAN CHAIN RULE.

This rule, called by the Germans *Ketten-Regel*, *regula multiplex*, and sometimes De Rees' rule, from its inventor, K. F. de Rees, is of vast use in commercial calculations, and greatly preferable to the common methods taught in England, on account of its simplicity, its brevity, and its correctness.

By it any operation of arithmetic required in commerce may be performed: but its superiority to the Rule of Three is most conspicuous in the arbitration of exchanges, and other complicated questions requiring several distinct statements by the latter.

In order to render the principles of this rule clear to my reader, I must commence by giving the simplest examples of it that I can select; and I request his earnest attention to these, assuring him, that when he has overcome the difficulty of stating his question, he will be amply repaid for his trouble, as he will then be possessed of a rule by which he may solve any arithmetical problem that can arise in business.

In the first place, let us consider what we seek to know when we put a common question, as for example: If 1 cwt. of sugar cost 56s. what does 1 lb. cost? We want to know, in this case, what proportion of the money will be equivalent to the given portion of the sugar. Knowing one pound to be the 112th part of a hundred weight, we have only to find the 112th part of the whole price, and that must be the value of the pound.

In like manner, if we reverse the question, and say, If 1 lb. cost 6d., what will 1 cwt. cost? we need only multiply the price of the pound by the number of pounds in a hundred weight, and we have the answer.

Thus, in all calculations our object is to find the relative proportions of things.

This is accomplished in the simplest manner by the chain rule, in which the divisors and dividends, be they ever so numerous, are classed together and intermultiplied, so as to produce one common divisor and one common dividend.

The only difficulty in this rule is, as I before hinted, in stating the question, and the mode of doing this will, perhaps, be best seen by contrasting it with that of the Rule of Three. The simple example above given may serve us again. If 1 cwt. cost 56s. what will 1 lb.

GERMAN CHAIN RULE.

cost? This in the statement by the rule of three. In the chain rule we must reverse this, and commence with the last term, thus:

What will . . . . 1 lb. cost?
there being . . 112 lb. in 1 cwt.
and . . . . . 1 cwt. costing 56 shillings
      1 shilling   12 pence.

Here we have the first and second terms alike, the third and fourth alike, the fifth and sixth alike, and the *last expresses that denomination in which the answer is to be*. The question being correctly stated, multiply the divisors and dividends into each other, and it will stand thus:

  Divisor.   Dividend.
  112     $56 \times 12 = 672$
       112) 672 (6

Reverse the question. Required to know what 1 cwt. will cost, at 6d, per lb?

   ? . . . . . 1 cwt.
  1 cwt. . . . . 112 lb.
  1 lb. . . . . 6 pence.
  Divisor.   Dividend.
  (none) $112 \times 6 = 672$ pence.

Add another term, and we have the answer in shillings.

  ? . . . . 1 cwt.
  1 cwt. . . . . 112 lb.
  1 lb. . . . . 6 pence.
  12 pence . . . . . . 1 shilling.
  Divisor.   Dividend.
  12   672   Answer 56s.

The above and the following examples are given merely to explain the *principles* of the rule, not to prove its *utility*, which will be seen hereafter.

What is the value of 1650 lb. of rice, at $2\ 1/2 d$. per lb.?

  ? . . . . 1650 lb.
  1 lb. . . . . $2\ 1/2\ d.$
  12 pence . . . . 1 shilling.
  20 shillings . . . . 1 pound.
  Divisor.   Dividend.
  $12 \times 20 = 240$ $1650 \times 2\ 1/2 = 4125.$
      Answer, 17l. 3s. 9d.

APPENDIX.

The fraction in this case might be differently treated, by reducing the 2 ½ to 5 halves, and adding a 2 on the side of the divisors as an equivalent.

What is the value of 7680 francs, at 25 francs 45 centimes per pound sterling?

Here the 45 centimes are so many hundredths, and two cyphers must be added to the dividend; to render this clear I will give the chain.

? . . . . 7680 francs.
1 franc . . . . 100 centimes.
2545 centimes . . . . 1 pound.
Divisor.   Dividend.
2545   7680 × 100 = 768,000

Having 250l. currency to remit from Quebec to London, at a premium of 8l. per cent., what is the amount in sterling to be purchased?

? . . . . 250 currency.
100 currency . . . . 90 sterling
108 sterling . . . . 100 sterling.
Divisor.   Dividend.
100 × 108 = 10800   250 × 90 × 100 = 2250000
            Answer, 208l. 6s. 8d.

Having, I trust, rendered the rule intelligibile, I will preceed to shew how to effect a great saving of time and figures in working it, by previously reducing the divisors and dividends as much as possible.

If we multiply by a given number, and then divide by the same, we do nothing, since the division neutralises the multiplication. Multiply 12 by 12, and we have 144: divide 144 by 12, and we have 12 again. Now, in the example last given, there is the same sum, 100, on each side, therefore both may be struck out; the 108 may then be divided by 2, leaving 54, and the 90 by 2, leaving 45. The chain, reduced in this way, will stand thus:

Divisor.   Dividend.
54   250 × 45 = 11250 *

Now revert to the first example.

? . . . . 1 lb.
112 lb. . . . . 56 shillings.
1 shilling . . . . 12 pence.

Divide the 112 by 56; strike out both, and set down 2 for a divisor; there will then remain but 12 to be divided by 2.

---

* By a more complicated process, this example may be reduced still more, thus: Strike out on cypher of the 100 and of the 250, leaving 10 and 25; divide the 90 on the right by the 10 on the left, leaving 9; divide the 108 by the 9, leaving 12 as the sole divisor, the dividend being 25 × 100 = 2500.

GERMAN CHAIN RULE. 253

Again, in the example at page 231, the 2 ¹/₂ may be divided into the 20, when both will become annihilated, and an 8 be set down as a divisor, thus:

    Divisor.   Dividend.
   12 × 8 = 96   1650

I will now give a few examples of the use of the chain in Exchange operations, showing the reduction in each case.

Hambro' remits to London 1691. 13s. 6d. at the exchange of 13.14. How much is paid for the bill ?

   ? . . . . L. 169 ²⁷/₄₀
   L. 1. . . . . 13 ⁷/₈

Reduce the sterling into sixpences, and the banco into eighths, placing as a divisor,

   40 × 8 = 320   6787 sixpences
                    111 eighths of a mark

                    6787
                    6787
                    6787

         320) 753357 (2354 marks
              640

             1133
              960

             1735
             1600

             1357
             1280

         20) 77 (3 shillings
             60

             17
              3

          5)51 (10 pfennings.

The only reduction practicable in this example, is in working the remainders.

The first, 77, would, by the rule of three, be multiplied by 16, and the product divided by 320; but here the 320 is divided by that 16, and the divisor reduced to 23. The second remainder would, in like manner, be multiplied by 12, and divided by 320; but here both are first reduced by dividing by 4.

APPENDIX.

A merchant of London, having to receive 3000 marks banco at Hamburg, requests his correspondent to remit that sum to Frankfort on the Maine, at 138 rix-dollars, with directions to invest the value in a bill on London. This being effected at 151 $^1/_4$ batzen, how much sterling money does he receive?

? . . . . 3000 marks
300 marks. . . . . . . 138 rix-dollars
1 rix-dollar . . . . . . 22 $^4/_5$ batzen
151 $^1/_4$ batzen . . . . . 1 pound.

Multiply the 151 $^1/_4$ by 4, making 605; the 22 $^1/_5$ by 5, making 45; place as equivalents a 4 on the right, and a 5 on the left. Then strike out the 300 and 3000, adding 10 on the right; divide that 10 by the 2, leaving 5; divide the 605 and 10 by that 5, leaving as a

  Divisor.   Dividend.
  121   138 × 4 × 45 = 24840
        Answer, 205*l.* 4*s.* 7*d.*

Hambro' remits to Amsterdam 4000 marks banco, at the exchange of 34 stivers, with directions to invest the proceeds in a bill on London; which is done at the exchange at 12 12 $^1/_2$. What will be the amount in sterling?

? . . . . 4000 marks banco
2 marks . . . . 34 stivers
Fl. 12 12 $^1/_2$ . . . . 1 pound.

The 12 12 $^1/_2$ must be reduced to stivers, and then multiplied by 2; the same figure being placed as an equivalent on the right side. The sum will then stand thus:

    2   4000
    505   34
           2

Strike out the 2 on each side; divide both the 505 and the 4000 by 5, leaving the

  Divisor.   Dividend.
  101   800 × 34 = 27200
        Answer, 269*l.* 6*s.* 1*d.*

A bill is drawn at Lisbon on London for 600 milreis, and negotiated first to Vienna at 366 reis per florin; thence to Frankfort at 100 florins currency of Vienna for 58 florins of Frankfort; thence to Paris at 80 florins for 300 francs; and from Paris to London at 24 50 What is the amount paid in London?

? . . . . 600 milreis
1 milrea . . . . 1000 reis
366 reis . . . . 1 florin of Vienna
100 florins of Vienna . . . . . . 58 florins of Frankfort
80 florins of Vienna . . . . . . 300 francs
24 $^1/_2$ francs . . . . 1 pound

GERMAN CHAIN RULE.

Multiply the 24 1/2 by 2, making 49, and add a 2 on the opposite side; then proceed to reduce the chain, as follows. Divide the 600 by the 100; strike out both, and place a 6 on the right side; divide the 366 by that 6, leaving 61 as a divisor. Divide the 80 by the 2; strike out the latter, and leave 40 on the left side. Annihilate the cypher of the 40 and one of the 300, leaving 4 and 30; get rid of the 4 by dividing it into the 1000, and the sum will stand thus:

Divisor.   Dividend.
49 × 61 = 2989   58 × 30 × 250 = 435000
         Answer. 143l. 10s. 8d.

In exchange operations, charges are incurred for bank commission, interest, brokerage, stamps, postage, etc. which may be estimated at 1/4 to 1 per cent. In buying bills, for instance, every 100l., will cost 101l.; in selling them, every 100l. sold will produce only 99l.

To include these charges in the chain, consider whether the quotient will be increased or diminished thereby.

If to be increased, state it thus:
        100   101
If to be diminished, thus:
        100   99

A single example of this may suffice.

A merchant of Hamburg remits to his correspondent at Rotterdam 6,500 marks banco, at the exchange of 34 stivers, requesting him to invest the produce in a bill on London. The exchange on London is 12 12, and the charges are one per cent. What is the value of the bill purchased?

        ? . . . . 6500 marks
        2 marks. . . . . 34 stivers
        252 stivers . . . . 1l.
        100 . . . .   99 for charges.

Commence by annihilating the two cyphers on each side; then divide the 34 by the 2, leaving 17 in lieu of the former, and striking out the latter. The two sums of 252 and 99 being divisible by 3, reduce them to 84 and 33, when you will have the following figures to work with.

        Divisor.   Dividends.
        84   65 × 17 × 33 = 36465
        Result, 434l. 2s. 1d.

In the computations connected with marine insurance the chain rule may be employed advantageously, and I will give one example of this kind to explain the manner of ascertaining the amount to be insured, to cover the expenses in case of loss.

What is the amount to be insured to cover 2,560l. invoice value

APPENDIX.

of a parcel of goods, with the cost of insurance and the expenses attending the recovery of a loss?
The expenses are reckoned at 3l. 5s. per cent: viz.

Policy	0	5	0
Commission on effecting insurance	0	10	0
Do. on recovering loss	2	0	0
Brokerage on do	0	10	0
L.	3	5	0
To which add premium, say 60s.	3	0	0
Total	6	5	0

Which deducted from 100l. leaves 93l. 15s. Then: —

? 2560
93 ³/₄ 100

Reduce the divisor into 375 quarters, and place a 4 on the side of the dividends. You may then either proceed at once to work the sum, or reduce it by dividing by 5 three times successively, which will leave the statement as follows:

Divisor.   Dividend.
   3   4 × 512 × 4 = 8192
               Answer, 2731l.

In conclusion, I will express a hope that I have here presented my readers with some valuable information, and have said enough to show the utility of the German Chain Rule. By selecting more complicated problems, I might have rendered that utility more apparent: but my object was to employ easy examples, in order that the principles of the rule might be the better comprehended.

If it be asserted that in many cases this rule is not preferable to the rule of three, it must, on the other hand, be admitted that in very many it is, *while it is inferior in none;* it has, therefore, higher claims to consideration, and I will venture to say, that few who have once made themselves masters of it, will hesitate to give the preference to the German Chain Rule.

THE END.

NDERSON'S Practical mercantile correspondence, collection of modern letters of business, with italian notes by *John Millhouse.* Milano, 1873, in 16°, III.ᵃ edizione . . . . Ital. L. 2. 70
GUIDE to the *SCIENTIFIC KNOWLEDGE* of things familiar, by *Dr. J. Brewer,* with italian notes by *John Millhouse.* Milano, 1881 in 16°. . » 1. —
ELECT COMEDIES by *R. B. Sheridan*: with explanatory italian notes by *John Millhouse.* Milano, 1881 in 16.°, II.ᵃ edizione . . . . . » 1. —
ENTAL CULTURE or *HINTS* on the cultivation of the mind by *W. Dealby;* with explanatory italian notes by *John Millhouse.* Milano, 1880 in 16° piccolo . . . . » — 80
'NNOCK'S BRITISH BIOGRAPHY and *DEALBY'S MENTAL CULTURE;* with plan. italian notes by *J. Millhouse.* Mil., 1888 ▅▅▅ 1. —
uddetti due Opuscoli, MENTAL CULT▅▅ *PINNOCK'S*, legati in un sol volume . . . . ., . . 80
CATECHISM of BRITISH BIOGRAPHY by *Pinnock;* with explanatory italian notes. Milano, 1844 in 16° piccolo . . . . » — 80
ratto del Prof. *J. MILLHOUSE* dipinto da Focosi, nciso in acciajo da J. Cochran, nel formato di 8°. » — 60

Milano, febbrajo 1873.

RAG. Francesco Resnati,
Amministratore dell'Eredità Millhouse.
Via Spiga, N. 28.

www.ingramcontent.com/pod-product-compliance
Lightning Source LLC
Chambersburg PA
CBHW031735230426
43669CB00007B/353